AIRCRAFT ACCIDENT REPORT 4/90

Air Accidents Invest

Department of Transport

**Report on the accident to
Boeing 737-400 G-OBME
near Kegworth, Leicestershire
on 8 January 1989**

LONDON : HMSO

© Crown copyright 1990
First published 1990

ISBN 0 11 550986 0

LIST OF RECENT AIRCRAFT ACCIDENT REPORTS ISSUED BY AIR ACCIDENTS INVESTIGATION BRANCH

1/89	Airmiss between Tristar G-BBAH and Tupolev 154 LZ-BTE near Lydd, Kent on 6 February 1988	February 1989
2/89	Incident involving BAC 1-11 G-AYWB and Boeing 737 EI-BTZ at Gatwick Airport on 12 April 1988	May 1989
3/89	Sikorsky S61N helicopter G-BDII near Handa Island off the north-west coast of Scotland on 17 October 1988	June 1989
4/89	Boeing 747 N605PE at Gatwick Airport on 1 February 1988	August 1989
5/89	Boeing 747-136 G-AWNM on approach to Runway 27L at London (Heathrow) Airport on 11 September 1988	December 1989
6/89	Concorde 102 G-BOAF over the Tasman Sea, about 140 nm east of Sydney, Australia on 12 April 1989	December 1989
1/90	Sikorsky S61N G-BDES in the North Sea, 90 nm north-east of Aberdeen on 10 November 1988	May 1990
2/90	Boeing 747-121, N739PA at Lockerbie, Dumfriesshire, Scotland on 21 December 1988	
3/90	Sikorsky S61N, G-BEID 29 nm north east of Sumburgh, Shetland Isles on 13 July 1988	
4/90	Boeing 737-400, G-OBME near Kegworth, Leicestershire on 8 January 1989	

Department of Transport
Air Accidents Investigation Branch
Royal Aerospace Establishment
Farnborough
Hants GU14 6TD

25 August 1990

The Right Honourable Cecil Parkinson
Secretary of State for Transport

Sir,

I have the honour to submit the report by Mr E J Trimble, an Inspector of Accidents, on the circumstances of the accident to British Midland Airways Boeing 737-400, G-OBME, which occurred near Kegworth, Leicestershire, on 8 January 1989.

I have the honour to be
Sir
Your obedient servant

D A COOPER
Chief Inspector of Air Accidents

CONTENTS		Page
GLOSSARY OF ABBREVIATIONS		(xii)
SYNOPSIS		1
1	FACTUAL INFORMATION	3
1.1	History of the flight	3
1.2	Injuries to persons	7
1.3	Damage to aircraft	8
1.4	Other damage	8
1.5	Personnel information	8
	1.5.1 Commander	8
	1.5.2 First Officer	9
	1.5.3 Cabin Attendants	10
1.6	Aircraft information	11
	1.6.1 Leading particulars	11
	1.6.2 Description of engines	12
	1.6.3 Engine instrument system (EIS)	12
	1.6.4 Airborne vibration monitoring (AVM) system	14
	1.6.5 Engine fire and overheat detection system	15
	1.6.6 Air conditioning system	16
	1.6.7 Cabin floor structure	17
	1.6.8 Seats	18
	1.6.9 Overhead stowage bins	20
	1.6.10 Maintenance records	20
1.7	Meteorological Information	22
1.8	Aids to navigation	23
1.9	Communications	23
1.10	Aerodrome information	23
1.11	Flight recorders	24
	1.11.1 Flight Data Recorder (FDR)	24
	1.11.2 FDR data analysis	25
	1.11.3 Cockpit voice recorder (CVR)	27
	1.11.4 CVR transcript significant events	27
	1.11.5 CVR frequency analysis	29

1.12	Wreckage and impact Information		30
	1.12.1 On site		30
	1.12.2 Subsequent detailed examination		37
1.13	Medical and pathological Information		53
	1.13.1 Injuries		53
	1.13.2 Types of injury		54
1.14	Fire		55
1.15	Survival aspects		55
	1.15.1 On-board emergency preparations and impact effects		55
	1.15.2 Rescue operations		56
1.16	Tests and research		57
	1.16.1 Engine tests to identify the cause of fan blade fatigue		57
	1.16.2 Trials to establish fuel leak characteristics		60
	1.16.3 Tests of the engine instrument system (EIS)		60
	1.16.4 KRASH computer simulation		62
	1.16.5 Computer simulation of occupant response		63
1.17	Additional information		65
	1.17.1 Pilot training		65
	1.17.2 The aircraft Operating Manual and checklist		66
	1.17.3 Pilot opinion of the EIS		69
	1.17.4 Engine vibration monitors in aircraft		69
	1.17.5 Actions by Air Traffic Control		70
	1.17.6 Development of the CFM56-3 engine		72
	1.17.7 Subsequent fan blade fractures on Boeing 737-400 aircraft		81
	1.17.8 Incidents involving fan blade damage from bird ingestion		84
	1.17.9 Fatigue initiation and growth		86
	1.17.10 Cracked fan disc		87
	1.17.11 Changes in seat and cabin structural requirements		87
	1.17.12 Crash dynamics research		89
	1.17.13 Aft-facing seats		89
	1.17.14 Child restraint systems		90
	1.17.15 Loading of overhead stowage bins		92
	1.17.16 Requirements for fuel tank protection		92
	1.17.17 Other survivable accidents		93
	1.17.18 Analysis of deceleration data		94
	1.17.19 Airborne closed circuit television monitoring		94
	1.17.20 AAIB Special Bulletin S2/89		96
1.18	New investigation techniques		96

2	ANALYSIS		97
2.1	Crew actions		97
	2.1.1	The reaction of the flight crew to the engine problem	97
	2.1.2	Crew co-operation	105
	2.1.3	The influence of stress	107
	2.1.4	Flight crew training	108
2.2	Engine failure analysis		111
	2.2.1	General	111
	2.2.2	No 1 engine failure sequence	113
	2.2.3	Cause of fatigue initiation in fan blade No 17	117
	2.2.4	Source of vibratory stresses	118
	2.2.5	Failure of the certification process to reveal vibration	119
2.3	Fire		120
	2.3.1	Source of fire	120
	2.3.2	Potential effects of fire	122
	2.3.3	Fuel tank integrity	123
2.4	Aircraft systems		124
	2.4.1	Aircraft systems - general	124
	2.4.2	Air conditioning system	124
	2.4.3	Engine fire and overheat detection system	124
	2.4.4	Performance of the AVM system	125
	2.4.5	Engine instrument system	126
	2.4.6	Airborne close circuit television monitoring	127
2.5	Flight recorder design requirements		128
2.6	Survival aspects		129
	2.6.1	Injuries	129
	2.6.2	Occupant simulation	130
	2.6.3	Assessment of deceleration	131
	2.6.4	Seating	132
	2.6.5	Alternative seating configurations	135
	2.6.6	Cabin floor structure	137
	2.6.7	Future floor requirements	138
	2.6.8	Infant and child restraint systems	138
	2.6.9	Overhead stowage bins	139

3	**CONCLUSIONS**	142
	3 (a) Findings	142
	3 (b) Cause	148
4	**SAFETY RECOMMENDATIONS**	149
5	**APPENDICES**	153

Appendix 1 Engines

        Fig 1 Engine cross-section
        Fig 2 Fan assembly damage (G-OBME)
        Fig 3 Microsection through fatigue origin on blade 17
        Extract 1 JAR and FAR blade vibration requirements
        Fig 4(a, b) Fan assembly damage (G-BNNL and G-OBMG)
        Fig 5 Fan blade fatigue fracture (G-OBME)
        Fig 6 Fan blade fatigue fracture (G-BNNL)
        Fig 7 Fan blade fatigue fracture (G-OBMG)
        Fig 8 Comparison of fan blade fatigue fracture lines.

Appendix 2 Systems

        Fig 1 Boeing 737 flight deck with hybrid EIS
        Fig 2 Boeing 737 flight deck with solid-state EIS
        Fig 3 Solid-state electronic EIS
        Fig 4 Location of fire/overheat detection elements
        Fig 5 Air conditioning system schematic
        Appendix 2.6 AVM interrogation read-out for last 20 flights
        Appendix 2.7 Engine instrument system assessment
        Appendix 2.8 Latch up condition

Appendix 3 Structures and Computer Impact Simulation

        Fig 1 Seat-track, forward fuselage
        Fig 2 Seat-track, aft fuselage
        Fig 3 G-OBME seating configuration
        Fig 4 Passenger triple seat
        Fig 5 Overhead stowage bin attachments
        Fig 6 Impact sequence
        Fig 7 Structural disruption
        Fig 8 Passenger seat damage summary
        Fig 9 Seat 3L (Area I)
        Fig 10 Seat 15L (Area II)

Fig 11   Seat 18L (Area III)
Fig 12   Seat 22R (Area III)
Fig 13   Seat 25L (Area IV)
Fig 14   Floor structure at Station 867 (Area IV)
Fig 15   Floor panel fasteners (Area IV)
Fig 16   Floor beam at Station 807 (Area IV)
Fig 17   Seat track at Station 727D (Area III)
Fig 18   Seat track and Seat 5R (Area I)
Fig 19   Seat track and seat 3L (Area I)
Fig 20   Floor beam at Station 460 (Area I)
Fig 21   (a) Stowage bin attachments
         (b) Stowage bins
Fig 22   KRASH decelerations - Run 2
Fig 23   KRASH decelerations - Run 3
Fig 24   Other survivable accidents - summary

Appendix 4   Flight Recorders

Fig 1   Block diagram of EIS signal path
Fig 2   G-OBME track plot
Fig 3   FDR engine parameters record
Fig 4   FDR engine vibration record
Fig 5   FDR engine parameters at Event 1
Fig 6   FDR final flight parameters record
Fig 7   G-OBME final flight path
Fig 8   CVR area mic frequencies before/after Event 1
Fig 9   CVR area mic frequencies before/after Event 2
Fig 10   FDR initial engine parameters comparison(G-OBME: G-BNNL: B-OBMG)
Fig 11   Variation of throttle lever angle during Event 1

Appendix 5   Injuries and computer occupant simulations

Fig 1   Seat positions of fatalities and survivors
Fig 2   Injury severity scores (ISS) of occupants
Fig 3   Distribution of injury extent (ISS $\gtrless 16$)

Fig 4   Occupant displacement simulation (braced, lap belt)
Fig 5   Occupant displacement simulation (lap +upper torso restraint)
Fig 6   Occupant displacement simulation (aft-facing standard seat)

Appendix 5.7   References

Appendix 6   AAIB Special Bulletin S2/89

GLOSSARY OF ABBREVIATIONS

AAIB	Air Accidents Investigation Branch
AFS	Airport Fire Service
agl	Above ground level
amsl	Above mean sea level
APU	Auxiliary Power Unit
ATA	Air Transport Association
ATC	Air Traffic Control
AVM	Airborne Vibration Monitor
BCD	Binary coded decimal
BCAR	British Civil Airworthiness Requirements
BITE	Built in Test Equipment
BMA	British Midland Airways
CAA	Civil Aviation Authority
CAMI	Civil Aeromedical Institute
CAS	Calibrated Airspeed
CATO	Civil Air Traffic Organisation
CG	Centre of Gravity
CIC	Cranfield Impact Centre
CID	Controlled Impact Demonstration
CVR	Cockpit Voice Recorder
EAS	Equivalent Airspeed
EGT	Exhaust Gas Temperature
EIS	Engine Instrument System
EMA	East Midlands Airport
EUROCAE	European Organisation for Civil Aviation Electronics
FAA	Federal Aviation Administration
FDAU	Flight Data Acquisition Unit
FDR	Flight Data Recorder
FF	Fuel Flow
FL	Flight Level
FMS	Flight Management System
FOD	Foreign Object Damage
fps	Feet per second
FSM	Flight Service Manager
ft	Feet or foot
g	Acceleration due to gravity
GE	General Electric
GPWS	Ground Proximity Warning System
Hg	Mercury (Chemical Symbol)
HIC	Head Injury Criteria
HP	High Pressure
HPC	High Pressure Compressor
HPT	High Pressure Turbine
IAM	Institute of Aviation Medicine
ILS	Instrument Landing System
ISS	Injury Severity Score

JAR	Joint Airworthiness Requirements
kg	Kilogram(s)
K_1	Stress Intensity Factor
kt	Stress Concentration Factor
kts	Knots
LATC(C)	London Air Traffic Control (Centre)
LE	Leading Edge
LED	Light Emitting Diode
LP	Low Pressure
LPC	Low Pressure Compressor
LPT	Low Pressure Turbine
MAC	Mean Aerodynamic Chord
MATO	Military Air Traffic Organisation
MATS	Manual of Air Traffic Services
mb	Millibar(s)
MEC	Main Engine Control
MHz	Mega Hertz
MLG	Main Landing Gear
MM	Maintenance Manual
MMEL	Master Minimum Equipment List
N1	Fan Speed
N2	High Pressure Compressor Speed
NATS	National Air Traffic Service
NDB	Non Directional Beacon
nm	Nautical miles
OAT	Outside Air Temperature
OGV	Outlet Guide Vane
PLA	Power Lever Angle
PMC	Power Management Controller
QNH	Pressure setting to indicate height above mean sea level
RAE	Royal Aerospace Establishment
RAF	Royal Air Force
RAM	Random Access Memory
RCC	Rescue Coordination Centre
RPM	Revolutions per minute
RT	Radio Telephony
SEM	Scanning Electron Microscope
SNECMA	Societe Nationale d'Etude et de Construction de Moteurs d'Aviation
TAI	Thermal Anti-ice
TAT	Total Air Temperature
TOD	Top of Descent
UFDR	Universal Flight Data Recorder
UTC	Universal Time Coordinated
VBV	Variable Bleed Valve
VHF	Very High Frequency
VOR	Very High Frequency Omni Range
VSV	Variable Stator Vane

FIG 1: SHOWING CRASH-SITE OF G-OBME

Air Accidents Investigation Branch

Aircraft Accident Report No: 4/90
(EW/C1095)

Registered owner		Kommanditbolaget 11, Malmo, Sweden,
Operator:		British Midland Airways Ltd
Aircraft	*Type:*	Boeing 737
	Model:	Series 400
	Nationality:	British
	Registration:	G-OBME
Place of accident:		½ nm east of East Midlands Airport
		Latitude: 52° 49' 54" N
		Longitude: 001° 20' 54"W
Date and time:		8 January 1989 at 2025 hrs
		All times in this report are UTC

SYNOPSIS

The accident was notified to the Air Accidents Investigation Branch during the evening of the 8 January 1989 and the investigation was initiated on-site at 0040 hours on the morning of the 9 January. The AAIB Investigating Team comprised Mr E J Trimble (Investigator in Charge), Mr J D Payling (Operations), Mr C G Pollard (Engineering, Powerplants), Mr S W Moss (Engineering, Systems), Mr R D G Carter (Engineering, Structures), Wing Commander D Anton, RAF Institute of Aviation Medicine (IAM) (Survivability), Mr P F Sheppard and Miss A Evans (Flight Recorders). In addition Mr R Green, Head of the Psychology Department of the RAF IAM, was co-opted to investigate the human factor aspects of this accident and Captain M Vivian of the Civil Aviation Authority (CAA) Flight Operations Department was co-opted to assist the final assessment of the operational aspects.

G-OBME left Heathrow Airport for Belfast at 1952 hrs with 8 crew and 118 passengers (including 1 infant) on board. As the aircraft was climbing through 28,300 feet the outer panel of one blade in the fan of the No 1 (left) engine detached. This gave rise to a series of compressor stalls in the No 1 engine, which resulted in airframe shuddering, ingress of smoke and fumes to the flight deck and fluctuations of the No 1 engine parameters. Believing that the No 2 engine had suffered damage, the crew throttled that engine back and subsequently shut it down. The shuddering caused by the surging of the No 1 engine ceased as soon as the No 2 engine was throttled back, which persuaded the crew that they had dealt correctly with the emergency. They then shut down the No 2 engine. The No 1 engine operated apparently normally after the initial period of severe vibration and during the subsequent descent.

The crew initiated a diversion to East Midlands Airport and received radar direction from air traffic control to position the aircraft for an instrument approach to land on runway 27. The approach continued normally, although with a high level of vibration from the No 1 engine, until an abrupt reduction of power, followed by a fire warning, occurred on this engine at a point 2.4 nm from the runway. Efforts to restart the No 2 engine were not successful.

The aircraft initially struck a field adjacent to the eastern embankment of the M1 motorway and then suffered a second severe impact on the sloping western embankment of the motorway.

39 passengers died in the accident and a further 8 passengers died later from their injuries. Of the other 79 occupants, 74 suffered serious injury.

The cause of the accident was that the operating crew shut down the No 2 engine after a fan blade had fractured in the No 1 engine. This engine subsequently suffered a major thrust loss due to secondary fan damage after power had been increased during the final approach to land.

The following factors contributed to the incorrect response of the flight crew:

1. The combination of heavy engine vibration, noise, shuddering and an associated smell of fire were outside their training and experience.

2. They reacted to the initial engine problem prematurely and in a way that was contrary to their training.

3. They did not assimilate the indications on the engine instrument display before they throttled back the No 2 engine.

4. As the No 2 engine was throttled back, the noise and shuddering associated with the surging of the No 1 engine ceased, persuading them that they had correctly identified the defective engine.

5. They were not informed of the flames which had emanated from the No 1 engine and which had been observed by many on board, including 3 cabin attendants in the aft cabin.

31 Safety Recommendations were made during the course of this investigation.

1. FACTUAL INFORMATION

1.1 History of the flight

The aircraft was engaged on a double shuttle between London Heathrow Airport and Belfast Aldergrove Airport. It landed at Heathrow at 1845 hrs on completion of the first shuttle flight and took off again for Belfast at 1952 hrs, with the first officer handling the aircraft. After take-off the aircraft climbed initially to 6,000 feet where it levelled-off above a layer of stratocumulus cloud for 2 minutes, before receiving clearance to climb to flight level (FL) 120. Soon afterwards, at 1958 hrs, clearance was passed to climb to FL 350 on a direct track to the very high frequency omni-range beacon (VOR) at Trent.

At 2005.05 hrs, as the aircraft was climbing through FL283 some 20 nm south-south-east of East Midlands Airport, the crew experienced moderate to severe vibration and a smell of fire. The area microphone for the cockpit voice recorder (CVR) picked up a sound of vibration or 'rattling' at this time and the flight data recorder (FDR) showed significant fluctuations in lateral and longitudinal accelerations. There was no fire warning or any other visual or aural warning on the flight deck. The commander stated afterwards that he saw and smelt air conditioning smoke. The first officer later remembered only a strong smell of burning. Replay of the FDR showed that severe vibration had occurred in the No 1 (left) engine at this time, accompanied by marked fluctuations in fan speed (N1), a rise in exhaust gas temperature (EGT) and low, fluctuating, fuel flow.

The commander took control of the aircraft and disengaged the autopilot. He later stated that he looked at the engine instruments but did not gain from them any clear indication of the source of the problem. He also later stated that he thought that the smoke and fumes were coming forward from the passenger cabin, which, from his appreciation of the aircraft air conditioning system, led him to suspect the No 2 (right) engine. The first officer also said that he monitored the engine instruments and, when asked by the commander which engine was causing the trouble, he said 'IT'S THE LE ... IT'S THE RIGHT ONE.', to which the commander responded by saying 'OKAY, THROTTLE IT BACK'. The autothrottle was then disengaged and the No 2 engine was throttled back. The first officer later had no recollection of what it was he saw on the engine instruments that led him to make his assessment. The commander's instruction to throttle back was given some 19 seconds after the onset of the vibration when, according to the FDR, the No 2 engine was operating with steady engine indications. During the 11 seconds that elapsed between the disengagement of the autopilot and the throttling back of the No 2 engine, the aircraft rolled slowly to the left through 16 degrees but the commander made no corrective movement of aileron or rudder.

Within 1 to 2 seconds of the closure of the No 2 throttle the aircraft rolled level again, the fluctuations in lateral and longitudinal accelerations ceased, the No 1 engine fan speed settled at a level 3% below its previous stable speed, and the EGT stabilised at 50°C above its previous level. These engine parameters remained fairly stable for a further minute until the commander reduced power on that engine for the descent. However, the indicated vibration remained at maximum and the indicated fuel flow behaved erratically. The commander later stated that the action of closing the No 2 engine throttle reduced the smell and the visual signs of smoke and that he remembered no continuation of the vibration after the No 2 throttle was closed.

Immediately after throttling back the No 2 engine, the first officer advised London Air Traffic Control (LATCC) that they had an emergency situation which looked like an engine fire. The commander then ordered the first officer: 'SHUT IT DOWN'. This order was given 43 seconds after the onset of the vibration but its execution was delayed when the commander said 'SEEMS TO BE RUNNING ALRIGHT NOW. LETS JUST SEE IF IT COMES IN'. The shutdown was further delayed as the first officer responded to radio messages from LATCC which advised the crew of the aircraft's position and asked which alternate airfield they wished to go to. The first officer said that it looked as if they would take it to Castle Donington (East Midlands Airport) but LATCC were to stand by. At about this time a flight attendant used the cabin address system to advise the passengers to fasten their seat belts. The first officer then told the commander that he was about to start the 'Engine Failure and Shutdown' checklist, saying at the same time 'SEEMS WE HAVE STABILISED. WE'VE STILL GOT THE SMOKE'. Again, action on the checklist was suspended as the commander called British Midland Airways (BMA) Operations at East Midlands Airport to advise his company of the situation. 2 minutes 7 seconds after the start of the vibration and during a short pause in radio communications with BMA Operations, the fuel cock (start lever) of the No 2 engine was closed and the auxiliary power unit (APU) was started. Shortly afterwards BMA Operations transmitted to the aircraft: 'DIVERT TO EAST MIDLANDS PLEASE'.

The commander later recollected that, as soon as the No 2 engine had been shut down, all evidence of smell and smoke cleared from the flight deck, and this finally convinced him that the action he had taken was correct. Shortly afterwards power was further reduced on the No 1 engine, which continued to operate at reduced power with no symptoms of unserviceability other than a higher than normal level of indicated vibration and increased fuel flow. This high level of vibration continued for a further 3 minutes and then fell progressively until it reached a level of 2 units on the cockpit indicator, still a little higher than normal. After the accident, the commander stated that during the remainder of the flight the indications that he had from the engine instruments, or any other source, were such as to indicate that the emergency had been successfully concluded and that the No 1 engine was operating normally.

In the cabin, the passengers and the cabin attendants heard an unusual noise accompanied by moderate to severe vibration. Some passengers were also aware of what they described as smoke, but none could describe its colour or density. They described the smell of burning as 'rubber', 'oil' and 'hot metal'. Many saw signs of fire from the left engine, which they described variously as 'fire', 'torching' or 'sparks'. Several of the cabin attendants described the noise as a low, repetitive thudding, 'like a car backfiring', and one described how the shuddering shook the walls of the forward galley. The three flight attendants in the rear of the cabin saw evidence of fire from the No 1 engine, and two of them briefly saw light coloured smoke in the cabin. Soon after the No 2 engine was shut down the commander called the flight service manager (FSM) to the flight deck and asked him 'DID YOU GET SMOKE IN THE CABIN BACK THERE?', to which the FSM replied 'WE DID, YES'. The commander then instructed the FSM to clear up the cabin and pack everything away. About one minute later the FSM returned to the flight deck and said 'SORRY TO TROUBLE YOU .. THE PASSENGERS ARE VERY VERY PANICKY'. The commander then broadcast to the passengers on the cabin address system that there was trouble with the right engine which had produced some smoke in the cabin, that the engine was now shut down and that they could expect to land at East Midlands Airport in about 10 minutes. The flight attendants who saw signs of fire on the left engine later stated that they had not heard the commander's reference to the right engine. However, many of the passengers who saw fire from the No 1 engine heard and were puzzled by the commander's reference to the right engine, but none brought the discrepancy to the attention of the cabin crew, even though several were aware of continuing vibration. The smell of smoke, however, had dissipated by the time the commander made this announcement.

The No 2 engine was shut down approximately 5 nm south of East Midlands Airport. Having cleared the aircraft to turn right and descend to FL 100, London ATC passed control to Manchester ATC, who passed headings to steer for the aircraft to descend to the north of East Midlands Airport (EMA) and to fly to the centreline of the localizer of the instrument landing system (ILS) for runway 27. During the descent the commander did not re-engage the autopilot but flew the aircraft manually, whilst the first officer dealt with radio communications. Flight deck workload remained high as the first officer obtained details of the actual weather at East Midlands and attempted without success to programme the flight management system to display the landing pattern at East Midlands. This last activity engaged the first officer's attention for 2 minutes. At 2012.28 hrs the commander attempted to review their situation, saying 'NOW WHAT INDICATIONS DID WE ACTUALLY GET (IT) JUST RAPID VIBRATIONS IN THE AEROPLANE - SMOKE ...'. His discussion with the first officer was then interrupted by ATC messages passing a new radar heading, further descent clearance to FL40 and instructions for the aircraft to change radio frequency to East Midlands (Castledon) approach control. As soon as contact was established on the new frequency the first officer began to read the one-engine inoperative descent and approach checklist. Radio calls again interrupted this activity when the Castledon approach controller asked the commander to make a test call to the aerodrome fire service, which he did, but received no response. The approach checklist was finally completed at 2017.33 hrs, when the aircraft was 15 nm from touchdown, descending through 6,500 feet above mean sea level (amsl). One minute later the commander accepted a new radar vector of 220° to take the aircraft south of the extended runway centreline in order to increase his distance from touchdown, and shortly afterwards called for the wing flaps to be selected to 1°. Throughout the descent there were distractions from a small number of other aircraft making radio calls on the same frequency as that being used by G-OBME.

When the aircraft was 13 nm from touchdown on this new heading, and descending to 3,000 feet amsl, ATC advised a right turn to bring the aircraft back to the centreline. At 2020.03 hrs, during this turn, power was increased on the No 1 engine to level the aircraft momentarily at 3,000 feet and maximum indicated vibration was again recorded on the FDR. The aircraft was then cleared to descend to 2000 feet and the commander began a slow descent, calling successively for 2° and then 5° of flap. After joining the centreline, at 2000 feet above ground level (agl), the commander called for the landing gear to be lowered and, as he passed the outer marker at 4.3 nm from touchdown, called for 15° of flap. One minute later, at 2023.49 hrs, when the aircraft was 2.4 nm from touchdown at a height of 900 feet agl, there was an abrupt decrease in power from the No 1 engine. The commander called immediately for the first officer to relight (ie restart) the other engine and the first officer attempted to comply. The commander then raised the nose of the aircraft in an effort to reach the runway. 17 seconds after the power loss the fire warning system operated on the No 1 engine and 7 seconds later the ground proximity warning system (GPWS) glideslope warning sounded and continued with increasing repetitive frequency as the aircraft descended below the glidepath. The commander ordered the first officer not to carry out the fire drill. At 2024.33 hrs the commander broadcast a crash warning on the cabin address system using the words 'PREPARE FOR CRASH LANDING' (repeated). 2 seconds later, as the airspeed fell below 125 kts, the stall warning stick shaker[1] operated, and continued to operate until the

---

[1] Stick shaker. An artificial stall warning device that causes both control columns to vibrate when the airspeed falls within not less than 7% of the actual stall speed.

aircraft struck the ground at 2024.43 hrs. The last airspeed recorded on the FDR was 115 kts. No power became available from the No 2 engine before the aircraft struck the ground.

The initial ground impact was in a nose-high attitude on level ground just to the east of the M1 motorway. The aircraft then passed through trees and suffered its second and major impact 70 metres to the west and 10 metres lower, on the western (*ie* northbound) carriageway of the M1 motorway and the lower part of the western embankment. The fuselage was extensively disrupted, and the aircraft came to rest entirely on the wooded western embankment approximately 900 metres from the threshold of runway 27 and displaced 50 metres to the north of the extended runway centreline.

Several of the passengers described heavy vibration immediately prior to the impact and one passenger, in the rear of the aircraft, described the vibration as being severe enough to open the overhead lockers and cause them to spill contents. Passengers in the rear of the aircraft described two distinct impacts; those in the front appeared only to have been aware of the final impact.

Ground witnesses who saw the final approach saw clear evidence of fire associated with the left engine. The intake area of the engine was filled with yellow/orange fire, and flames were observed streaming aft from the nacelle, pulsating in unison with 'thumping noises'. Metallic 'rattling' was also heard, and flaming debris was seen falling from the aircraft.

After the aircraft crashed, a BMA engineer entered the flight deck and switched off the main battery switch and the standby power switch. He later returned to the flight deck and switched off the engine ignition (engine start switches) and the fuel booster pumps. The engine start levers (fuel valves) were found in the cutoff position. No witness was found who could testify to having moved them.

1.2 Injuries to Persons

	Crew	*Passengers*	*Others*
Fatal	nil	47	Nil
Serious	7	66 + 1 infant	Nil
Minor/none	1	4	

5 firemen suffered minor injuries during the rescue operation.

1.3 Damage to aircraft

G-OBME suffered severe impact damage and the fuselage broke into 3 main sections (Fig 1). The nose section travelled the greatest distance up the western embankment of the M1, the centre-section remained upright with the wings attached and the tail-section buckled over, and to the right of, that section of fuselage just aft of the wing.

Both engines were found at their wing stations, although they had suffered ground impact damage. Most of the components which had separated were found around the impact site. Several small pieces of the No 1 engine were recovered from a site about 3 kilometres to the east, under the final flight path.

1.4 Other damage

During the crash sequence the rear fuselage underside and main landing gear of the aircraft scraped the surface off a small area of a grass field next to the eastern embankment of the motorway. The aircraft then demolished a 10 metre section of wooden fencing at the crest of the eastern embankment, before cutting a 40 metre swathe through the tops of trees growing on the embankment.

As the aircraft descended across the carriageways it destroyed one central lamp standard and a detached landing gear leg struck and deformed the central reservation barrier. The aircraft then slid up the western embankment, destroying trees over an area approximately 40 metres square.

1.5 Personnel information

1.5.1

Commander:	Male, aged 43 years
Licence:	Airline Transport Pilot's Licence first issued 9 August 1977, valid until 8 August 1997
Aircraft ratings:	Auster, Dakota/C47, BAC 1-11, Viscount, DC-9, F 27, Boeing 737 Series 200, 300 and 400
Medical certificate:	Class One issued 24 August 1988 with no limitations, valid until 31 March 1989
Instrument rating:	Valid until 15 November 1989
Last base check:	16 October 1988
Last route check:	12 November 1988
Last emergencies check:	26 April 1988

Flying experience:	Total all types:	13,176 hours
	Total on B737:	763 hours
	Total last 90 days:	112 hours
	Total last 28 days:	12 hours
Duty time:	On leave from 17 December 1988. On duty 1430 hrs 8 January 1989	

The commander underwent initial flying training at The London School of Flying in 1964/65 before joining BMA in 1966. He was employed as a first officer until he passed a command course in 1974, and then as a captain successively on Viscount, F27 and DC9 aircraft until 1987. He completed a conversion course to the Boeing 737 Series 300 on 13 December 1987 and a further short course on the Series 400 aircraft on 17 October 1988. He had flown 23 hours on the Series 400 aircraft.

1.5.2 *First Officer* Male, aged 39 years

Licence: Airline Transport Pilot's Licence first issued 12 August 1986 and valid until 11 August 1996

Aircraft ratings: PA 28, Cessna 402B, 402C and 404, Shorts SD 330 Series 100 and 200, Shorts SD 360 Series 100 and 200, Boeing 737 Series 200, 300 and 400

Medical certificate: Class One issued 25 August 1988 with no limitations, valid until 31 March 1989

Instrument rating: Valid until 13 August 1989

Last base check: 22 December 1988

Last route check: 5 November 1988

Last emergencies check: 20 July 1988

Flying experience:	Total all types:	3,290 hours
	Total on B737:	192 hours
	Total last 90 days:	104 hours
	Total last 28 days:	37 hours
Duty time:	On duty 1200 hours 8 January 1989 (positioning to London / Heathrow from Belfast.)	

The first officer underwent flying training at Simulated Flight Training at Hurn Airport in 1983. He was then employed by several independent public air transport companies before joining BMA in 1988, where he was initially employed as a first officer on the Shorts SD 360. He received conversion training on the Boeing 737-300 from his company during June and July 1988. He was checked as competent to act as a first officer on the B737 Series 300 on 28 July 1988 and on the B737 Series 400 on 17 October 1988. He had flown 53 hours on the Series 400 aircraft.

1.5.3   *Cabin attendants (listed in order of joining BMA)*

    Flight Service Manager: Male, aged 27 years
    Date joined BMA: 5 May 1986
    Qualified on B737:   4 November 1987
    Last emergencies check: 5 January 1989
    Rest period before flight: 14 hours 10 minutes

    Cabin attendant 1:   Female, aged 24 years
    Date joined BMA: 11 May 1987
    Qualified on B737:   20 April 1988
    Last emergencies check: 25 August 1988
    Rest period before flight: 16 hours 50 minutes

    Cabin attendant 2:   Female, 27 years
    Date joined BMA: 30 March 1988
    Qualified on B737:   25 August 1988
    Last emergencies check: 29 September 1988
    Rest period before flight: 15 hours 20 minutes

    Cabin attendant 3:   Male, aged 29 years
    Date joined BMA: 5 October 1988
    Qualified on B737:   14 December 1988
    Last emergencies check: 21 December 1988
    Rest period before flight: More than 2 days

    Cabin attendant 4:   Female, aged 22 years
    Date joined BMA: 23 November 1988
    Qualified on B737:   14 December 1988
    Last emergencies check: 21 December 1988
    Rest period before flight: 19 hours 10 minutes

    Cabin attendant 5:   Male, aged 23 years
    Date joined BMA: 19 October 1988
    Qualified on B737:   14 December 1988
    Last emergencies check: 21 December 1988
    Rest period before flight: 19 hours 30 minutes

1.6 Aircraft information

1.6.1 *Leading particulars*

Type:	Boeing 737 Series 400
Constructor's number:	23867
Date of Manufacture:	1988
Certificate of Registration:	Registered in the name of British Midland Airways Ltd.
Certificate of Airworthiness:	Issued on 3 November 1988 in the Transport Category (Passenger) and valid until 2 November 1989.
Total airframe hours:	521
Engines (2):	CFM 56-3C high by-pass turbofan engines No 1 Serial No:- 725-127 No 2 Serial No:- 725-130
Maximum weight authorised for take-off:	64,636 kg (142,496lb)
Actual take-off weight:	49,940 kg (110,098 lb)
Maximum weight authorised for landing:	54,884 kg (120,997 lb)
Estimated weight at the time of the accident:	48,900 kg (107,805 lb)
Estimated fuel remaining at the time of the accident:	4,210 kg (9,281 lb)
Centre of gravity (CG) limits at accident weight:	8-27.6% mean aerodynamic chord (MAC)
CG at time of accident:	15.7% MAC

1.6.2   *Description of engines*

General features   (See sectional view of engine at Appendix 1, fig 1)

The CFM 56-3C-1 is a two shaft, high by-pass ratio turbofan engine of modular construction, rated at 23,500 lbs thrust for take-off. The 38 blade fan and 3 stage low pressure compressor (LPC or booster) are driven by a four stage low pressure turbine (LPT) powered by the exhaust gases of the core engine. The 60 inch diameter fan produces about 80% of the total engine thrust, which is almost directly related to fan speed (N1). The thrust is regulated by control of the core engine which has an annular type combustion chamber and a 9 stage axial flow high pressure compressor (HPC) driven by a single stage high pressure turbine (HPT). The fuel and airflow control of the core engine is governed by a Woodward hydromechanical main engine control (MEC) which, in conjunction with the electronic power management controller (PMC), adjusts the core speed (N2) to give the fan speed/thrust demanded by the pilot via the thrust lever. The MEC and fuel pump are driven by the core engine via an accessory gearbox, mounted on the lower left side of the fan case, which also drives a generator and hydraulic pump to provide electrical and hydraulic power for aircraft services. High pressure air is bled from the core compressor to provide cabin air conditioning and other aircraft pneumatic services.

A brief development history of this engine type is given at paragraph 1.17.6.

1.6.3   *Engine instrument system (EIS).*

The EIS provided a solid-state display of engine-related parameters which replaced the earlier array of individual hybrid electro-mechanical instruments with two display units. One unit displayed the primary parameters and the other displayed the secondary parameters (see Appendix 2, figs 1, 2 & 3).

1.6.3.1   *EIS primary display*

The following engine parameters were displayed:-

> fan speed (N1)
> exhaust gas temperature (EGT)
> core speed (N2)
> fuel flow (FF)

These parameters were presented in both analogue and digital form by the use of light-emitting diodes (LEDs). The analogue presentation utilised 81 bars of LEDs, arranged radially around the outside of each display scale. The bars illuminated one at a time, in sequence, to simulate the movement of the end of a pointer sweeping around the outside of the display scale. Other design features concerning the movement of the LED 'pointer' were also incorporated, in order to mimic the behaviour of an electro-mechanical indicator.

The digital presentation, which was common to both the EIS and the earlier hybrid instruments, was situated in the centre of each indicator and also used LEDs. These simulated the rolling drum mechanism used on conventional electro-mechanical indicators by making the display digits appear to 'roll' past the viewing aperture, with half of each adjacent digit visible in the last 'window'. This preserved the rate and direction of motion cues available to the pilot. Red exceedance warning lights were positioned above each N1, N2 and EGT display and were designed to illuminate whilst the affected parameter remained above the 'red-line' limit. Exceedance information was stored in a non-volatile memory which could be interrogated by maintenance personnel.

Both N1 displays also featured movable LED cursors to indicate 'target N1', which could be set manually by using two knobs located in the lower corners of the display bezel, or automatically by the flight management computer. When set manually, this information was repeated in digital form in two windows at the top of the display. A button at the bottom of the display bezel was used to change the reading of fuel flow rate to fuel used. After 10 seconds the displays automatically reverted to 'fuel flow'.

A three-character display at the top of the primary EIS annunciated the thrust mode as selected through the flight management computer.

An 'abnormal start' algorithm was incorporated which would cause the EGT digits to flash if the unit detected conditions such as incipient 'hot', or 'hung', starts.

1.6.3.2   *EIS secondary display*

The secondary EIS displayed the following parameters for both engines, in analogue form only:-

> engine oil pressure
> engine oil temperature
> engine vibration
> A and B system hydraulic pressure

The system of scales and LED 'pointers' was similar to that used in the primary display but there were no digital repeaters and, since the secondary displays were smaller (see Appendix 2, fig 3), there were 31 bars of LEDs to simulate the pointer. There were digital readouts of engine oil quantity, hydraulic quantity (% full) and total air temperature (TAT). In common with normal practice on engine instruments classified as secondary, there were no exceedence lights on the secondary EIS.

1.6.3.3   *Features common to both EIS displays*

Both primary and secondary displays were fitted with numerous sensors which varied the LED brightness according to the amount of ambient light falling on the display. Thus the displays were designed to remain legible under all conditions, including situations where the ambient light fell differentially across the displays. For night operation the scales were edge-lit and their brightness was controlled by the crew, through the normal panel lighting control.

Both displays featured built-in test equipment (BITE), activation of which would cause the unit to run through a test programme. Use of BITE was restricted to ground maintenance only.

Engine parameters were received by the EIS direct from the sensors on the engines with the exception of vibration, where signals from the sensors were processed by the airborne vibration monitor (AVM) before being passed to the EIS (see paragraph 1.6.4). The EIS fed its output of these parameters (except vibration and engine oil temperature) to the flight control computers, the flight data acquisition unit (FDAU) and the stall warning computer, as required.

The EIS was connected to the aircraft wiring through 4 connectors located on the back of each unit. The input and output wiring associated with each engine was fed through a discrete connector, which had a baulk system known as 'clocking'. This physically prevented inadvertent cross-connection.

The EIS reacted to input system failures in different ways, depending upon the type of input and the nature of the failure. In all cases where a definite system failure was detected, the EIS would delete the affected parameters from the display.

1.6.4   Airborne vibration monitoring (AVM) system

The AVM system continuously displays engine vibration levels via the indicators on the secondary EIS. This information is also output to the FDAU for transmission to the digital flight data recorder and stored as 'peak per flight' values in the non-volatile memory of the AVM module in the electronics bay.

The AVM module will, however, only output up to a certain maximum value, equivalent to a reading of 5 units on the EIS scale. Vibration levels above this value are displayed as 5 units and there is no additional indication if the true vibration level exceeds 5 units.

Two piezoelectric-type vibration sensors are fitted on each engine; one on the No 1/No 2 (front) bearing support and one on the turbine rear frame, both sensing engine rotor vibration - see Appendix 1, fig 1. The AVM is also supplied with information concerning the rotational speeds of the low pressure (LP) and high pressure (HP) spools (N1 and N2). It uses this information to 'track' any vibration signals and to filter out those not associated with either N1 or N2 speeds. This has helped to considerably reduce problems encountered with earlier systems whereby spurious vibration signals from a source other than the rotating assemblies could be indicated to the crew.

Although genuine vibration signals from both sensors monitoring both spools are output to the FDR, only those from the No 1/No 2 bearing sensor are actually displayed to the crew on the EIS. The higher value of HP or LP shaft vibration will be indicated.

The nominal reading of 5 units is not only the maximum the EIS would display but is also the maximum the AVM will output. Any fault condition which could cause the AVM to output more than 522.5 microamps nominal (equivalent to 5.25 vibration units) will be interpreted by the EIS as an interface failure and the display pointer will be driven to the zero position, held for 2 seconds and then disappear.

The vibration units are non-dimensional and the figure of 5 units represents a level at which vibration should be apparent through the airframe, but of itself should not jeopardise the integrity of the engine.

1.6.5 *Engine fire and overheat detection system*

The engine fire and overheat detection system used a continuous loop method as the basis for the detector elements. Each element had a heat-sensing device consisting of an inconel sheath which contained a ceramic-like thermistor material in which two fine wire conductors were imbedded. As the temperature of the element rose, the electrical resistance between the conductors fell and, at a set threshold, the appropriate warnings were activated by the control module located in the electronics bay.

There were two 'loops', A and B, comprising each element. Both loops normally worked together, although either loop A or B could be selected individually to cater for unserviceability of one loop. There were four elements mounted on support tubes located in each engine nacelle and positioned to cover those areas most at risk from a fire or overheat condition (see Appendix 2, fig 4). Each element differed not only with respect to its length and formed shape, but also three of the four elements used a different composition of the Thermistor core, thus allowing the system to trigger at different alarm temperatures.

The purpose of the system was not simply to detect engine fires but also to provide warnings of overtemperature conditions, such as bleed air duct leaks. In the latter case, an overheat condition would cause illumination of the MASTER CAUTION light, OVHT/DET annunciator and the associated engine OVERHEAT light. An engine fire condition would be indicated by illumination of the master FIRE WARNING, the associated engine fire switch light and the sound of the alarm bell. Whilst the FIRE WARNING light and the bell could be cancelled by the crew, the fire switch light would remain illuminated until the element temperature had dropped below its threshold.

The system could be tested from the flight deck by activating a test switch. This would switch both loops from their normal monitoring circuits to a test circuit which simulated the pattern of falling resistance induced by a fire. During such a test, the crew would expect to receive all of the above warnings, in addition to others associated with APU and landing wheel well protection, if the system was serviceable.

The continuous loop system had the inherent ability to detect overheats and fires, even if an element was severed, since both ends of the element would continue to function. The function test described above would indicate such a fault. False warnings were catered for by a discriminator circuit which was designed to recognise the instantaneous drop in resistance caused by a short circuit, compared with the pattern of falling resistance over a finite time associated with a genuine warning.

1.6.6 *Air conditioning system*

The air conditioning and pressurisation system used pneumatic air drawn from the compressor stages of the engines (see Appendix 2, fig 5) or from the APU. The main supply was obtained from the 5th stage of each engine compressor, but at low engine thrust settings or at idle, the 9th stage bleed automatically opened to maintain the supply.

The pneumatic supply from each engine was ducted to its associated air conditioning pack, which used the energy of the hot, high pressure, pneumatic air to cool it to a level suitable for use in the passenger cabin and the flight deck. In normal operation, the two systems operated virtually independently as far as the conditioned air mix manifold (Appendix 2, fig 5), although a normally closed isolation valve could be opened to cross-feed pneumatic air, or to duct APU air into the right-hand system.

A relatively small amount of un-conditioned air was, however, bled off both systems upstream of the packs and mixed together to provide a source of 'trim air'. This air was used to raise the ambient temperature locally in any of the three zones into which the passenger cabin/flight deck was divided for air-conditioning purposes.

As shown in Appendix 2, fig 5, conditioned air from the right engine was ducted into the mix manifold only and thence to the forward and aft passenger cabin zones. Conditioned air from the left engine was also ducted into the mix manifold, but a tapping was taken before this to direct unmixed air to the flight deck. The reason for this was that the passenger cabin also received filtered, recirculated air driven by two recirculation fans which discharged into the mix manifold. With this arrangement, and both systems operating, the crew would receive mostly fresh, unrecirculated air.

A separate subsystem circulated air from the flight deck around the equipment in the electronics bay and the flight deck for cooling purposes. Air used in this subsystem was not, however, a source of transfer from such zones into the flight deck.

1.6.7 *Cabin floor structure*

The structure of the cabin floor in the Boeing 737-400 is typical of this class of aircraft. It consists principally of a series of transverse floor beams which are mechanically attached, at each end, to the circumferential fuselage frames. The floor beams are, in general, placed at 20 inch spacing. The cabin flooring panels and longitudinal seat track members are secured on top of these beams. Thus the vertical inertial loads from the passenger seats and other track-mounted furnishings are supported by the beams and the longitudinal loads are carried out to the cabin sidewalls through the flooring panels. The lateral loads from the track-mounted seats are carried out to the fuselage frames both by the floor panels and by the transverse floor beams. The only area of passenger seating which differs from this scheme is the over-wing section (fuselage station 540 to 727) where the loads from the seat tracks are reacted directly by intercostals attached to the upper surface of the wing centre-section.

In the forward section (station 360 to 540) the seat track member is of an I-section, heavily tapered (Appendix 3, fig 1) to pass across the transverse floor beams. In the aft section (station 727 onwards) the arrangement is similar but the bottom flange of the I-member passes through a cut-out in the floor beam (fig 2).

1.6.8. *Seats*

1.6.8.1 *Flight deck crew seats*

The pilots' seats were type 3A090 units built by Ipeco Europe Ltd. These crew seats were designed to be positioned on floor-mounted tracks and the complete seat assembly comprises two basic light-alloy structures: the upper structure contains the controls for the back cushion and lumbar support and the seat base contains the controls for the vertical seat height and horizontal track lock. The harness is conventional, with a buckle on one of the 2 lap straps, 2 shoulder straps each controlled by an inertia reel and with a crotch strap mounted on the seat pan.

Height adjustment is achieved by a parallelogram linkage of four lift-arms connecting the seat pan to the seat base and the height is locked by two height lock pins which engage in any pair of a series of holes in the height lock plates. Horizontal adjustment is effected by the motion of four bogie assemblies along the floor-mounted tracks and the fore-aft position is locked by a single track lock pin which engages in any one of a series of holes in the top of one of these tracks.

This seat type was approved by the CAA as meeting the appropriate Joint Airworthiness Requirements (JARs), which included the inertial loading provisions (paragraph 1.17.11), and was approved by the Federal Aviation Administration (FAA) in July 1986 as meeting the '9g static' provisions of TSO-C39a. This model of seat had, however, undergone development testing to the dynamic '16g' level of Federal Airworthiness Requirement (FAR) Amendment 25-64.

1.6.8.2 *Cabin attendant seats*

The aircraft had seating for 5 cabin attendants, arranged as 2 double seats and 1 single seat, all of which were aft-facing (Appendix 3, fig 3). Both double seats were mounted on the left-hand side of the aircraft, one just forward of the forward/left passenger door and the other just forward of the rear/left passenger door. The single attendant seat was mounted just forward of the rear/right passenger door.

These cabin attendant seats were model 2501 units, built by Trans-Aero Industries. The design includes full lap and shoulder harness and the seat pan automatically folds to the vertical position when the seat is not occupied. This model of seat was tested and approved in 1988 to the standards of FAA TS0-C39b and British Civil Airworthiness Requirements (BCAR) sections D3-8 and D4-4.

1.6.8.3   Passenger seats

At the time of the accident, G-OBME was configured with 156 passenger seats in a single class cabin with a total of 26 rows of pairs of triple seats as shown in Appendix 3, fig 3; the seats were of a type designated as the Model 4001 tourist seat by the manufacturer, Weber Aircraft, Inc. The seat rows were numbered conventionally from 1 to 27 (no row 13) from the front to the back of the aircraft. The seat pitch ranged from a maximum of 38 inches, for the 2 seat rows (12 and 14) next to the overwing emergency exits, to a minimum of 30 inches for row 27L. The remaining seat pitches were either 31 or 32 inches.

A typical Model 4001 triple seat is shown in Appendix 3, fig 4. The upholstered seat backs are pivoted at the lower end to break-over forward to ease emergency evacuation and to recline for passenger comfort. The exceptions in the G-OBME configuration were the seats adjacent to the overwing exits, rows 11, 12 and 14, where the seat backs were fixed. The detachable flotation cushions are supported on an alloy sheet suspended between the front and rear horizontal spars; these spars are mounted on a welded lower structure of hollow steel members of square section. Longitudinal locking to the seat tracks is at the rear attachments only and both the front and rear leg attachments are designed to allow for some angular deformation of the seat tracks in an impact. At the rear leg this flexibility is achieved by incorporating a pivot, and at the forward leg a U-strap, at the track attachment. The intent of the U-strap is principally to make the seat structure compliant with floor deformations and also to provide some load attenuation through the buckling mechanism.

The Model 4001 seats were approved by the FAA in December 1985 as meeting the performance standards of TSO-C39a and were approved by the CAA in February 1986 as meeting the more stringent requirements of BCAR Sections D3-8 and D4-4.

However, in addition to meeting the static loading criteria required by the above performance standards, the Model 4001 seat was tested at the FAA's Civil Aeromedical Institute (CAMI) in 1987 to the standards of FAR Part 25 Amendment 25-64, (paragraph 1.17.11). Although these 'Amendment 25-64' (dynamic loading criteria) tests were for development rather than certification, the results indicated that the seat would probably meet the certification criteria, although the testing was done prior to the issue of the requirements for seat deformation. Longitudinal impact tests on the front legs had shown buckling loads of around 4800 lbs for the U-strap at the base of the front leg; load cell measurements on the test leg showed, for the 16g / 44 feet per second (fps) decelerations, vertical loads in excess of this (4800 lbs) load.

1.6.9 Overhead stowage bins

The aircraft was equipped with a total of 30 overhead stowage bins in the passenger compartment. Of these, 26 were of 60 inch length and fully available for passenger hand baggage. The remaining two end pairs were shorter and partly used for cabin safety equipment.

The support system for a typical bin is shown at Appendix 3, fig 5. The forward inertial load is reacted by a diagonal tie, mounted at one end to stringer 6 or 7 in the fuselage crown and at the other end to a fitting on the upper surface of the bin. The vertical and lateral loads are reacted by short tie rods attached to the fuselage.

Certification to FAR 25 (paragraph 1.17.11) was based on substantiating tests performed by the manufacturer and witnessed by the FAA. Subsequent certification to the requirements of BCAR Section D3-8, which required combinations of loading to 9.0g resultants, was achieved by load analysis. The assumed baggage loading of the bins for certification and placard purposes, was 3 lbs per inch of length. Thus a 60 inch bin would be assumed to contain a maximum of 180 lbs of baggage.

1.6.10 Maintenance records

The aircraft was delivered from the Boeing Commercial Airplane Company to British Midland Airways (BMA) on 25 October 1988 and it entered revenue service on 4 November 1988.

At the time of the accident, it had accumulated some 521 total flying hours and 519 landings. The Certificate of Maintenance Review had been issued on 3 November 1988 and was valid to 2 March 1989.

The CAA approved BMA maintenance schedule, in addition to the usual daily and pre-flight checks, called for a 'minor service check 1' as the first scheduled maintenance inspection at 300 airframe hours. This had been accomplished on 9 December 1988 at 273 hours, and would have been repeated after a further 300 hours. No major component changes or rectification work had been required, or carried out, since delivery.

1.6.10.1 Aircraft Technical Log

This document is carried on the aircraft and one page is completed by the flight crew for each sector flown. In addition to routine information such as fuel uplift, sector times etc., any defects noticed are entered by the crew for action by the ground engineers. Defects which cannot be rectified at the time but which are considered acceptable for further flight(s) are also entered in the 'carried forward defect' (C/FD) section of the log until rectification can be accomplished. Where the nature of the defect is such that it involves unserviceability of a component or system, acceptability is assessed with regard to the 'Master Minimum Equipment List' (MMEL). The MMEL is approved by the CAA and lists system deficiencies with which the aircraft may still fly. It also details any special maintenance or operational procedures which must be observed as a result.

The Technical Log from G-OBME was examined with particular regard to those defect entries which related to the engines, or associated systems. There were no entries in the Air Transport Association (ATA) 100 engine chapters listing of relevance to this accident apart from Chapter 77 - Engine Indicating. These are reprinted verbatim below.

DATE	DEFECT	RECTIFICATION
11.12.88	At TOD[2] as power levers moved to flight idle, No 2 eng. vib.rdg.increased to approx.3.2 units and then reduced to 0.5 units.	BITE check of AVM carried out. SATIS; Trans. to c/fwd 15306/1 for monitor on the next few sectors and further reports.
11.12.88.	Ref. c/fwd 15306/1 No 2 eng. vib. rdg.at TOD increased to approx 2.8 units and then decreased to 0.5 units.	Noted with thanks. C/fwd remains open for fan blades to be cleaned and lubed i.a.w. MM[3]. BITE check carried out AVM limits found not exceeded.

No further flight crew comment was made on the subject of vibration of either engine until 17.12.88 when the following entry was recorded:-

| 17.12.88 | Re. cfd. 15306/2. When power levers moved to flight idle No 2 engine vibration increased to 3.2 units then reduced to 0.5 units. | Engine 2 fan blades removed/cleaned/ inspected iaw MM 71- 00-47 page 103 item 150. Re-installed after lubrication. Opportunity taken to action same lubrication to No 1 engine fan blades. All found satis. nil damaged. Vibration survey actioned as per MM 71-00-00 page 564 test 7 OAT +7°C (1024 Mb) (30.23 Hg.). No 2 found to be |

---

[2] Top of descent
[3] Maintenance Manual

satisfactory. During vibration survey eng. posn.1 vibration noted as steady 1 unit when throttle retarded to idle - no noticeable buzz. Post engine shutdown inspection carried out - nil untoward noted. Suspect possible grease settling. AVM interrogation showed nil problem. CFD 15307/3 raised for information/ flt. report. After flying day. (Vibration within limit).

The 'action taken' column also recorded the fact that the blade lubricant used was Molykote Rapid G RV D 61075. The above work was carried out on the night of 17/18 December and the first sector flown thereafter generated the following comments in the log:-

18.12.89.	No problems noted with either engine vibration after work carried out.	Noted. Based on flight evaluation and AVM interrogation-nil problems recorded considered satisfactory for service. CFD 15307/3 clrd.

No further comments concerning vibration of either engine were made prior to the accident. The results of the AVM interrogation covering the last 20 flights may be found in Appendix 2, fig 6.

Although there appeared to be no other entries relevant to this investigation, it was noted that a number of entries relating to the serviceability state of the No 1 engine cowl thermal anti-ice system (TAI) were made between 7 and 9 December 1988. Whilst it appeared at first that these entries could have indicated a possible source of ice ingestion into the No 1 engine, for reasons stated in part 2 of this report it does not now seem likely that this was the case and it is unnecessary to discuss them.

1.7 **Meteorological information**

1.7.1 *General situation*

The route from London to East Midlands lay within a moist west-south-westerly airstream, with a marked temperature inversion around 3,000 feet. The 0°C isotherm was at 10,000 ft. There was scattered stratus and stratocumulus cloud between 1,000 feet and 3,500 feet over the southern part of the route and a small probability of scattered stratocumulus up to 6,500 feet to the north, with thin patches of altocumulus/altostratus between 14,000 and 17,000 feet.

1.7.2   Actual weather conditions

The weather at Heathrow at 1950 hrs was reported as: wind velocity 230°/6 kts; visibility 6,000 metres; cloud 8 oktas stratus, base 500 feet; temperature +9° C; dew point +9° C; occasional light rain.

The actual weather at East Midlands Airport, reported to the pilot by ATC at 2011 hrs was: wind velocity 250°/10 kts; visibility 10 km; cloud 7 oktas, base 1,700 feet; temperature +9° C; QNH 1018.

1.8   Aids to navigation

A non-directional locator beacon (NDB), transmitting on 353.5 MHz and coded EME, was situated at the outer marker for runway 27 at East Midlands Airport, 4.3 nm from touchdown. The height of the 3° glideslope at the beacon was 1,710 feet amsl. Localizer and glidepath guidance for aircraft landing on runway 27 was provided by an instrument landing system (ILS); the localizer frequency was 109.9 MHz and the coding was I-EME. The NDB and the ILS were checked after the accident and found to be operating normally.

After the commander declared an emergency, the aircraft was given radar guidance from Manchester ATC and later East Midlands approach control for it to intercept the localizer for runway 27 at 6 nm from touchdown.

1.9   Communications

All communications were on very high frequency (VHF) radio and were satisfactory. Tape recordings were available of all frequencies used during the flight.

1.10   Aerodrome information

East Midlands Airport was a licensed public transport aerodrome constructed and equipped to international standards and operated by East Midlands International Airport plc. Runway 27 had a landing direction of 273° M, a threshold elevation of 280 feet amsl and a landing distance available of 2,280 metres. It had high intensity approach lights, with 5 crossbars, extending for 900 metres from the landing threshold; and low intensity centreline lighting, with one crossbar, extending for 420 metres. High intensity green lights with wing bars illuminated the threshold. Precision approach path indicators were installed for a 3° glideslope. All these lights were illuminated at the time of the accident.

The approach to runway 27 was over level terrain and passed over the M1 motorway, 1500 metres from touchdown. The southern edge of the village of Kegworth lay beneath the approach path to the east of the motorway.

1.11 Flight recorders

1.11.1 Flight Data Recorder (FDR)

The aircraft was fitted with a Sundstrand Universal Flight Data Recorder (UFDR) with a recording duration of 25 hours on magnetic (kapton) tape, and a Teledyne flight data acquisition unit (FDAU). A total of 63 parameters and 90 discrete events were recorded. In addition, the FDAU was equipped with a computer type 3½ inch 'floppy' disc which recorded 'snapshots' of routine information and data associated with specific exceedances. The FDR was located in the rear passenger cabin above the cabin roof, in line with the rear passenger exits.

The UFDR takes flight data into one of two internal memory stores, each holding about one second of data. When one memory store is full, the data flow is switched to the other store. While the data is being fed to this other store, the tape is rewound and the previous second of data is checked. A gap is left on the tape and the data in the first store is then written to the tape, and the first memory store emptied. This whole 'checkstroke' operation takes much less than one second to complete so that once the other store is full, data is switched back to the first store, and the other store is written to tape using the 'checkstroke' operation again to check its data. The procedure is then repeated.

Thus the UFDR tape is not running continuously. The tape first accelerates from stationary to 6 inches per second to read the previous data block, leaves an inter-record gap and then writes the new data block. The tape then slows and rewinds ready to begin the next 'checkstroke' operation. A total of 0.48 inches of tape is used to record one block of data and inter-record gap.

Data is formatted by the FDAU into one second subframes, each subframe begins with a synchronisation code, and is followed by the other parameters in a 64 word set format. The start of a block of data stored in the internal memory may not coincide with the start of a subframe, so when a block is recorded onto tape it is preceded by 'pre-amble' data bits and followed by 'post-amble' data bits. These bits of data are recognised during replay and removed, producing a continuous datastream. The start of a frame is identified from the synchronisation code.

When power is lost from the recorder, the data held in the volatile memory which has not been recorded on the tape is lost. As can be seen from the way in which data is temporarily stored on this UFDR and then recorded, this can mean that up to 1.2 seconds of data may be lost just before impact. Analysis of the raw signal on the UFDR tape from ME showed that the recorder had completed writing the contents of one memory store to tape, and this stopped at word 30 subframe 2. It was not possible, in this case, to know exactly how much data had been lost, and obviously as this was the last information prior to impact, such data could have been important to the investigation.

Where the parameters recorded were those presented to the crew on the EIS system, with the exception of vibration and engine oil temperature, the UFDR derived its information from the EIS. Each parameter from the EIS was treated in a similar way. Analogue signals from the sensors were supplied to the EIS where they underwent some signal conditioning and were digitised. The average of 8 samples was taken and passed through a software filter which provided a simple exponential lag. The filter output was subjected to a hysteresis level in order to improve the display stability. This hysteresis output was converted back to an analogue signal and fed to the FDAU then to the UFDR. The hysteresis output was also taken through further minor processing before being used to drive the counter display. It was converted to binary coded decimal (BCD) and stored in random access memory (RAM) in the required format for the counter display. The RAM contents were transferred to the display board under interrupt control.

The pointer display was also derived from signals taken from the filter output which were subject to a different hysteresis level before being scaled for the pointer, stored in RAM, and fed to the display under interrupt control. A simplified block diagram of the signal path is shown in Appendix 4, fig 1.

The vibration signals to the UFDR came directly from the AVM. All four vibration levels (LP compressor, LP turbine, HP compressor and HP turbine) were taken from the AVM and fed to the FDAU. They were then recorded at a sampling rate of once every 64 seconds. The route to the secondary EIS vibration displays was different in that the AVM sampled only the two compressor levels for each engine, it then detected the higher of these two levels and output only that signal to the EIS.

1.11.2   *FDR data analysis*

Appendix 4, fig 3 shows a plot of the engine parameters from 20.04 hrs as the aircraft was passing 26,000 ft at 300 kts calibrated airspeed (CAS) on the climb, until the final impact. The initial problem with the No 1 engine occurred at 28,300 ft, 295 kts CAS. The No 2 engine was throttled back as the aircraft began a descent from 30,000 ft and was then shut down at 20.07 hrs, 2 minutes and 7 seconds after the start of the first fluctuations of N1 on the No 1 engine. Power was reduced on the No 1 engine, and during the descent this engine was at flight idle for a period of 10 minutes. The power on the No 1 engine was increased at 20.20 hrs, at an altitude of 3000 ft, as the aircraft approached EMA.

Appendix 4, fig 4 shows the engine vibration parameters for the same period. These are recorded once every 64 seconds, but it can be seen that although the initial N1 fluctuations on No 1 engine lasted only some 22 seconds, the N1 compressor vibration levels on this engine remained at maximum for about 3 minutes. They decreased significantly once the No 1 engine was brought back to flight idle for the descent. Because of the low sampling rate for the vibration levels, it was not possible to determine exactly when the high vibration levels started. (see paragraph 1.16.3)

The maximum value which could be recorded by the FDR for vibration levels was 5 units. The values recorded for the N1 turbine and compressor levels on the No 1 engine corresponded to this maximum value after the initial engine vibration problem, and returned to this level some 4 minutes before impact as power was increased during the final approach. The actual level of vibration could have been much higher.

The No 1 engine N2 compressor and turbine vibration levels also showed a slight increase as the initial problem occurred and again when the power was increased on the No 1 engine during the final approach, although the levels were lower than those associated with the N1 compressor and turbine. The vibration levels on No 2 engine were normal throughout, and fell to zero once this engine had been shut down. The vibration level displayed to the crew on the vibration gauge would have been the N1 compressor level.

Appendix 4, fig 5 shows a more detailed plot of the initial engine parameters during the 'first event'. It shows that the No 1 engine fluctuations in N1, from the steady climb value of 99% to a minimum value of 74%, lasted for 22 seconds. There was also a slight rise and then fall in N2 from the steady climb value of 96%, to almost 97%, and back to around 93%. The EGT on No 1 engine also rose from the steady climb value of 780°C to a maximum of 900°C and then remained constant at around 830°C. No 1 engine fuel flow also dropped during this period. Just before the end of these fluctuations the autothrottle was disconnected and the power lever of the No 2 engine was moved to idle. At this time the No 1 engine stabilised at 96% N1, where it remained until it was throttled back for the descent. Throughout this time all indications on the No 2 engine remained steady and normal.

Appendix 4, fig 6 shows the final seconds of data from the FDR. The final sample of pressure altitude was 192 ft, based on 1013 mb. This corresponded to a height of 328 ft above mean sea level (amsl). The first impact of the aircraft with the ground occurred at 265 ft amsl. The last sample of radio altitude recorded was 30 ft above ground level (agl), and was recorded in word location 29, just before the recorder stopped at word 30.

The final second of data recorded on the FDR showed the aircraft in a nose-up pitch attitude of 15.1°, and a roll attitude of 4.8° to the right. The speed was 115 kts CAS. The final vane angle of attack recorded on the FDR was 26.4°, equivalent to 20.2° body angle of attack. The stick shaker was set to operate at body angles of attack above 16.7° and this angle was first exceeded 7 seconds before the FDR stopped. The recorded speed at this point was 124 kts CAS. This is shown in Appendix 4, fig 7 which gives the final flight path from a distance of 6 n.m. to the end of data. Stick shaker operation is not recorded on the FDR.

The actual speed at which the stick shaker operated would have depended on the rate of approach to the stall. In a steady stall entry, the stick shaker angle would correspond to a speed of 116.7 kts equivalent airspeed (EAS). The final speed on the FDR of 115 kts CAS was equivalent to 115 kts EAS for the prevailing flight conditions. For the configuration before impact the 1g stall alpha body angle of attack was 20.4°, which would correspond to a speed of 114.4 kts EAS in a normal stall entry.

1.11.3 *Cockpit voice recorder (CVR)*

The aircraft was equipped with a Fairchild model A100 CVR which was mounted at the rear of the aft baggage hold, on the right side. It was a slightly unusual installation in that it used a Sundstrand microphone monitor. This monitor contained the cockpit area microphone and was mounted in the overhead instrument panel on the flight deck.

The Fairchild CVR was of the usual 30 minute duration, endless loop type. It recorded on 4 tracks, the allocations of which were as follows:-

TRACK 1 - Commander's 'live' microphone (mic) and headset signals
TRACK 2 - Flight deck area mic.
TRACK 3 - Cabin address
TRACK 4 - Co-pilot's 'live' mic. and headset signals

The recorder was recovered from the aircraft on site. It was undamaged and a satisfactory replay was obtained using the AAIB's replay equipment. The audio quality of the CVR was good and a full transcript was produced for the period from the later stages of the climb until the end of recording.

1.11.4 *CVR transcript significant events*

From the CVR it was apparent that the first indication of any problem with the aircraft was as it approached its cleared flight level when, for a brief period, sounds of 'vibration' or 'rattling' could be heard on the flight deck. There was an exclamation and the first officer commented that they had 'GOT A FIRE'. The autopilot disconnect audio warning was then heard, and the first officer stated 'ITS A FIRE COMING THROUGH'. The commander then asked 'WHICH ONE IS IT?', to which the first officer replied, 'ITS THE LE..ITS THE RIGHT ONE'. The commander then said 'OKAY, THROTTLE IT BACK.'

London ATC was then called by the first officer, advising them of an emergency, after which the commander asked for the engine to be shut down. The first officer began to read the checklist for 'Engine Failure and Shutdown' but was interrupted by ATC calls and the commander's own calls to the operating company during which the decision was made to divert to East Midlands. Approximately 2 minutes after the initial 'vibration' the final command was given to shut down the engine. The first officer then recommenced the checklist and 2 minutes 7 seconds after the initial engine problem he moved the start lever of the No 2 engine to 'OFF'. He then started the APU. Throughout this period no fire audio warning was heard.

The aircraft then started the descent to East Midlands Airport and the commander made his first announcement to the passengers during which he mentioned that they had had a problem with their right hand engine which had produced some smoke in the cabin. The flight crew were then fully occupied with the relevant checklists, calls to the operating company and ATC, who were routeing them into East Midlands, and reprogramming the flight management system (FMS) for an East Midlands diversion, with which they had some difficulty. During this period they also briefly discussed the symptoms that had occurred initially and the commander mentioned 'RAPID VIBRATIONS IN THE AEROPLANE - SMOKE'.

The flight proceeded until the aircraft was on final approach with the landing checklist completed. Just after they had confirmed with East Midlands ATC that the right engine had been shut down, there was a crackling noise on the CVR, possibly due to electrical interference. This occurred 54 seconds before the first ground impact. Leading up to this event there were significant changes in the frequency content of the background noise on the CVR area microphone, which are discussed in paragraph 1.11.5. These changes would probably not have been audible to the crew.

Immediately following this, a transmission was made to the tower indicating that the crew was having trouble with the second engine as well and the commander asked the first officer to 'TRY LIGHTING THE OTHER ONE UP - THERE'S NOTHING ELSE YOU CAN DO'.

36 seconds before impact the (No 1 engine) fire bell sounded. The first officer asked the commander if he should shut this engine down. The commander

replied in the negative. The CVR recording then indicated their intention to 'stretch the glide', but at 29 seconds before impact the ground proximity warning system (GPWS) 'glideslope' warning commenced and continued with increasing repetition rate, indicating that the aircraft was steadily diverging below the glidepath. The commander twice said 'TRY OPENING THE OTHER ONE UP' and each time the first officer said 'SHE'S NOT GOING'. At 10 seconds before the impact the commander made an announcement to the passengers to 'PREPARE FOR CRASH LANDING' (repeated). The stick shaker was then heard operating, followed by the sounds of impact.

Relevant comments from the CVR transcript are shown in relation to the FDR information in the Appendix 4, figs 2, 5 & 7.

1.11.5   *CVR frequency analysis*

An analysis was carried out of the frequency content of the background noise from the area microphone. This was done to identify any changes in the frequency signatures that might have indicated an engine problem before the crew became aware of it.

This analysis was carried out using a Hewlett-Packard model 13561A dynamic signal analyser. The first significant change in the frequency signature occurred just after the onset of the initial vibration and smoke, when harmonics of the frequency associated with 'once per revolution' of an LP shaft became detectable. This was indicative of either vibration of the shaft, damage to a limited number of blades on the shaft, or a combination of the two. The amplitude of the dominant frequencies changed with the variations in power taking place, but became particularly high just before the No 1 engine was throttled back to flight idle for the descent. Thereafter, and up until power was increased for the final approach, the frequencies associated with the LP shaft were not detectable. Appendix 4, fig 8 shows comparisons of the signatures of frequencies up to 625 Hz for the start of the CVR tape (aircraft level at 6,000 ft); the climb; and significant points immediately after the first event.

As the No 1 engine power was increased on the final approach, the frequencies associated with the LP shaft once again became detectable, and varied with the changes in engine speed. They became increasingly audible during replay of the area microphone track in the AAIB audio laboratory until the point at which the 'crackle' was heard, when they were no longer detectable. This was indicative of this second event also having been associated with the LP shaft (the FDR data showed a sudden drop in the No 1 engine N1 coincident with this point). These changes in audio content were probably not detectable by the crew within the flight deck environment. Appendix 4, fig 9 shows a comparison between the signatures just before, and just after, this second event.

1.12 Wreckage and impact information

1.12.1 *On site*

The AAIB on-site inspection of the wreckage and site started shortly after midnight on 9 January. The salvage of the wreckage commenced on 10 January and the site was cleared by 1700 hrs on 13 January, at which time the Leicestershire Constabulary re-opened the closed section of the M1 motorway.

The positions of all controls and switches on the flight deck were recorded. Those relevant to the investigation were:

Engine start levers	CUTOFF
Fire handles	not pulled
No 1 engine start switch	OFF
No 2 engine start switch	OFF
Igniter select switch	L (left ignition system)
Left air conditioning pack switch	AUTO
Right air conditioning pack switch	AUTO
Isolation valve switch	AUTO
No 1 engine bleed air valve switch	ON
No 2 engine bleed air valve switch	ON
APU bleed air valve switch	OFF

1.12.1.1 *Impact sequence*

Appendix 3, fig 6 shows a cross-section of the final flight path of the aircraft and the impact sequence. The angles and attitudes of the first impact were derived from the ground and airframe markings and compare closely with the final data available from the FDR, approximately 1 second before the first impact (paragraph 1.11.2).

The first ground contact was made just before the eastern embankment of the M1 by the tail-skid and aft fuselage, and started 29 metres east of the embankment boundary fence. The marks created by the two main landing gears started at 14.6 metres (right) and 12.5 metres (left) from this fence, showing that the main landing gear touched almost simultaneously with the tail. Analysis of the marks showed that at first impact the aircraft's attitude was:

Pitch	13° nose up ±1°
Roll	4° right wing low ±1°
Yaw	4.5° nose left ±1°
Track	266°M

The impact velocities were extrapolated from the final FDR readings:

Airspeed	113 knots CAS
Ground speed	between 104 kts (CAS corrected for wind) and 111 kts (from the aircraft Inertial Reference Unit)
Rate of descent	between 8.5 feet/sec (barometric rate of descent) and 16 feet/sec (radar altimeter rate corrected for terrain)

These velocities combined to give an aircraft final flight path angle of between 2.5° and 5°, consistent with the entry angles to the ground marks.

The first impact was sufficiently severe to separate the tail-skid and APU door, and the drag loads on the two main landing gears failed both legs rearwards. The airframe was otherwise intact after the first impact. The aircraft had then cut a swathe through the trees on the eastern embankment. The debris found in this area was almost exclusively from the wing leading edges and the engine cowlings.

As the aircraft descended across the motorway it made no contact with the eastern (ie southbound) carriageway or the central reservation barrier, although the left wing struck a central lamp standard, fracturing it at its base and removing the outboard 6 feet of the wing. The only major component to strike the central barrier was the right main landing gear leg, but its position showed that this was after it had separated from the airframe.

The second, and major, impact occurred when the nose contacted the base of the western embankment. The first contact was made by the nose wheel on the road surface, followed, within approximately 0.1 seconds, by the nose radome striking the embankment and the engine nacelles striking the road surface. The nose landing gear failed rearwards, the nose crushed against the embankment and both engine support structures failed upwards. For this second impact, analysis of the marks indicated an attitude of:

Pitch   between 9° and 14° nose down

Roll   2.5° right wing low ±1°

Yaw   0° ±2°

Track   266°M

There was no indication of velocity at the second impact from either the FDR or the aircraft instrumentation. Initially, to give boundary values for the impact simulation (paragraph 1.16.4) a simple calculation of the ballistic trajectory from the first impact was made, giving velocities at the second impact of:

Resultant   50.0 metres/sec   (97.2 knots)

Horizontal   48.9 metres/sec   (95.1 knots)

Vertical   14.4 metres/sec   (28.0 knots)

Flight path   16.4° below horizontal

A first-order aerodynamic calculation using lift coefficient data from the aircraft manufacturer and mid-trajectory values of airspeed and angle-of-attack gave a lower boundary approximation of velocities at the second impact:

Resultant   39.4 metres/sec   (76.6 knots)

Horizontal   37.9 metres/sec   (73.7 knots)

Vertical   11.1 metres/sec   (21.6 knots)

Flight path   16.4° below horizontal

The above values were used for, respectively, 'Run 2' and 'Run 3' of the KRASH impact simulation (paragraph 1.16.4). At a later stage in the investigation, the Boeing Company contributed an analysis of the impact sequence to provide a set of parameters for the second impact. This analysis used a non-linear dynamic finite element model to simulate the aeroplane response in the first impact and the 737-400 engineering simulator at Boeing for the analysis of the trajectory between the impacts. This analysis gave parameters at the second impact of:

Resultant: 51 metres/sec   (99 knots)

Flight path   12° below horizontal

Pitch attitude 14° below horizontal

The velocity change in the second impact can only be estimated. For example, based on the measured crush distance of approximately 2.6 metres along the direction of motion in the nose area, a 25% change of velocity (from 51 m/sec) in the second impact would give a pulse with a mean deceleration of about 22g, lasting about 60 milliseconds.

After the second impact the forward fuselage separated from the centre section and both structures decelerated as they cut through the trees on the western embankment; the tail section buckled over, and to the right of, the centre section. The forward fuselage came to rest 27 metres from its position at the second impact whereas the centre section, attached to the wing, came to rest in 21 metres.

1.12.1.2   Airframe structural damage

Two major structural failures of the fuselage occurred in the impact, one slightly forward of the wing leading-edge (approximately stations 500B to 500D) and one aft of the trailing-edge (approximately stations 727G to 827). These failures left the structure in 3 principal sections (Appendix 3, fig 7). In addition, all 3 landing gear legs and both engine supports failed (paragraph 1.12.1.2.1), without rupturing the fuel tanks.

The nose section sustained considerable crushing in the lower flight deck area and the belly skin disintegrated along the length of the passenger cabin. The floor of the forward passenger cabin was entirely disrupted (paragraph 1.12.2.7). Inspection of the stubs of floor beams which were still attached to the fuselage frames indicated that the failures were, aft of body station 380 (ie.seat row 1 and aft), in a forward and downward sense. The nose landing gear failed rearwards and the lower portion of this landing gear leg, including both wheels, became detached. Forward of station 380 the cabin floor was deformed upward by the presence of this detached nose landing gear leg and the forward electrical equipment.

The centre-section remained intact and the wings remained attached, although the leading-edges of both wings were extensively damaged by contact with the trees on both embankments. The outboard 6 feet of the left wing separated, but this did not affect the wing fuel tank, which was inboard of the failure. Part of the centre-section keel beam was displaced upward and exhibited ground contact evidence which corresponded with ground marks on the western carriageway.

The tail section was almost inverted, but had sustained less damage than the other fuselage sections. The lower lobe had suffered an upwards compressive displacement of some 14 inches in the first impact and the tail-skid had been torn out, without displacement of the crushable cartridge. This failure had caused detachment of the grounding point for the tailplane jackscrew, releasing the tailplane from its trimmed position.

1.12.1.2.1 *Separation of main landing gear legs and engines*

On the Boeing 737-400 both the engine and main landing gear (MLG) attachments were designed so that, in otherwise survivable accidents, separation of the engines or MLGs would not cause rupture of the wing fuel tanks. Calibrated 'fuse pin' bolts were, therefore, incorporated into the design of the attachments to ensure maintenance of the structural integrity of the wing box spars and skins during ground impact conditions.

In this accident, examination of the MLG legs and the associated wing attachments showed that both legs had separated cleanly at the initial impact. The forward trunnion fuse bolts had failed first and the aft trunnions had then rotated out of their respective main landing gear beams.

The engines were intended to separate cleanly from the wing at the junction between the engine pylon and the wing leading-edge. The No 1 engine was found to have separated benignly (*ie* without rupturing the wing fuel tank). All the fuse pins were found intact, however, and the major break had occurred within the pylon itself, approximately in the vertical plane of the forward wing spar. The pylon attachment at the upper wing skin had also failed.

The No 2 engine pylon failures on the right wing were almost identical and the wing fuel tank had not been ruptured by the pylon failure. On this (No 2 engine) side the attachment at the upper wing skin had 'lifted' but had not completely separated.

1.12.1.3 *Initial engine examination*

Both engines had remained partially attached to their respective pylons and these in turn were still partially attached to the aircraft wings. The nacelles of both engines had been severely crushed and large sections of their forward parts had detached during ground impact before the aircraft came to rest.

Right (No 2) engine

The right engine intake had been fragmented during the groundslide from the motorway to the final position. Only the rear left segment of the intake liner had remained attached to the fan frame. The only other forward cowling parts which had remained attached to the engine were the upper hinge support beam and fragments of the clamshell doors on either side. The remainder of the forward cowlings and intake was spread in fragments between the point of engine impact on the motorway and where the engine came to rest.

The core exhaust duct had been crushed between the pylon and the ground and the rear engine frame was severely distorted. The forward end of the engine was heavily clogged with earth and tree debris, but none of the fan blades had suffered significant leading edge damage. The fan case had been severely distorted, pushed aft and crushed towards the engine axis over its lower arc. In this sector the fan blades had been severely bent, both in and against the normal direction of rotation and some were broken with their detached fragments retained, generally adjacent their respective blades. The fan case distortion had also trapped and bent blades at various places around the fan periphery. The fan blade tips had been driven into the fan casing abradable liner, with little or no evidence of fan rotation. These blade contacts had left sharp imprints of blade tips in the abradable material, which was otherwise generally in its normal condition. The accessory drive gearbox on the lower left of the fan case had been severely ruptured and the accessories themselves, including the fuel control and lubrication systems, badly disrupted. There was no evidence of fire on the outside of the engine, nor on any of the nacelle sections.

Left (No 1) engine.

The left engine nacelle had suffered similar ground impact damage to that of the right, except that there was a greater portion of the forward cowling still attached to the hinge beam and a segment of the intake lip from the upper right quadrant was still attached to the engine by the intake lip anti-icing air duct. The intake duct had been fragmented and only a short stub remained attached to the fan frame. The core exhaust duct was similarly crushed, but the rear frame was rather less distorted than that on the right engine. The forward end of this engine was also clogged with earth and tree debris. There were, however, two major differences in the appearance of the left engine; one being the condition of the fan and the other, the presence of fire damage.

The fan blades of this engine had been very severely damaged by hard object ingestion and a large number of blade fragments were found lying forward of the fan disc. Most of the blades had fractured at part span positions and many were in two or more fragments. A number of blade fragments were recovered from the area between the impact point of the left engine on the motorway and the final position of the engine. As in the case of the right engine, the lower quarter of the fan case had been crushed upwards, driven aft and several blades were trapped between the fan disc and the case. It was observed that the fan case abradable seal material was completely missing and the acoustic panels, both fore and aft of the fan, were either missing or badly scarred.

The engine had also suffered severe fire damage to its forward outboard region. The fire appeared to have emanated from the base of the engine fan case, around the fuel system, and had affected the entire left side of the outside of the fan case including the associated components and pipework. The fire resistant outer covers of the main low pressure fuel feed flexible hose from the pylon, and a section of the metered fuel pipe to the fuel flow meter, had both been burned away. Only the reinforcing braid and decomposed parts of the inner liners of both fuel hoses remained. There was a localised clean area on one of the component attachment brackets below the fuel flow unit which had the appearance of having been 'fuel washed' as a fire had burned around it, or had been masked from the flame. There was also an area around the front of the fan case, where the electrical power cables from the generator were routed, which appeared to have been subjected to a more intense fire than the rest of the fan case area. The fire had burnt the left side forward clamshell cowling and had extended up to the hinge beam. It had also entered the fan case, and had affected about two thirds of the case in the left hand and upper segments. Many of the blades in this sector of the fan were heavily sooted. None of the fire damage in this area was indicative of having occurred in a flight speed slipstream.

There was a second area of fire damage, which appeared to be separate from the main zone. This area was on the trailing edge of the left side of the fan duct. There were some black streaks which extended diagonally aft and upwards to this fire affected area, from a position on the underside of the cowling where the forward clamshells fasten together at the cowling firewall bulkhead. The forward cowling sump and drain was located in this area.

1.12.1.4   Engine wreckage trail

Most of the engine components which had broken free were located between the point at which the engines had struck the motorway and where the engines came to rest. However, witness reports had described burning pieces falling from the aircraft when it had been above Sutton Bonnington, some 2 nm. short of the accident site. Ground searches of this area produced a number of fragments which appeared to be parts of titanium alloy fan blades and several pieces of fan case acoustic liner, liner attachment bolts and washers. These were all found in a well defined area close to the piggery of the Sutton Bonnington agricultural college.

1.12.2   *Subsequent detailed examination*

1.12.2.1   *Engines*

Both engines, complete with their remaining cowlings and pylons, were removed from the wings and taken to the operator's base. Here, the filters and magnetic chip detectors of the left engine lubrication system were examined and the core engine compressor of No 1 engine and the high pressure turbines (HPTs) of both engines examined by borescope. (The right engine lubrication system had not been located and identified at this time.) These inspections did not reveal significant evidence of internal distress on either engine. The engines were then transported to the manufacturer's factory for detailed examination under AAIB supervision.

1.12.2.1.1   *Right(No 2) engine*

Initial external examination of the engine after removal of the cowlings and core exhaust duct showed that, apart from the obvious deformation of the fan frame and case, rear frame and low pressure turbine case, the basic engine structure was only superficially damaged. The lower quadrant of the fan case had suffered the greatest distortion and had also ingested a substantial quantity of earth and tree debris. The distortion of the cowlings and crushing from below, which had resulted from the engine being partially trapped between the wing and ground at impact, had caused some damage to the pipework. However, all of this damage was considered consistent with the effects of ground impact. There was also considerable damage to the linkages controlling the variable stator vanes and variable bleed valves (VSVs and VBVs). No evidence of any external fire on the engine was revealed on removal of its cowlings.

After removal of the earth and wood debris from the fan case, it was evident that the fan blades within the lower outboard quadrant had been severely damaged and were trapped between the fan case and the booster section intake. The fan blade fragments were recovered and it was found that, apart from very small pieces from the tips of two blades, the complete fan had been contained within the case after impact. Eight of the 38 blades had minor 'nicks' in their leading edges and these blades were all from the lower quadrant of the fan case where there had been the greatest distortion and ingestion. Examination of the fan case abradable liner, after removal of the blades, showed that there was no evidence of tip rubbing on the abradable surface between the fan blade tip penetrations, indicating that the latter had occurred with the fan effectively stationary. There was no evidence of any heat effects on the fan blade tips. A metallurgical examination of the fan blade fractures showed that they had all failed as a result of bending overload. The fan case acoustic lining panels showed no evidence of pre-impact damage and the fan outlet guide vanes showed no evidence of having been struck by high energy fragments.

The position and rigging of the VSVs and VBVs was measured. They were found to be consistent with each other and were in the positions to be expected either with the engine running at sub-idle speed, or shut down.

The core, booster and LPT modules were completely disassembled. It was evident that there was some crushing distortion of the lower quadrant of the booster inlet which had only affected the inlet guide vanes. The other stator stages and all the rotor stage blades of the booster were undamaged. There was evidence, from static impact marks on the case liners and internal seals, of an aft and upward movement of the LP shaft relative to the core. The rear bearing support housing had also been forced aft, causing failure of its retaining bolts.

Apart from these features the internal condition of the engine was consistent with that of a fully serviceable, low time engine which had had very little or no rotational energy at impact. There was no evidence of overheating of either the HP or LP turbines, nor of any distress or malfunction in the combustion section. There was no evidence of hard foreign object ingestion on any of the compressor or turbine blades, nor of abnormal rubbing of blade tips or rotating seals whilst the engine had been turning. Examination of all bearings showed that none had any significant wear or sign of overheating, nor was there any evidence of failure or internal leakage of the engine lubrication and cooling air systems. Examination of the lubrication system filters and magnetic chip detectors showed no evidence of pre-crash distress.

1.12.2.1.2 *Left (No 1) engine*

After removal of the cowlings and exhaust duct it was observed that, apart from the difference in fan damage and the evidence of fire around this engine, it had suffered very similar external mechanical damage to that on the right engine.

The position and rigging of the VSVs and VBVs was measured. They were found to be consistent with each other and were in the positions to be expected with the engine running within ±4% of 71% core speed.

Disassembly of the booster, core and LPT modules revealed considerable evidence of rotation of both shafts at moderate speed on impact. Earth had been ingested through both compressors and there was baked earth on the HPT nozzles. There was evidence throughout the engine of severe, and circumferentially uniform, rubbing of blades on their tip paths and of all rotating seals. The LPT rotor blades had also suffered considerable tip rubbing as a result of the LPT casing having been distorted during ground impact. Although there was only slight evidence of hard object ingestion within the booster section, all stages of the core compressor had some hard object damage. Apart from these features, this engine was also in relatively good condition, with no evidence of any pre-crash bearing distress nor of overheating of the turbine blades. Checks on the combustion system revealed no evidence of malfunction.

In addition to the evidence of fire already noted in the fan case zone, there was also considerable sooting of the underside of the core, centred around a damaged combustion nozzle attachment. Considerable sooting was also found on the inside of the HPC case and inside the LP shaft. The appearance of both of these areas was consistent with the effects of small, rich mixture, convective fires.

The cowling assembly was reconstructed to establish the fire pattern. It was observed that the bottom, outboard and upper sections of the forward cowling had been severely affected by the ground fire, with damage to the inner and outer skins and the interposed Nomex honeycomb. Over much of its area, the cowling panels had been almost totally reduced to their fibrous content and metal fittings. There was one fragment, however, in the region of the fan case forward flange and just above the 9 o'clock position (viewed from aft - looking forward), which had broken away from the cowling at impact, and which showed no evidence of fire damage on its outer surface, but had a discrete area of such damage on the Nomex. This area was adjacent to the position where the generator power cables crossed the front of the fan case. Another fragment, which was identified as having come from the area immediately adjacent to the MEC, had no evidence of fire damage. No evidence was found anywhere on the cowling to suggest that the fire had been driven by a fierce airstream, as in flight.

1.12.2.1.3   *The No 1 engine fan and fan case*

(All radial position descriptions are given as clock hours viewed from the rear, looking forward.)

Examination of the fan and case revealed the greatest differences in the condition of the left engine compared with that of the right. The most obvious difference on the left engine was the severe fire damage which extended on the outside of the fan case from circumferential position 6, through 9 to 12 and on the inside from about 7.30 through 9 to 2. Most of the fire damage was biased towards the rear of the fan case and appeared to have entered the inside through a split in the fan case to frame joint, at about the 7.30 position, caused by crushing distortion. Many of the acoustic lining panels, (*ie* all of the forward and some of the mid and aft panels) had been torn out of the case, their attachment bolts having been either severely bent or sheared off in the normal direction of fan rotation. The fire had severely affected the remaining pieces of acoustic lining panels and their underlying panels in the fire affected zone. The fan blades which came to rest in the outboard and upper sectors of the case were very heavily sooted. The whole of the abradable lining of the fan tip path around the fan case was missing and there was little evidence of circumferential scoring of the underlying case. A number of dents in the casing were observed within the abradable path, consistent with impact effects from fan blade fragments released from the fan whilst it was rotating.

All the fan blade root ends had remained attached to the fan disc. They were removed from the disc and the fragments which had spilled from the front of the fan case at the accident site were correlated with them by fracture matching. After all these pieces had been matched and those fan blades which had sections missing had been identified, the small blade fragments which had fallen from the aircraft at the piggery were matched with their respective blades, where this was possible. Two small fragments were identified as having come from blade Nos 4 and 5. Two larger pieces were identified, by thickness mapping, as having come from a blade outer panel. At this time, the complete outer panels of four blades (Nos 9, 17, 31 and 34) had not been identified and there were only sufficient fragments to account for one of these. Chemical content analysis of the two large pieces showed that they were more consistent with the composition of blade No 17. Appendix 1, fig 2 shows the fan fragmentation and identifies the missing pieces.

A general survey of the fan blades revealed that all had suffered considerable hard object damage, particularly to the leading edges, with considerable bending and folding damage to several blades. Of the 38 blades, only 9 had retained their full length, 5 had a single failure outboard of the mid-span shroud and 11 were broken into 2 or more major fragments; one blade (No 23) had suffered a single failure near the root end and was the only such blade to exhibit major trailing edge damage over its whole span. There was evidence of blade/case and blade/blade collisions, with 'shingling'[4] of the mid-span shrouds and root platforms. There was a group of 6 blades (Nos 22 to 17) which had some indications of bulged leading edges but these bulges were not all at similar or progressively changing spanwise locations through the group. Blade No 6 had failed just inboard of the mid-span shroud and the released outer portion had 3 areas of severe abrasion and overheating, 2 on one side and one on the other. The two overheated areas on one side were separated by a distance which matched the spacing of the containment flanges of the fan-case abradable liner and the overheated area on the other side lay between them. Examination of the containment flanges showed them to be heavily scored and worn down, with areas which had been 'blued' due to the effects of frictional heating.

---

[4] Shingling: The overlapping of root platforms or mid span shrouds as a result of peripheral blade lean.

The fractured surfaces of all fan blade failures were examined metallurgically and, with the exception of the failure of blade No 17 above the mid-span shroud, were all found to be overload failures, consistent with either bending or a combination of tension and bending. The failure of blade No 17 was observed to be very flat over the forward half chord, and exhibited several features consistent with fatigue, but was covered by a carbonaceous deposit which was very resistant to chemical cleaning. This deposit was analysed in the scanning electron microscope (SEM) and samples taken for chemical analysis. These analyses showed that the deposit was consistent with an amalgam of the materials present in the fan case, intake, acoustic liners and the fan abradable liner.

The bulged fan blades (Nos 17 to 22) were examined under ultra-violet light and subjected to forensic analysis for evidence of bird ingestion (blade No 17 was also examined as it had a bend near the failure point). No evidence of bird ingestion was found, but a slight deposit consistent with acoustic panel material was detected.

1.12.2.1.4 Metallurgical examination of blade No 17

The fracture surface of this blade was cleaned of the chemical deposit by sputter erosion[5] followed by chemical cleaning in a sodium hydroxide bath. It was then examined, both optically and in a scanning electron microscope. The characteristics of the fracture were those of high cycle fatigue which was deduced to have originated from a point on the concave (pressure) face of the blade, about 1 to 1.5 mm aft of the original leading edge (LE). The fatigue extended aft to about mid chord (ie above the mid-span shroud), where the fracture mechanism had changed to overload in tension.

The true origin could not be determined with certainty because the LE area had suffered severe mechanical damage and the pressure face portion in which the fatigue appeared to have originated was locally deformed over the fracture face. This area of the pressure face appeared to have suffered a hard blow in a rearwards direction which had obliterated the original blade surface and as a result there was no feature which could be associated with the fatigue origin. (See Appendix 1, fig 3 for section of damage to LE) A section through the blade just below and parallel to the fracture face revealed that the general microstructure and cleanliness of the blade material was satisfactory. However, in the region of the damage around the LE and close to the fatigue origin, the normal microstructure of this titanium alloy had been altered by the effects of high strain shear deformation.

---

[5] Sputter erosion: Erosion of the deposit by an ionic particle beam

Evidence was sought of possible grinding abuse or other damage resulting from the blending of foreign object damage (FOD). It was established that the alteration of the material structure caused by grinding, filing or polishing differed from that observed at the LE of blade No 17. A trial showed that a similar deformation of the microstructure to that observed on blade No 17 could be produced by a high energy blow. It had been noted that several blades had clashed their LEs against the surfaces of adjacent blades and sections through some of these blades revealed that similar alterations had occurred to their microstructure. There was clear evidence of high energy clashing of blade No 17 against both blades Nos 16 and 18. Indeed, the part of the LE of blade No 17 from in front of the fracture zone was found friction-welded to the pressure face of blade No 16 in a position which was consistent with the anticipated contact location when allowance for blade distortion during the impact sequence had been made.

Samples were taken from blade No 17 for analysis of microstructure, chemical composition and mechanical properties. These analyses revealed no deficiencies from specification, when allowance for the effects of ingestion of intake fragments released by break up at impact and the fire were taken into account.

1.12.2.1.5   *Main engine controls (MECs)*

Both MECs had been severely damaged during the aircraft's groundslide. Neither MEC was in a condition to be tested as a unit.

The No 2 engine MEC was completely stripped and all components examined for signs of abnormal operation. Although many components had been badly damaged or distorted during the break-up of the MEC at ground impact, no evidence was found, on any part, of a pre-impact defect. As found, the fuel shut-off lever was in the closed (fuel off) position and the power lever angle (PLA) was found in a position which was slightly less than the full power setting. However examination of the input cables showed that both had been subjected to bending and tension loads during the accident sequence and had severed close to their throttle box attachments . The result of tension on the cables would have been to close the fuel shut-off and increase the PLA. Many of the pipe fittings attached to components had been damaged and some had been torn out.

The No 1 engine MEC was less damaged than the No 2 MEC, but was heavily 'sooted' as a result of the fire around the No 1 engine. It was noted, however, that one sub-assembly which had become completely detached after impact with the motorway, and had come to rest clear of the engine, was unsooted and showed no evidence of fire damage. After inspection of the external condition of the No 1 MEC it was decided that the main speed governor mechanism was in sufficiently good condition to attempt a bench functional test of this part of the unit. The sub-assemblies which had either been separated or substantially loosened from the governor block were completely disassembled and no evidence of pre-crash failure or malfunction was found. Examination of the mating faces and fasteners which had attached these components to the main governor showed no conclusive evidence of pre-impact failure or of fretting due to long term looseness. There was, however, evidence that the seal around the high pressure fuel supply port had been distorted outwards over a limited arc and the governor discharge fitting seal showed evidence of low clamping pressure. The throttle and fuel shut-off cables had not been subjected to tensile loading, but the lower projection of the throttle cable outer sleeve, below the input arm, had been bent and the inner cable seized. The positions of the levers as found were fuel 'on' and PLA at maximum. Several of the pipe fittings on this MEC were also found to be torn out or damaged and some unions were loose, although they showed no evidence of mechanical damage.

The governor portion of the No 1 MEC was returned to the manufacturer for functional tests. The damaged pipe unions were reworked to minimise fuel leakage and the mating faces to which sub-assemblies attached were cleaned of soot. New production examples of those sub-assemblies which had already been strip examined were fitted as slave units to check the overall governor operation and the sub-functions of VSV and VBV positioning. The tests showed that, after making allowances for the non-standard configuration resultant from the accident damage, the unit functioned satisfactorily.

1.12.2.2. *Engine instrument system (EIS) and associated wiring*

The primary and secondary EIS units were still in position within the centre instrument panel but the secondary unit had suffered some distortion which had caused the glass face to crack. Prior to removal, the wiring and connectors to and from both units were checked for left/right sense and found to be satisfactory.

Upon removal of the EIS display units it could be seen that, whilst the primary unit was virtually undamaged, the secondary unit had received an impact on the upper rear case due to contact with deformed structure behind the panel. Loose items, which were later found to be a small screw, nut and washers broken from the bezel, could be heard rattling within the case.

Both EIS units were examined at the manufacturer's premises under AAIB supervision. Power was applied to the primary display and, as the unit appeared to function normally, it was subjected to a BITE check which revealed no faults. The exceedance memory was interrogated and it was established that no exceedances had been recorded. When the unit was subjected to a full acceptance test, it met all the requirements of this test satisfactorily.

Despite the damage to the case of the secondary display, an internal inspection suggested that the unit should function. However, when power was applied a malfunction was apparent within the right-hand (No 2 engine) channel. The engine oil pressure and hydraulic pressure displays on this side at times displayed multiple pointers whilst the digital oil quantity indication also displayed in an obviously faulty manner. The other parameters on this No 2 side (including the No 2 vibration display) read correctly, as did all the parameters on the No 1 left engine side. The fault was correctly diagnosed as a defective hybrid integrated circuit associated with the display drive. The board containing this part was removed and the defective component replaced. Thereafter the secondary EIS worked normally and fully met the acceptance test requirements.

The defective microchip appeared to have broken and, since it was located close to the sheared screw mentioned above, it was suspected that it had received an impact at the same time as the screw. When the microchip was examined by the manufacturer in the USA, it was confirmed that it had broken due to mechanical shock.

It was concluded from these tests that both EIS units were functioning at the time of impact and correctly displaying the input information.

1.12.2.3.   *Engine fire and overheat detection system*

The fire detector elements located in the engine nacelle were examined to establish their serviceability. It was found that, with the exception of the lower fan detector elements, they had suffered little impact damage although those located around the forward part of No 1 engine had been subjected to heat which had damaged the associated wiring. Those elements which had not been mechanically damaged beyond meaningful test were subjected to resistance and continuity checks, followed by an improvised function test. It was concluded that these elements had been capable of normal operation at the time of the accident.

The control module had been badly damaged by impact but, upon detailed inspection at the manufacturer's premises, it was found that the internal components were largely intact. After replacement of a few electrical components it was possible to run a functional test on the unit. Although the module functioned in these tests it was found to exhibit a condition known as 'latch-up' (Appendix 2.8). Inspection showed that the module from ME was fitted with the type of microcircuit which could cause this condition. When this module was tested, a latch-up condition occurred on 2 occasions out of 20 when power interruptions were included in the test programme.

This module was later subjected to further testing using the Boeing 737 electrical system test rig at Seattle. This test-rig replicated the aircraft electrical system and, in particular, the characteristics of power supply changes on the battery bus bar, from which the module is powered. The tests involved connecting the module to a test box with variable resistors which simulated the detector elements and represented the cockpit visual and audio warnings. An ultra-violet chart recorder was used to measure the voltage 'spike' which each power transfer imposed on the bus bar. Essentially, each test simulated the situation where power supplied by the No 2 engine or APU generators was switched to, or from, the battery bus. Following each transfer, the fire detection test switch was pressed every few seconds to determine whether the system was operative. Latch-up was evidenced by failure of one or both system warning lights to illuminate when the TEST button was pressed. This more realistic test caused the module to latch-up far more frequently than had been apparent during bench testing. In fact, after a total of 19 power interruptions, one or both systems latched up 13 times. It was also found that latch-up did not occur immediately after the power interruption but at intervals varying between 18 and 44 seconds afterwards. The time during which a system stayed latched also varied widely, ranging from 18 seconds to in excess of 8 minutes.

Having established these characteristics, it was decided to check the response of the system to a simulated fire detected by the elements whilst the system was latched-up. The module reacted in one of two different ways. In the first, the system did not respond to the stimulus and no warning was generated. However, contrary to expectations, the system would also sometimes react to the stimulus, giving a warning for a period ranging from 7 to 19 seconds before self-cancelling and reverting to a dormant mode.

As expected, a latched-up system with a simulated fire present did not generate a fire warning when the latch-up ceased. This was because the module instantly sensed a low resistance on the detector elements as it unlatched, and interpreted it as a short-circuit, illuminating the FAULT light in the cockpit (the module is programmed to recognise a pattern of falling resistance). Removal of the simulated fire cancelled the fault indication and any subsequent fire warning was correctly detected and indicated.

1.12.2.4 *Flight deck crew seats*

At the accident site, both pilots' seats were found still on their tracks and they were left in place in the flight deck until the wreckage had been moved to AAIB at Farnborough. The seats were then removed and examined in detail.

Despite the heavy impact damage to the lower flight deck area, all 4 bogies on both seats had remained engaged with their seat tracks and the sections of seat track had remained attached to the floor. The small amount of deformation to the flight deck floor under each seat had been within the allowed articulation of the bogies. On both seats the track lock pins had remained engaged within their respective seat tracks, restraining the seats from longitudinal movement during ground impact.

It was evident that, during the final ground impact, the centre of the flight deck floor had been forced upwards by the nose landing gear leg, which had produced a symmetrical pattern of damage between the seats. Associated bending fractures had occurred close to the inboard forward bogie pivot point on the forward crossbeam of both seats.

Examination of both restraint systems showed them to be almost undamaged. However, the first officer's crotch strap had detached from his seat due to failure of its anchoring bracket. The commander's crotch strap was fully serviceable, indicating that it had not been in use at the time of impact.

Both seats were found with their respective seat pans at the bottom of their vertical travel and this downwards stroking onto the seat bases had fractured both forward lift arms on both seats by allowing the lift arms to strike the forward cross beams. This stroking had been caused by the failure of the height lock mechanisms. On each seat the inboard height lock pin had sheared through the material between the height adjustment holes; the outboard pin had overcome its retaining spring, come out of engagement and had not re-engaged any of the remaining holes in its height lock plate.

Previous dynamic testing by the manufacturer indicated that the failure of the forward lift arms would not have occurred at deceleration levels up to, and including, the separate 14g 'vertical' and 16g horizontal pulses defined in Amendment 25-64 (paragraph 1.17.11.1).

1.12.2.5   *Cabin crew seats*

All 5 attendant seats had been occupied at ground impact. The aft attendant seats (1 double seat, 1 single) remained intact, with some downwards distortion of the seat pan of the aft double-seat. However, the aft/left toilet module, to which this double seat was attached, had partially separated from the airframe. This had allowed the toilet aft bulkhead, with this double seat, to rotate through approximately 90° into the centre aisle.

The seat pan of the forward double seat had failed downwards in the impact, although it was still attached to the remainder of the seat assembly. The movement of the seat pan pivot at each side was limited by a physical stop. In this instance, the inboard stop had sheared, loading the outboard pivot which in turn broke away from the seat frame. The out-of-plane loading at the inboard arm had then sheared the pop rivets which held the seat pan onto this inboard arm.

1.12.2.6   *Passenger seats*

A total of 21 of the 52 triple seats remained fully attached to the cabin floor: 14 of these were in the over-wing area (Area II in Appendix 3, fig 7) and 7 in the aft fuselage (Area IV in fig 7). During the rescue operations a total of 35 triple seats were removed from the aircraft, either intact or, in most cases, after being cut to allow the release of injured passengers. A further 3 were removed during the salvage operation.

After delivery of the wreckage to AAIB Farnborough, the cabin seating arrangement was reconstructed as completely as possible. There were 14 triple seats still in place (7 cut out during recovery) and the position of the remaining seats, by row number, was determined by the following primary methods:

(i) part numbers and features of unique seats;
(ii) distinctive construction features between left-hand and right-hand seats;
(iii) matching patterns of cutting made by rescuers and salvage crews;
(iv) for seats which still had a length of track attached to the floor fittings, the distance between the rear floor fittings and the nearest transverse floor beams could be related to the identical layout in G-OBMF;
(v) in cases where method (iv) above gave an ambiguous result, the pattern of the floor panel attachment studs was used as the determinant.

Some secondary checking was also possible by relating the final passenger seating arrangement against personal effects remaining in the seat-back pockets, impact damage on the rear face of the seat-backs and the seat-belts which were found to have been cut by rescuers. Using all these methods, an arrangement of the seats was finally generated, with a high level of confidence, and this arrangement was then related to the pattern of damage to the cabin floor structure (paragraph 1.12.2.7).

The seats were examined in detail. Although there was some variation in damage due to, for instance, differing weights of occupants, some distinctive patterns were identified These are summarised in Appendix, 3 fig 8 & figs 9 to 13 which show triple seats representative of typical seat damage sustained in different areas of the cabin. In each case, all 3 seats were occupied.

Area I - Rows 1L/R to 9L/R

Area I (fig 7) corresponded to Rows 1 to 9 (a total of 18 triple seats) and all of these seats were totally separate from any floor structure. The rescue personnel who entered the forward section early in the rescue operation found that the seats and occupants had, in general, remained upright or tipped forward and had compressed together at the front of this section, with the occupants' heads at approximately the level at which the cabin floor had been before it had collapsed.

Examination of the rear track attachments of these seats showed that, of the 33 (out of 36) attachments identified, 27 (82%) were still attached to segments of the seat track and that in no instance had the seat structure failed at the rear track attachment. A number of separations were found within the welded lower support structures of the seats but these were found, in each case, either to be bending failures which had occurred after the seat to floor geometry had been disrupted or as a result of cutting by rescue personnel.

35 of the 36 front legs in this area were identified. 17 of these legs (49%) had remained fully attached to the horizontal front spar of the seat pan, 12 legs (34%) were partially detached and 6 (17%) had become detached entirely. The associated failures had generally occurred at the welded junction with the front spar and as a result of rearward loads applied to the front legs after the floor failure. The 'U'-shaped steel straps at the front leg track attachments displayed a wide range of deformation: of the 35 identified, 4 (11%) appeared undeformed; 18 (51%) were slightly deformed and 13 (37%) had collapsed. The deformation of these straps gave some indication of the loads which had been applied to the front legs of the seats and comparison between the front legs of individual seats indicated that such collapse was generally not symmetrical.

Almost all of the seat backs showed damage which appeared to have been induced by contact from the occupant seated behind. Only 8 (15%) of the seat backs were found detached.

Of the seats in Area I, triple seat 3L (fig 9) may be considered representative, and had segments of seat track attached to both rear track attachments, both front legs still attached, though bent, and some deformation of the 'U'-straps at the front leg track attachments.

Area II - Rows 10L/R to 17L/R

Area II (fig 7) corresponded to Rows 10 to 17, (a total of 14 triple seats), and these seats had remained attached to the cabin floor in the centre-section with the exception of seats 11F and 12F, which both suffered complete bending failures of their horizontal front spars. Although these were the only seats where the front spar had separated, deformation and, in some cases, failure of the front spar had occurred in several places in Area II. The failures had occurred in a forward-downward sense and, in every case, had occurred just outside the forward leg attachments.

In all cases both rear track attachments had remained properly engaged within the seat tracks which, in the centre section, were attached directly to intercostals mounted on the upper surface of the wing-box.

All 28 front legs were identified. Of these, 23 (82%) had remained fully attached to the front spar and the remaining 5 (18%) were partially detached. The 'U'-straps at the front leg track attachments were considerably more deformed than in the forward (Area I) section: 27 'U'-straps were identified and 20 (74%) of these had suffered full collapse, 2 (7%) showed lesser degrees of deformation and 5 (19%) appeared undeformed. In those instances where the collapses displayed any lateral displacement it was in the inboard direction both for left-hand and right-hand triple seats, indicating that the associated impulse had been essentially in the longitudinal direction, with negligible lateral component.

Triple seat 15L (fig 10) may be considered representative of those seats in Area II, having remained essentially intact and with fully-collapsed 'U'-straps at the forward track attachments.

Area III - Rows 18L to 23L and 18R to 24R

Area III (fig 7) corresponded to Rows 18 to 23/24, a total of 13 triple seats. In this area the seats had suffered varying degrees of disruption. Some seats (such as 18L - fig 11) were almost intact whereas others (such as 22R - fig 12) were very extensively damaged. These highly damaged seats were from rows 19R to 24R on the right-hand side and row 23L on the left-hand side. Some of this disruption appeared to have been caused by the buckling of the upper fuselage as the tail section moved forward and rotated over, and to the right of, the section of fuselage just aft of the wing. Further disruption of these seats was caused by the rescue personnel working to extricate the occupants from this portion of the wreckage.

Damage to the rear track attachments in Area III was very similar to that in the forward fuselage (Area I). 25 (out of 26) attachments were identified: of these, 18 (72%) were still attached to segments of seat track. In many cases there had been considerable damage to the lower support structure of the seats (similar to Area I) and this was attributed to a combination of bending failures, which had occurred after the floor had failed, and cutting by the rescue personnel.

Of the 24 front legs identified (out of 26), 7 (29%) had remained fully attached to the horizontal front spar, 13 (54%) were partially detached and 4 (16%) were detached entirely. The pattern of damage to the front legs was found similar to Area I with the failures principally caused by rearward loading, typically through the welds at the junction of the front leg, diagonal brace and the front spar. The greatest severity of front leg damage was to the seats in the buckled area (19R to 24R and 23L). The remaining seats were similar to Area I.

The deformation of the 'U'-straps was more evenly distributed throughout this area than was the damage at the upper end of the front legs. Of the 24 examples, 5 (21%) appeared undeformed, 14 (58%) were slightly deformed and 5 (21%) had collapsed. This showed a slightly lower degree of initial deformation than was present in Area I.

The pattern of seat-back damage was distinctive in Area III. Of the seat-backs in the buckled area (19R to 24R and 23L) only 1 seat-back remained attached to the seat. On the remaining seats (18L to 22L and 18R) only 1 seat-back had become detached.

Area IV - Rows 24L to 27L and 25R to 27R

Area IV (fig 7) corresponded to rows 24L to 27L and 25R to 27R, a total of 7 triple seats. The seats in this area showed less damage and disruption than in any other part of the cabin. All the seats were intact when the aircraft came to rest, although the legs of triple seats 25R and 26R were cut during the rescue operation.

All 14 rear track attachments had remained properly engaged with the seat track and, despite the seat track failures from the front legs (paragraph 1.12.2.7), the floor surface around 13 (93%) of these rear track attachments was complete.

The front leg attachment to the front horizontal spar of the seat pan appeared undamaged on all 14 legs. Of the 12 'U'-straps identified, only 1 (24L, outboard) had suffered any deformation.

Triple seat 25L (fig 13) may be considered representative.

1.12.2.7   *Cabin floor structure*

The cabin floor which supported passenger seats in G-OBME extended from station 380 (seat row 1) to station 927 (seat row 27) as shown in Appendix 3, fig 7. Of this length, two areas of floor had survived the impact sequence well, with almost all of the seats still completely attached, and two areas had suffered substantial or total disruption of the floor structure. These are designated Areas I, II, III and IV in fig 7.

In the forward section (Area I) the floor was totally disrupted between stations 380 and 520 and had folded downwards between stations 520 and 540. All of the floor beams had failed in this area and were mostly moved away from the fuselage by the rescue services during the night of the accident.

In the section of fuselage behind the wing and forward of the aft fuselage (stations 727 to 787 - Area III) the floor structure was disrupted, but to a lesser degree than that forward of the wing (Area I). In some places, such as Row 17, the seats had been retained by the floor beams which had remained intact, although separated from the fuselage wall.

The two surviving areas of floor were the overwing area (station 540 to 727 - Area II) and the aft fuselage section (station 787-807 to station 927 - Area IV). In the overwing area (II) there was considerable evidence of very high deceleration loads but the floor structure in this area was built up on intercostal members from the wing centre section and was thus more robust than the floor areas immediately forward and aft. In the aft fuselage section (Area IV) there was less evidence of high deceleration, although the floor structure had sustained some inertial damage before the tail unit had rotated forwards into its final, inverted, position.

Because of the degree of disruption in Areas I and III, the actual sequence of failure of the floor structure was not readily apparent. The floor failures in Area IV were, therefore, examined closely to identify possible similarities in the pattern of damage.

Within the aft fuselage (Area IV) there were several places in which the seat tracks had fractured due principally to the downloads applied by the front legs of the occupied passenger seats. Fig 14 shows an example, corresponding to seat row 26R, where the section of seat track has been displaced out of the plane of the cabin floor. At other locations, such as row 27L, the track had cracked but not moved.

The longitudinal inertial loads from the passenger seats are carried to the fuselage wall through the floor panels. It was evident in the aft fuselage (Area IV) that where the fractured sections of seat track had been displaced, the out-of-plane loads had prised the fasteners out of the floor panels (fig 15).

It was also noted in the aft fuselage that some of the floor beams had suffered transverse cracks (*eg* at row 24L, station 807, shown in fig 16) although the floor beams had, in this section, remained in position. It was evident that these cracks had occurred when the beams had been subjected to longitudinal loading from the passenger seats, following failure of the floor panels to transmit the seat loads to the fuselage wall.

In the section of fuselage behind the wing (Area III) these patterns of damage, observed in Area IV, were repeated. For example, fig 17 shows a typical seat attachment (row 19R at station 727D) to a length of seat track. The track fracture mode is similar to that found in Area IV and the track is still attached to a segment of the upper cap from the floor beam at station 727D. In this area the floor panels were not matched against their retaining studs, but it was noted that the fasteners had remained in position and that, in almost all cases, the floor panels had been separated from the fasteners by out-of-plane forces.

The floor structure in the forward fuselage section (Area I) had been so extensively disrupted by the impact sequence, and by the rescue services, that the positions of the sections of floor beam recovered from the wreckage could be determined only by comparing them with detailed engineering drawings supplied by the manufacturer. Typical seat track failures occurred at row 5R and 3L (figs 18 & 19), and showed very similar failure modes to the aft fuselage (Area IV). A large download had been applied by the front seat legs as a result of both the longitudinal and vertical inertial loads. Both of these examples also showed a lack of apparent damage to the floor panel fasteners. fig 18 shows strips of floor beam upper cap still attached to the row 5R seat track, consistent with the beam having failed under a combination of vertical and longitudinal loads. Fig 20 shows the floor beam failure at station 460, from a combination of vertical and longitudinal loads.

1.12.2.8   *Overhead stowage bins*

All the overhead stowage bins were recovered from the wreckage and their respective cabin positions determined. Photographs taken during the rescue operation on the night of the accident did not show any of the bins in the forward and centre sections (Areas I and II) still to be attached at their fuselage attachments, apart from the forward bin on the right-hand side (1R), which was partially detached. Interview evidence with rescuers indicated that this had been caused by the aircraft impact and not by rescue personnel. The bins in the remaining sections (Areas III and IV) were also found detached and although there was no photographic evidence to show when this had occurred, the evidence from the rescuers again indicated that these detachments had been caused by the impact.

After the rescue, all the bin doors except 1R were found detached from their hinges. There was no conclusive evidence that this had occurred during the accident and there was no apparent pre-impact damage to the latching mechanisms.

The pattern of damage to the bins themselves reflected the cabin damage, with the least damaged bins (15L, 15R, 7L & 7R) in the aft and overwing areas and the most damaged being those creased and crushed in the fold-over area aft of the wing.

On all the bins (except 1R) the initial failure appeared to have occurred when the diagonal tie fitting pulled out of the bin upper surface. The lateral and vertical tie-rods had then failed when they were subjected to the added longitudinal inertial load for which they were not designed. A typical failure of the upper surface attachment is shown in figs 21a & b, with the corresponding fuselage attachments. The failure sequence was consistent in the bins which had detached and appeared to have been caused by a combination of the inertial loading of the bins themselves and the distortion of the fuselage attachments induced by the second impact.

1.13 Medical and pathological information[6]

39 passengers died at the scene of the accident, 8 more died in hospital at times up to 22 days later. 79 passengers and crew survived.

The acute medical care of the 87 passengers and crew removed from the site alive was undertaken by hospitals in Nottingham, Leicester, Derby and Mansfield. The response of the Ambulance Services and the Health Authority to this incident has been documented by the Trent Regional Health Authority[1]. The pathological investigation was conducted by a team of civilian pathologists and by a multidisciplinary team from the Royal Air Force Institute of Pathology and Tropical Medicine, including the RAF Dental Branch.

1.13.1 *Injuries*

All passengers and crew suffered varying degrees of injury during the aircraft impact. Information on the severity of the injuries sustained by the passengers and crew is displayed anonymously in Appendix 5, figs 1 & 2. The impact damage sustained by the aircraft is shown to assist in the understanding of the mechanism and degree of injury.

Appendix 5, fig 1 shows the distribution of ultimate survivors and fatalities from the accident. Appendix 5, fig 2 shows the Injury Severity Score (ISS) that was coded for the injuries that each passenger and crew member sustained[2]. The ISS is a scheme for denoting the magnitude of the injury suffered in a manner that permits an assessment of outcome. The American Association for Automotive Medicine Abbreviated Injury Score[3] (1985 revision) was used. The injury score

---

[6] All superscripts in this section denote references listed in Appendix 5.7

was calculated using the system of Baker et al[4] as the sum of the squares of the three highest regional Abbreviated Injury Scores. It can be seen that the most severe injuries occurred in rows 6-8 in the region of the forward fuselage break, with serious injuries occurring in the whole of the area forward of the wing where the floor structure failed. Further serious and fatal injuries occurred in the region of the failure of the rear fuselage and floor, and in the area where the tail structure had swung over, and into, the rear fuselage. The least injuries occurred in the rear of the aircraft. Appendix 5, fig 3 shows the distribution of the survivors and fatalities in the aircraft, coded according to whether their ISS was above or below 16; this figure represents the ISS at which an approximately 10% fatality rate has been reported[4].

1.13.2 *Types of injury*

Head injury

All but one of the 39 fatalities at the scene of the accident sustained head injuries of varying severity. 43 non-survivors had facial injuries. 74 of the 83 patients removed to hospital had suffered head or facial injury. 31 cases of facial injury required treatment. 17 patients showed clinical evidence of a strike to the head from behind. 43 of the patients presenting at hospital had suffered an episode of impairment of consciousness. 5 of the 83 patients removed to hospital had suffered severe head injuries.

Neck injury

21 non-survivors and 6 survivors sustained injuries to neck structure.

Upper limb and shoulder injury

19 fatalities and 28 survivors sustained fractures and dislocations of the upper limbs and shoulders.

Chest injury

Some degree of generally major chest injury was found in all but one of the fatalities. 18 of the 79 survivors also suffered major chest trauma.

Abdominal injury

36 fatalities suffered abdominal trauma compared to only 2 of the survivors who suffered a major abdominal injury.

Lower limbs and pelvis

22 survivors and 13 non-survivors sustained pelvic injuries. A considerable number of lower limb injuries also occurred. 22 survivors and 13 non-survivors sustained fractured femurs; 18 survivors and 5 non-survivors sustained knee injuries; 31 survivors and 38 non-survivors sustained lower leg fractures; 26 survivors and 24 non-survivors sustained fractures/dislocations of the ankle; and 22 survivors and 6 non-survivors sustained fractures of the bones of the feet. Many of those affected suffered fractures of more than one area. Only 18 surviving passengers and 6 non-surviving passengers had no injury to the lower limbs and pelvis.

1.14 Fire

There were two separate areas on the No 1 engine which had been affected by fire and these were the only areas where there was evidence of fire on the aircraft. The most seriously affected zone was on the fan case within the forward engine cowling, and the less serious zone was on the rear edge of the reverser duct, on the outboard side.

Ground witness reports indicated that immediately after the ground impact of the aircraft the only fire visible was relatively localised and centred around the forward end of the No 1 engine, but that after a short time the fire suddenly grew in intensity. Upon the arrival of the airport fire service, the fire was quickly extinguished using a combination of aqueous film forming foam (AFFF) and fluoroprotein foams.

1.15 Survival aspects

1.15.1 *On-board emergency preparations and impact effects*

Following the initial engine problem the cabin attendants collected the in-flight meals, which had not long been served. After the diversion to the East Midlands Airport was announced, the attendants checked the passengers' seat belts and stowed all the loose carry-on luggage in the overhead bins. Approximately 10 seconds prior to the first impact the commander warned the passengers to prepare for a crash landing.

Some, but not all, of the passengers adopted a crash position prior to the aircraft striking the ground. One young child was secured on his mother's knee using a supplementary lap belt (seat 3F). Both the mother and child were injured during the impact, the mother sustaining a greater degree of injury, as evidenced by the ISS score, than other passengers sitting around her.

Several of the passengers described heavy vibration immediately prior to the impact and one passenger, in the rear of the aircraft, described the vibration as being severe enough to open the overhead lockers and cause them to spill contents. Passengers in the rear of the aircraft described two distinct impacts; those in the front appeared only to have been aware of the final impact.

During the impact the fuselage broke into 3 main sections, with 4 distinct areas of damage (paragraphs 1.12.2.6 & 7): the area forward of the wing (rows 1-9), where the floor structure was completely disrupted and all the seats became detached, the centre section (rows 10-17), where the majority of the seats remained attached to the floor; and the area behind the wing (rows 18-23L/24R), where the floor failed and the fuselage was disrupted, both circumferentially and from above, by the overturning tail section, in which seat rows 24L/25R-27 remained attached.

In the forward area where the seats became detached, passengers were trapped by the seats moving forward, compressing their occupants. A number of passengers in this area sustained severe crushing injuries.

Following the impact the majority of the passengers were trapped due to injury, seat failure or debris from overhead. Only 14 of the passengers were able to make a significant contribution to effecting their own escape.

Both pilots were trapped, as was one of the two stewardesses in the front flight attendant seat. One stewardess, seated on the rear flight attendant double seat, reported that she had been injured and trapped by a food service cart. The other occupant of this seat was released by the steward, who had been seated on the single seat adjacent to the right rear door.

1.15.2 *Rescue operations*

ATC at East Midlands Airport declared a full emergency at 2008 hrs, alerting the Airport Fire Service (AFS) and the civil emergency services. Vehicles of the AFS deployed immediately to two holding points alongside the mid-section of the runway. Whilst in this position, the AFS attempted to speak to the aircraft on their emergency frequency but were unable to make contact. Vehicles from the Leicestershire Fire Service moved to a pre-arranged rendezvous point at the airport, arriving at 2023 hrs. The AFS crews in the vehicles near the runway saw the aircraft descend below the motorway embankment and moved immediately to the crash site, two vehicles proceeding via the runway and the eastern crash gate and the other via the airport main entrance. The AFS identified and broadcast the exact location of the aircraft at 2029 hrs and were in action extinguishing the fire at 2033 hrs. The vehicles of the Leicestershire Fire Service, travelling via the main entrance, reached the motorway intersection 200 metres north of the site at 2032 hrs and joined the AFS at the scene of the crash shortly afterwards. Immediately afterwards additional vehicles from the Nottinghamshire and Derbyshire Fire Services arrived at the site to assist in rescue work.

At 2012 hrs the police notified the emergency to the Leicestershire Ambulance Service, who immediately despatched ambulances to the airport rendezvous point. These vehicles followed the fire vehicles to the scene. At 2020 hrs the Leicestershire Ambulance Service requested support from the Derbyshire and Nottinghamshire services, whose vehicles were moving towards the airport before the crash occurred. In addition, when they heard news of the accident, the Staffordshire Ambulance Service volunteered assistance. During the rescue operation, the 3 adjacent counties provided 69 ambulances, and 5 were provided by the Staffordshire service. Royal Air Force helicopters and Mountain Rescue Teams also moved to the site when alerted by the Rescue Coordination Centre (RCC) (see paragraph 1.17.5.2). Further assistance was provided by the Army and the Derbyshire Miners' Rescue Team. The Salvation Army provided a mobile canteen service for the rescue workers.

After extinguishing the fire, the fire services laid a blanket of foam as fire protection against leaking fuel, and this blanket was constantly refreshed as the rescue operation continued. Fire and ambulance services, assisted initially by passing motorists, began to recover the survivors from the aircraft and move them to hospital with the minimum of delay. RAF helicopters were used to move some of the more seriously injured passengers to hospital.

The evacuation of the passengers was prolonged. The last passenger was not extricated from the aircraft until 0420 hrs. The survivors were taken to the University Hospital, Queen's Medical Centre, Nottingham, the Derbyshire Royal Infirmary, the Leicestershire Royal Infirmary and the Mansfield and District General Hospital.

1.16 Tests and research

1.16.1 *Engine tests to identify the cause of fan blade fatigue*

At first the cause of the fatigue on blade No 17 was uncertain, but it did not appear to be related to a material or geometric deficiency in the blade, or to any maintenance related actions. As a result, the manufacturer undertook a series of tests to determine whether discrepancies in the condition of the fan abradable liner could have given rise to vibratory excitation of the fan blades. No evidence of any such influence was found.

There was also another series of tests which was directed towards relating the observed imbalance, as recorded on the FDR of ME after the first event, to the loss of fragments of fan blades or to fan blade damage without material loss. During these tests, components mounted on the fan case were fitted with either strain-gauges or accelerometers in order to establish the degree of excitation experienced by these components due to fan imbalance. The results of this test series indicated that the fan imbalance recorded on the FDR of ME after the first event and on the BMA incident to G-OBMG (see paragraph 1.17.7.2) were consistent with that obtained on testing an engine with a single fan blade outer panel missing. During this test series, an engine with a fan in which one blade had no outer panel but the fan assembly was balanced, was run over the full speed range. This did not reflect a 'real' engine condition, as the fan imbalance resulting from the panel loss with its inevitable accompanying vibration levels and gas path degradation were absent. The test was conducted to measure the change of fan performance related purely to the absence of the blade outer panel. It was observed that, under these conditions, there was no measurable difference in thrust relative to that of a complete fan at the same conditions, and that overall engine performance was also unchanged. It was noted, however, that the engine made a peculiar sound in this condition.

After the second and third in-flight fan blade fractures (paragraph 1.17.7) another series of tests was performed with the objective of establishing the modes and degrees of excitation of the fan blades at very high corrected fan speeds[7]. These tests were done in three phases, the first in a ground test cell, the second in a Boeing 737 test pod on a Boeing 707 flying test bed aircraft and the third on a production Boeing 737-400. This final phase was done to check the engine response during various manoeuvres which were not possible on the Boeing 707, and to correlate Boeing 707 derived data with that from the Boeing 737-400.

A ground test engine was fitted with a set of fan blades, some of which were fitted with strain gauges. This fan blade set was selected so that all the blades had the same natural frequency of their second order bending mode. The fan disc to which they were fitted was also strain-gauged, particularly in the region of contact of the fan blade dovetail roots. The engine, with this 'tuned' blade set, was run on a test bed to very high corrected fan speed by combining high mechanical speed with the use of a variable area fan nozzle. This test showed that, under these conditions, there was an excitation of a non-synchronous system vibratory response but it did not produce vibratory stress levels greater than 50% of the endurance limit (paragraph 1.17.9). When the blade set was detuned, by substituting a number of the blades with blades of differing natural frequency, it was found that the response was reduced.

---

[7] Corrected fan speed: Actual fan speed must be factored for temperature to decribe airflow conditions.

Following these tests, the strain-gauged blade sets were installed in an engine on the Boeing 707 flying test bed. The ensuing flight tests showed that the vibratory response in flight was considerably stronger than that apparent during the ground tests. A weak response was observed whilst the engine was running at the −3B-2 rated climb power. When using −3C-1 rated climb power, a response was observed at altitudes above 10,000 feet which was at its most severe at altitudes between 25 and 30,000 feet; vibratory stress levels of up to about 80% of the endurance limit were observed.

It was noticed, during both the ground and flight testing, that the coefficient of friction of the mid-span shroud contact faces affected the vibratory response of the fan. It was found that, as these contact faces became more highly polished with use, the response reduced, and as the lubrication between the faces dried out, the response increased. A number of tests was done in which the shroud contact friction was deliberately changed and the change in excitation was observed to be in the predicted sense.

As a result of the information acquired during these tests, the manufacturer explored several possible ways to eliminate the excitation of this vibration mode. It was established that by installing blade dampers under the root platforms, a significant reduction in the vibratory response could be achieved. The improvement was, however, considered sufficient only to improve the safety margin of the -3B-2 but not to provide satisfactory safety margins at -3C-1 climb power. They therefore investigated methods of eliminating the excitation by a redesign of the fan blades.

Two techniques were considered, each of which had potential penalties. One approach was to alter the contact angle of the mid-span shrouds and thereby change the damping characteristics of the outer portion of the blade. Although this alteration was known to have the desired effect of eliminating the vibration excitation, it had the potential to adversely affect the birdstrike tolerance of the fan and, if this approach were adopted, the engine would have had to be recertificated to show compliance with the birdstrike requirements. The other approach was to recamber the blade outer panel, altering the spanwise thrust distribution on the blade and, consequently, the exciting forces so that the blades did not respond in this particular mode. This approach potentially had detrimental effects on fan efficiency. The manufacturers therefore elected to adopt the change to the shroud contact angle and to recertificate the engine at -3C-1 rating.

1.16.2 *Trials to establish fuel leak characteristics*

After the initial examination of the engines from the two later incidents, suffered by Dan Air and British Midland (paragraph 1.17.7), some tests were performed to establish if there was a relationship between the looseness of various types of fuel line joint and the pattern of the leak (*ie* dripping, continuous flow or fine spraying) at various fuel line pressures. These tests showed that, with the looseness observed on the various types of joint on the accident engine and both of the later incident engines, a fine high pressure spray might have been produced.

As a result of these trials, the engine manufacturer adopted improved self locking nuts for the MEC to fuel pump interface. These were introduced by a Service Bulletin (CFM 56 - SB 73-080 issued 4 May 1990) with a campaign to retrofit all engines by the end of 1992.

1.16.3 *Tests of the engine instrument system (EIS)*

As noted in paragraph 1.12.2.2, no pre-accident defects were found in either the primary or secondary EIS units. However, since the EIS logic requires some degree of processing of the input signals before displaying the parameters to the crew, it was considered necessary to evaluate the response of the system to rapidly changing parameters. It should also be noted that most of this processing occurs before the data is output to the FDAU and thence to the FDR and that therefore the data recorded on the latter has undergone such processing.

Initially, the data available from the FDR was fed into an EIS in a flight deck simulator at the Boeing Company's premises. The purpose of this test was to allow a real-time appraisal to be made of the FDR data on representative displays. During the test it was noted that the instrument which showed the most marked fluctuations of both the cursor and digital display was the No 1 engine N1 gauge. However, it was also apparent that, over a total period of 20 seconds of parameter fluctuations, there occurred a 6-second period of relative stability, some 9 seconds after their onset. Parameters which were not recorded on the FDR were either allocated representative values or left blank. Strictly for the purposes of this test, it was assumed that the No 1 engine vibration display rose to a maximum reading coincident with the primary parameter fluctuations and remained there until it dropped below 4 units when power on the No 1 engine was reduced to flight idle. Although some evidence for this behaviour could be deduced from the FDR data, the 64 second sample rate of the vibration parameter rendered precise timing impossible.

Substantiation for the behaviour of the EIS system was explored during a further series of tests conducted at AAIB using the actual hardware from ME. Data for these tests was obtained from the FDR records of a number of aircraft, including ME, and from engine test bed data. The operating range of the EIS was explored using computer-generated N1 and vibration signals. The vibration parameter is discussed separately in the following section. The AAIB tests on the primary EIS concentrated on the N1 speed parameter since this appeared to have undergone the most pronounced fluctuations during the first event.

The purpose of the AAIB tests was to confirm that:-

(i) the data recovered from the FDR was a subset of the information presented to the crew, and

(ii) no condition existed where the EIS display could differ from the output to the FDAU/FDR.

Both the above propositions were confirmed and no abnormalities were observed in the operation of the primary EIS.

Tests on the AVM/Secondary EIS.

The AVM module processes the raw accelerometer data from the engines to a high degree before a signal is output to the EIS and the FDR. In addition to the tracking filter, other features are incorporated to suppress transients and spurious data. It was decided to test the AVM module and the secondary EIS from ME together to determine:

(i) how rapidly a simulated signal from the accelerometers would be displayed on the vibration indicator.

(ii) whether the AVM tracking filter was able to track a rapidly fluctuating N1 signal and to what extent the output value might be modified.

It was found that, for massive rotor imbalances in the order of 20 scale units, the meter rose to full-scale deflection within 2 seconds of the event occurring (50 units being approximately that estimated as generated by loss of a single fan blade outer panel).

For lower values of vibration (*ie* less than 10 units), the recorded N1 fluctuations caused the displayed vibration parameter to be reduced by 1 to 2 units below the maximum 5 units over the period of the fluctuations.

1.16.4   *KRASH computer simulation*

As part of the structures and survivability aspects of the investigation, it was decided to attempt a computer-based modelling of the ground impact dynamics of ME. The primary objective was to refine the deceleration levels at the cabin floor throughout the impact sequence. Secondary objectives were to determine the efficacy of such a computer-based model and whether such a study could achieve useful results within the time-scale of the overall accident investigation.

The two broad groups of computer programs available for impact dynamics may be classified as:

(i)   'full' finite element programs, which model a vehicle structure in detail using only geometric and material-properties input data.

(ii) 'hybrid' programs, which use a simpler library of structural elements for the model and incorporate some test-derived data for the collapse properties of key members within the structure.

KRASH is a hybrid program and has been developed specifically for the analysis of aircraft impact problems. Because of its simpler modelling, and the availability of full-scale test data from previous FAA full-scale impact tests, Cranfield Impact Centre Limited was commissioned to perform the impact study, using the KRASH program.

1.16.4.1   *KRASH model for G-OBME*

As the 3 main sections of fuselage (forward, centre-section, tail) remained essentially complete, the wings, fuselage and empennage were modelled as 3 lumped-masses, divided by the 2 fuselage breaking points. The 2 engines, 2 main landing gears and nose landing gear were individually represented by mass-points, resulting in an 8-mass model. The effective masses and moments of inertia of the occupants, fuel and luggage were added at the appropriate mass-points.

A key assumption made in this approach was that the deformation of the aircraft had been limited to localised areas of structure - ie the fuselage break-points and the lower fuselage. 'Contact springs' were thus attached to the mass-points to represent the force/deflection properties of those parts of the structure which would make contact with the ground and a simple beam model represented the bending behaviour of the fuselage.

The impact parameters for the first impact were those in paragraph 1.12.1.1, derived from the impact markings and extrapolation of the FDR values. Aerodynamic forces and moments were not included in the basic KRASH model, so the trajectory between the 2 impacts was initially considered as ballistic. However, the second case analysed for the final impact was based on the more accurate aerodynamic considerations of paragraph 1.12.1.1.

1.16.4.2   *KRASH results*

Following the creation of the KRASH model, the impact sequence was run 3 times. In Run 1 the whole impact sequence was represented, allowing the aircraft a free ballistic trajectory between the 2 impacts and using an estimate of the coefficient of friction between the airframe and the soil. Although the model remained stable, the second impact was shown occurring further up the western embankment than was actually the case so, rather than fine-tuning the model, Runs 2 and 3 were started at the second impact and used the impact parameters shown in paragraph 1.12.1.1.

Run 2 represented the second impact after ballistic flight from the first impact, giving horizontal and vertical velocities of 48.9 metres/sec and 14.4 metres/sec respectively. Peak deceleration values for the centre section (Appendix 3, figs 22a and 22b) were 26.5g (longitudinal axis) and 23g (vertical axis): the peak resultant coincided with the 26.5g longitudinal peak.

Run 3 represented the second impact after a trajectory in which the wing was assumed to produce residual lift equivalent to approximately 40% of the weight of the aircraft. This gave horizontal and vertical velocities of 37.9 metres/sec and 11.1 metres/sec respectively. Peak deceleration values (figs 23a and 23b) were 19.5g (longitudinal axis) and 12.6g (vertical axis): again, the peak of the resultant deceleration coincided with the longitudinal peak (19.5g).

In Runs 2 and 3 the longitudinal deceleration signals (figs 22a and 23a) were composed of a vibratory component of about 60 Hz, superimposed on a fundamental signal of approximately sine-curve shape. The 60 Hz signal represented the low-amplitude elastic deformations, whereas the fundamental wave represented the actual plastic deformation. The maximum values of this fundamental signal were 19.5g (Run 2) and 15.5g (Run 3).

1.16.5   *Computer simulation of occupant response*

Using data derived from the impact analysis conducted at the Cranfield Impact Centre (CIC) a further computer analysis of the occupant response was carried out. The CIC KRASH analysis is described above in paragraph 1.16.4. This further study was undertaken by H W Structures Ltd[6] using the crash victim simulation program, MADYMO. Pre and post-processing was achieved using MADPREP and MADPOST. The occupant was simulated by a Hybrid 111 dummy data set. The simulation was conducted for an occupant seated in the rear of two rows at a 32 inch separation in the overwing area. An occupant was seated in the seat in front to give that seat the appropriate inertial characteristics for the rear occupant impact. No data was derived directly from the front seat occupant. The simulation permitted the evaluation of the dynamic response of the rear occupant, as well as generating information on the contact and inertial forces and accelerations experienced.

Appendix 5, fig 4 shows the results of a 1.4 second simulation which embraces all the significant events of the actual impact, using the dynamic pulse generated by Run 2 of the CIC KRASH simulation. The occupant experienced a double impact with the seat back which was clearly seen in the graphics of the animation. Head contact occurred early due to the deliberately preset brace position. In the case of 'breakover' capable seats (*ie* -424 type shown in Appendix 5, fig 4) the impact pulse was sufficient to release the seat backs before occupant contact occurred. In the case of emergency exit 'non-breakover' (*ie* -444 type) seats the impact of the occupant caused structural failure of the seat back frame at its base. The seat back was then only retained by trim and flailed for the remainder of the impact event.

Contacts, forces and accelerations were obtained from the simulation and these were found to be consistent with the injuries sustained by survivors and some of the deceased. Head injury criteria (HIC) values were consistent with consciousness for the braced occupant, and head injury and impairment of consciousness for the unbraced. Contacts representative of facial, pelvic and lower limb injuries were also demonstrated. High contact forces between the front spar of the seat and the femur were noted.

The simulation was also used to estimate the loads into the floor structure from the seat legs for four seating configurations: forward facing (braced), forward facing (unbraced), forward facing with three point harness (upper harness location on airframe) as shown in fig 5 and rearward facing as shown in fig 6. The peak loads, which were based upon loadings generated by a single occupant, were as follows:-

		Max resultant load
Forward facing seat	Front Leg	19.3kN
(occupant in brace position)	Rear Leg	20.8kN
Forward facing seat	Front Leg	16.5kN
(occupant upright unbraced)	Rear Leg	20.3kN
Forward facing seat	Front Leg	19.2kN
(three point harness)	Rear Leg	19.6kN
Rearward facing seat	Front Leg	22.9kN
	Rear Leg	21.3kN

1.17 Additional information

1.17.1 Pilot training

The Boeing Commercial Airplane Company provided technical training for pilots of the Boeing 737 series aircraft. This training was conducted either at the company facility at Seattle or by a Boeing instructor, using the same syllabus, at a facility in the customer's own country where a flight simulator was available. The commander completed a course on the Boeing 737 Series 300 given by a Boeing instructor in the United Kingdom. The first officer was trained by BMA on a course that followed the Boeing syllabus.

The Boeing course consisted of 12 days of academic instruction on the aircraft and its systems using audio-visual aids and a fixed-base flight simulator. This was followed by further training on a full flight simulator during which systems knowledge was revised and normal and non-normal procedures were practised.

Boeing training for non-normal situations was that pilots should evaluate all cockpit indications and should not take action until the problem had been positively identified. When it had been identified the appropriate non-normal procedure or checklist should have been completed. Emphasis was given to the need for pilots to avoid precipitate action.

The high vibration checklist (paragraph 1.17.2.4) had not been introduced when the commander completed his type training on the Boeing 737 Series 300. No special importance was given during this training to the engine vibration monitors and no instruction in the fixed base simulator or in the full flight simulator included the non-normal condition of high engine vibration. No reference was made during training to the possibility of ingress of smoke and fumes from the fan and LP compressor abradable seals in the event of fan blade failure.

Boeing also produced a study guide to the differences between the Series 300 and the Series 400 aircraft, which covered *inter alia* the differences in the air-conditioning systems of the two aircraft. Both the commander and the first officer underwent a one day course at BMA on these differences during which they were also introduced to the EIS. At this time, however, no EIS-equipped flight simulator was available for use by BMA.

Following type training, all pilots of BMA were required to complete currency training every six months. Each session consisted of 8 hours flight simulator training, shared between a captain and first officer, during which each pilot flew the mandatory six-monthly base check under the supervision of a training captain. Each pilot also completed a technical questionnaire to refresh his knowledge of the aircraft and its systems. Pilots renewed their instrument ratings annually during currency training. A substantial part of the flight simulator training that was not devoted to base checks and instrument rating renewals was used to practise emergency situations and non-normal procedures. In addition to the mandatory exercises specified in the company Training Manual, crews were exercised on further emergency drills selected by the training captain. Any additional time available in each simulator training period was used for particular drills that the pilots themselves wished to practise. BMA stated that all training captains employed by the company taught a deliberate and considered response to emergencies and the avoidance of precipitate action. Since the accident to ME the company has increased practice of fan blade failures but the flight simulators are not programmed to produce a combination of high vibration and fumes.

Training captains were appointed by the Chief Pilot and approved by the Operations Director. They were checked every 3 years by the CAA. Their performance was also checked by company inspectors, who included the Operations Director, the Chief Pilot and other specially appointed senior pilots.

1.17.2   *The aircraft Operating Manual and checklist*

1.17.2.1   *Non-normal procedures*

In the aircraft Operations Manual the introduction to non-normal procedures included the following instructions:

> 'Non-normal procedures are used by the trained flight crew to cope with system faults and other situations affecting safe flight. . . . . .

> 'Procedures that prescribe an engine shutdown must be evaluated by the Captain to ascertain if an actual shutdown or operation at reduced power is the safest course of action.'

1.17.2.2   *Air Conditioning Smoke*

The aircraft checklist included the following procedure to be followed in the event of air conditioning smoke:

AIR CONDITIONING SMOKE

Pilot oxygen masks and regulators	ON, 100%
Smoke goggles (if required)	ON
Crew communications	ESTABLISH
Recirculation fan switch	OFF

If smoke stops:
Continue flight with recirculation fan switch off.

If smoke continues:

    Isolation valve switch   CLOSE

    Right pack switch   OFF

If smoke stops:

    Continue flight with isolation valve closed and right pack switch off.

If smoke continues:

    Right pack switch   AUTO

    Left pack switch   OFF

If smoke stops:

    Continue flight with left pack switch off and isolation valve closed.

If smoke continues:

    Left pack switch   AUTO

If smoke continues:

    Land at nearest suitable airport

1.17.2.3   *Engine shutdown checklists*

Two engine shutdown procedures were given in the aircraft checklist. The 'Engine Failure and Shutdown' procedure was intended to be accomplished by reference to the checklist. The 'Engine Fire, Severe Damage or Separation' procedure was for more urgent situations and required the initial actions to be accomplished from memory (the 'recall' items). Only the latter procedure called for the use of the engine fire extinguishing system.

1.17.2.4   *High engine vibration*

In March 1988 Boeing issued an Operations Manual Bulletin on the subject of CFM 56-3 engine vibration. It defined 'high engine vibration' as a condition indicated by a reading on the vibration indicators in excess of 4.0 units accompanied by perceivable airframe vibrations. It introduced the following procedure:

    Thrust lever........   RETARD

    Flight conditions permitting, reduce N1 to maintain AVM below 4.0 units.

NOTE: Engine shutdown is not required as AVM indications will decrease with thrust reduction. If the AVM indication does not decrease when the thrust lever is retarded, other engine problems may be indicated.

This drill was incorporated in the Quick Reference Handbook in May 1988. Pending amendment of the Operations Manual, a copy of the Operations Manual Bulletin was issued to all Boeing 737 pilots employed by BMA.

The Operations Manual included another reference to vibration in the non-normal procedures section under the heading 'ENGINE FIRE, SEVERE DAMAGE OR SEPARATION'. The reference read:-

'This condition is recognised by the fire warning bell ringing and an engine fire warning light illuminated, and/or airframe vibration with abnormal engine indications with or without yaw.

'If the emergency is positively corrected, the Captain should evaluate the situation before proceeding with the next step. If any doubt exists as to the condition of the engine or fire warning system, complete all recall items.'

(The 'recall items' are the actions taken by the crew from memory for the emergency shut-down of an engine. (1.17.2.3))

1.17.2.5   *In-flight engine start*

The drill in the Quick Reference Handbook for engine starting in the air with airspeed outside the 'windmill' start envelope was as follows:

Thrust lever	CLOSE
Pack switch (affected side)	OFF
Duct pressure	MINIMUM 30 PSI
(If required, advance the thrust lever to increase duct pressure)	
Start switch	GRD
Start lever	IDLE

The Quick Reference Handbook also listed a drill for restarting the No 1 engine in the event that both engines had failed and the airspeed was below the 'windmill' start envelope. This drill was suitable only for the start of the No 1 engine and was as follows:

APU	START AND ON BUS
Isolation valve switch	CLOSE
Left air conditioning pack switch	OFF
Engine No 1 bleed air switch	OFF
APU bleed air switch	ON
Ignition select switch	BOTH
Engine No 1 start switch	GRD
Start lever	IDLE

1.17.3   Pilot opinion of the EIS

During May and June 1989 an informal survey of pilot opinion of the EIS among Boeing 737 pilots in UK airlines was conducted by AAIB. Replies were received from 120 pilots, representing over 90% of all pilots in the UK with experience of the EIS. When the results of the survey were received, it was noted that the replies of the 53 pilots of BMA were more critical of the EIS than those of other airlines.

The overall results, however, showed that a large majority of pilots considered that the EIS displayed engine parameters clearly and most considered that it also showed rate of change of parameter clearly. Fewer than 10% of pilots reported any difficulty in converting to the EIS from the earlier hybrid instruments and only a few reported minor difficulty in alternating between the EIS and hybrid displays. 64% of pilots stated that they preferred instruments with electro-mechanical pointers to the EIS (74% of BMA pilots and 58% of non-BMA pilots).

The most unfavourable assessments were received in response to the question 'Is the EIS effective in drawing attention to rapid changes in engine parameters?'. 64% of BMA pilots and 39% of non-BMA pilots thought it was not. 43 pilots (31 from BMA and 12 others) wrote additional comments in answer to this question in which they criticised the LED pointers of the EIS as too small, lacking in visual impact and not as conspicuous as the pointers on electro-mechanical instruments. These pilots considered that their attention was more likely to be attracted by the movement of full-length pointers than by changing numeric displays and the shorter LED pointers. An analysis of the human factors aspects of the EIS design is included at Appendix 2.7.

1.17.4   Engine vibration monitors in aircraft

When questioned after the accident both pilots said that they did not remember seeing indications of high vibration on the engine vibration gauges. The commander added that he rarely included these instruments in his scan because he believed them to be unreliable and prone to giving spurious readings. Accordingly, the background to the use of vibration monitors in turbo-jet aircraft was investigated.

Effective from 1 March 1974, the Federal Aviation Administration (FAA) introduced an amendment to Parts 25 and 33 of the Federal Aviation Regulations which introduced a requirement for turbojet powered aircraft to have fitted an instrument to indicate rotor system unbalance. The preamble to the amendment stated *inter alia*:

> 'The FAA is aware that the currently available vibration detectors are not as reliable as the engines they monitor and to that extent, they may impose an economic penalty; however, a rotor system failure can be catastrophic and the contributions to flight safety gained from a vibration monitoring system that provides the flight crew with an appropriate vibration warning far outweighs any difficulties that may be experienced.'

> 'The rule, however, does not require that a level of acceptable vibration be specified. It merely requires an indication of "rotor system unbalance'in the engine as installed in the aircraft. The indicator may be employed to sense a trend of vibrations over a period of time, rather than a specific level at a particular instant.'

On 30 August 1974, a similar requirement was added to BCARs, which were amended to include in the items of equipment to be installed on aeroplanes:

> 'On turbo-jet engine installations, a vibration meter for each engine to indicate the level of vibration in the engine unless serious out-of-balance of the engine would be otherwise evident to the flight crew.'

In compliance with the requirement in BCARs, vibration meters were installed in most turbo-jet powered aircraft operating on the British Register. Their serviceability was poor and, because they were sensitive to a broad band of vibration frequencies, they often indicated high vibration levels from sources other than the engines, particularly during take-off from uneven runway surfaces. They were subsequently removed from a number of aircraft types including the Boeing 707, Concorde, McDonnell Douglas DC9 and those Boeing 747s powered by Pratt and Whitney JT9D engines. In many cases where engine vibration meters were installed, master minimum equipment lists (MMELs) permitted aircraft to be despatched with no vibration monitors operating. Some UK companies were permitted to operate BAC 1-11 and MD83 aircraft with the vibration monitors disconnected at the circuit breaker. Another company was permitted to remove the vibration monitors from its Boeing 727 aircraft.

Newer airborne vibration monitoring systems, such as that fitted to the Boeing 737 Series 300/400, are more reliable and display only those vibration signals related directly to the rotating assemblies within the engines (see paragraph 1.6.4).

1.17.5 *Actions by air traffic control*

1.17.5.1 *Transfer of control from London to Manchester*

In the Manual of Air Traffic Services the following guidance is given to controllers on the selection of the controlling agency for an aircraft in an emergency:

'If the controller can offer immediate assistance the aircraft should normally be retained on the frequency. If necessary impose radio silence on other aircraft or transfer them to another frequency.'

'If a controller considers that another unit may be able to give more assistance than he can give himself, and in the circumstances it is reasonable to ask the pilot to change frequency, he shall .....alert the nearest suitable unit and transfer the aircraft to a common frequency, giving assistance to that unit as required.'

The decision to transfer control of G-OBME to Manchester was taken because communications between Manchester and East Midlands were by direct telephone line rather than the PBX line linking the LATCC Daventry sector controller with East Midlands. If the recovery of the aircraft to East Midlands had been undertaken by LATCC, authorisation would have been required from Manchester for the aircraft to penetrate the Manchester sub-centre's airspace and time could have been wasted. The Manchester Chief Sector Controller also considered that his radar controller, being well-versed in approach duties, would have been more practised in dealing with airfields than the LATCC en-route controller.

1.17.5.2 Alerting

The Distress and Diversion (D & D) Cell at LATCC is an RAF unit tasked primarily with the recovery of military aircraft. However, when they are advised by the LATCC supervisor of a civil aircraft emergency, they coordinate their activities with the civil operation and inform the appropriate Rescue Coordination Centre (RCC).

When this accident occurred the Chief Sector Controller (CSC) on the Daventry East sector at LATCC advised his supervisor but did not say that the aircraft had declared an emergency, stating only that the aircraft 'has got a fire in an engine and is diverting quickly to Castle Donington'. The supervisor treated the occurrence as a straightforward diversion and left the Daventry east sector controller to execute the necessary coordination. He took no further action regarding the flight until he was advised of the crash.

When notified of the crash the supervisor referred to the LATCC Emergency Orders and informed the authorities named therein. The correct ATCC alerting action is described in the Manual of Air Traffic Services (MATS) Part 1, Section 5, Chapter 6 and requires that in all emergency phases the ATCC informs the RCC. However, the emergency orders provided to the supervisor on this occasion included a copy of the Manual of Air Traffic Services (MATS) Part 1, Section 6, Chapter 2, para 4, which does not contain a specific instruction to liaise with the D & D Cell.

As a consequence of this the D & D Cell was not informed. They first heard of it when an RCC controller, who was off duty and heard of the accident on the radio, called the D & D Cell for information. The Officer Commanding the RCC then scrambled three helicopters and two mountain rescue teams.

In July 1988 it became apparent to the RAF Air Officer Scotland and Northern Ireland that the links between civil ATC agencies and RAF rescue services were not as good as they should be. He therefore requested the Military Air Traffic Organisation (MATO) to take up the matter with the Civil Air Traffic Organisation (CATO) and ensure that the appropriate RCC was informed of all aircraft accidents and of aircraft in distress. It was stressed as particularly important that the ATCC Supervisors should alert the appropriate D & D cell at the earliest opportunity so that information could be passed to the RCC. Although this matter had been discussed by CATO and MATO and the plan approved in principle, the appropriate administrative steps to ensure such notification had not been taken at LATCC at the time of the accident.

1.17.6   *Development of the CFM56-3 engine*

The engines of the CFM 56 family are high by-pass turbofans, which fall broadly into the 10 tonne thrust range. They have been designed and produced by CFM International, a company in which SNECMA of France and General Electric (GE) Aircraft Engines of the USA co-operate.

These engines are of similar design and have 2 shafts. The high pressure (HP) core is based on GE F101/110 military engine technology. This core is used as a gas generator to drive a low pressure (LP) system which comprises a multi-stage turbine driving a fan and LP compressor (booster) ahead of the core (see engine cross-section at Appendix 1, fig 1). The original production model, the CFM 56-2, had a fan diameter of 68.3 inches, with blades which had tip shrouds but no part span shrouds. This engine had a by-pass ratio of 6:1 in the cruise.

The CFM 56-3 was a derivative of this engine which was designed specifically for the Boeing 737 -300 & 400 models, and had a by-pass ratio of 5:1. The fan was to a new design, of a reduced 60 inch diameter, with blades which had part span shrouds, but no tip shrouds. The booster was also of a new design. The CFM 56-3 was originally certificated at a take-off thrust rating of 22,000 lbs, but it was derated to 20,000 lbs for the first production variant, which was designated -3-B1. Later, the 22,000 lbs thrust engine entered production and was designated -3B-2. Both these variants were fitted to Boeing 737-300 series aircraft.

The -3C-1 engine was a development for the Boeing 737-400 aircraft, and was rated at 23,500 lbs take-off thrust. The thrust increase to the -3C-1 rating was achieved by a control schedule change. This permitted an increase in core speed together with an increase to the rated temperature. In addition it included an alteration to the scheduling of the variable stator vanes (VSVs) of the core compressor at high corrected speed. This change to the VSV schedule slightly increased the LP to HP speed ratio (N1/N2) as the engine approached maximum rated power. The fan outlet guide vanes (OGVs) were also redesigned for greater efficiency, as were the fan blade tips. These last two changes were also introduced into the -3-B1 and 3B-2 engines

1.17.6.1   Fan blade development and testing

The general approach to the development of a new fan design must encompass two main requirements. One requirement is to achieve the maximum thrust and engine efficiency, optimised for a specific flight regime. The other is that the manufacturer has to ensure that the fan, and indeed the entire engine, will meet all the airworthiness criteria which include those for failure containment, foreign object damage tolerance and vibration characteristics.

The containment requirement for gas turbine engine design is that, if blades are sufficiently severely damaged that part or complete blades detach whilst the engine is running at its maximum speed, the detached parts shall not penetrate the engine casings and escape in a radial direction. It should be noted, however, that should the disc on which the blades are mounted break up, the energy of the fragments thus produced is so large that it is not a requirement that the engine casing shall contain them. The CFM 56-3 was subjected to the standard containment test where a complete fan blade was released at maximum take-off power and proved acceptable.

Damage tolerance requirements in turbofan engine design fall into two inter-related categories. The first is the requirement that the engine should retain the capacity to produce a specified proportion of its rated thrust for a limited time period after ingesting defined foreign objects such as birds of various sizes or hailstones, ice, sand and gravel. The second category of requirement is that, if the engine ingests smaller debris which does not result in a detectable change in performance, the damage to the aerofoil blades should not lead to their failure before the next normal inspection. To meet this requirement, designers endeavour to ensure that the stresses, particularly those arising from vibratory loading, are low in the region of the blade leading edge, where FOD is most likely to occur. In this way it is intended that the increased stresses induced by the presence of such damage will not be sufficiently high as to cause the initiation of fatigue cracking, before such damage is detected by normal inspection and blended-out.

In order to achieve this second requirement, CFMI adopted a design objective that the maximum allowable vibratory stress anywhere on the fan blades should not exceed 35% of the endurance limit[8] for the minimum material specification. In addition, they used an endurance limit which was reduced by a factor of 1.365 from the minimum material specification for the titanium alloy used. The manufacturers adopted this approach to provide a conservative margin of strength to allow for any typical in-service damage, deterioration and airflow distortion.

The fan blade stress tests were conducted in two phases. In the first phase, individual blades were tested to determine the various modes of blade vibration, their frequencies and nodal patterns, followed by tests using a dense strain-gauge array, to determine the stress distribution in the blades resulting from the various vibration modes. In the second phase, engine tests were conducted to determine the actual degree of excitation of these vibration modes in operation. Such tests were performed with a limited array of strain-gauges on some fan blades in an engine, placed in positions on the blades in positions which had been used during the individual blade tests, so that correlation between the two types of test could be made. In addition, during such engine tests further strain-gauges were placed on the fan disc, to enable any blade-to-disc interaction to be detected. There were thus two basic types of fan vibration excitation which were checked - ie blade only modes and combined blade and disc (system) modes, each of which could be directly related to the fan speed (synchronous mechanical or aerodynamic resonant excitation) or apparently unrelated to fan speed (aerodynamically induced, non-synchronous excitation). The vibration response of the fan was required to be examined over the full speed range of the engine and up to 102% of the maximum overspeed condition, with and without distorted inlet airflow. The inlet distortion for which the engine was demonstrated had to be equivalent to the maximum that the airframe manufacturer demonstrated to be possible, under all flight regimes. The requirements stated that these tests had to be performed either in a test bed or in an installation on an aircraft, provided that the certificating authority was satisfied that the complete operational envelope was adequately explored.

For the CFM 56-3 these tests were performed in a ground test cell over an engine speed range from ground-idle up to 103% of the red line speed[9] (109%). In order to reach this high speed, which in flight only occurs as a corrected speed at high altitude, a variable area fan nozzle was used. Since use of this technique altered the operating line of the fan, it was not a true test of the fan characteristics at high altitude. Up to the time of the accident to ME, however, the manufacturers were confident that this technique was sound as it had never failed to reveal any tendency for blades to be susceptible to excitation. As a result, it

---

[8] Endurance limit: See paragraph. 1.17.9
[9] Red line speed: maximum permissible physical speed in service

was accepted by them and the regulatory authorities as a satisfactory way to demonstrate compliance with the requirements. These tests did not reveal any unexpected vibration excitation at that time and all the vibratory stresses calculated from observations made during the tests, where the inlet distortion was within the agreed limits, were of such low amplitude that they did not reach 50% of the endurance limit for the material. Thus the testing appeared to indicate that the fan blades should have had infinite high cycle fatigue life.

The original fan blade design for the CFM 56-3 engine was a directly scaled-down version of that used in the General Electric CF6-80A engine. Initial performance and blade stress testing and analysis was conducted using this blade form.

The design of the blade was then developed through a series of modifications. The first modification introduced a general thickening of the aerofoil forward of mid-chord, to improve the bird ingestion capability of the blade. This was accompanied by an increase in thickness of the blade aerofoil in the vicinity of the mid-span shroud. The second modification was a refinement of the foil/shroud intersection and this design was further modified by a reduction in length of about 0.1%, to reduce tip rubbing. As a result of bird ingestion testing, one of several modifications was to change the mid-span shroud contact angle from 42° to 25° to improve the resistance to bird strikes. This reduced length / modified contact angle blade became the initial definitive -3 production blade known as the P08 blade. This blade type was fitted to all –3B and –3B2 engines until the –3C variant became available. At that time, a new design of blade, with a small change to the tip, was developed to improve fan efficiency. This new blade (designated P09) was fitted to all –3C engines from new and was available to be fitted to earlier engine variants, either in complete fan sets or mixed with P08s in a set.

At each stage of this fan blade development, the vibration characteristics were compared with those of the original blade by cross reference to test data and were not seen to have altered significantly. Furthermore, test bed running of engines with strain-gauged blades confirmed that the vibratory stresses remained the same, or decreased, compared with the original design. Particular attention was focused on any change in the vibration characteristics following the alteration to the mid-span shroud contact angle as the change from 42° to 25° was known to have the potential to reduce blade damping. Because there were no significant detected changes to blade characteristics from the time of the tests on the original blade design, no further engine tests with a strain-gauged fan were run up to 103% red line speed, up to the time of the accident to ME.

Shortly after this accident, a test bed run with a strain-gauged fan was run up to 103% red line speed as part of the testing of a redesigned airflow splitter at the booster intake. This modification was being tested as a development to improve the capability of the engine to ingest rain and hail. This test showed that the basic vibration response of the fan was very similar to that of the original fan. It was later noted, however, that in the maximum speed range there were indications of a very low level, non-synchronous, excitation. At the time of the test, however, the significance of this excitation was not appreciated because of its low amplitude (see paragraph 1.16.1).

After the two subsequent fan incidents (paragraph 1.17.7) further tests, conducted to a modified technique, revealed the existence of an hitherto unsuspected non-synchronous fan system excitation mode within the maximum fan speed range. With the benefit of this knowledge of the precise mode involved, the previously obtained data from the certification and modified splitter tests was critically reviewed. This showed that indications of the existence of this excitation had been present, but at such a low amplitude that it was not appreciated, without the foreknowledge of the exact mode to seek.

1.17.6.2 *Certification and CAA validation of the CFM 56–3C engine*

The primary type approval of aero engines is normally performed, in a similar manner to that for aircraft, by the certificating authority of the country of design and manufacture. Even after this has been obtained, each variant developed from the basic type must be type approved in its own right although that approval will depend largely on the previous one. When an engine type is first fitted to an aircraft type, the installation must also be approved and the aircraft is then approved with that particular installation. This approval enables the type or variant to be used legally in the country of origin.

When an operator wishes to introduce a new aircraft type onto the register of another country, the local airworthiness authority must validate the approvals for the aircraft, engine and installation. In countries in which the airworthiness requirements are identical to those of the primary certificating authority, this validation is straightforward. If, however, the local airworthiness requirements are different, the local authority must ensure compliance with its own requirements or satisfy itself that non-compliance in a certain area is not significant, before validating the primary approval.

Since the CAA had to validate FAA engine type approvals frequently, about ten years ago it conducted a major audit comparing the service histories of all engine types approved under FARs with those approved under British Civil Airworthiness Requirements (BCARs). The conclusion reached was that, from an airworthiness standpoint, there was no significant difference in the standards achieved using either set of requirements. They therefore entered into an agreement with the FAA concerning the mutual validation of engine type approvals given by the other authority. The CAA continued to monitor the airworthiness standards achieved but remained satisfied that there was no reason to alter this agreement. Thus the validation of engine type approvals issued by the FAA as the primary certificating authority are, to all intents and purposes, automatically given CAA type approval although the agreement provides for the CAA to audit the means of compliance as it considers necessary.

A comparison of the Federal and Joint Airworthiness Requirements (FARs and JARs[10]) for type certification of an engine shows that the factors which must be considered are largely common. As a general rule, however, FARs are less specific than JARs as to how a manufacturer should demonstrate compliance with the requirements. When considering the requirements for demonstrating that an engine type is free from damaging vibrations of rotor blades or discs within a gas turbine engine, this difference is apparent. (see Appendix 1, extract 1) In particular, it can be seen that JARs indicate the types of testing that a manufacturer may use to demonstrate compliance whilst allowing them the option to use other methods with the authority's agreement. However, FARs do not indicate the type of test that may be used but leave the determination as to what constitutes a satisfactory demonstration of compliance to the manufacturer. It is, however, implicit in both sets of requirements that the certificating authority must be convinced that the means of demonstration are both appropriate and sufficient for proof of compliance. Historically, it has not been a regular practice amongst US engine manufacturers to check for blade vibrations using a strain-gauged engine in a flying test bed, unless tests in a cell at sea level indicated that there was cause for concern. This factor was one which was considered by the CAA during their comparitive audit and the comparison did not show that US primary certificated engines had been any more prone to suffering unexpected damaging vibration modes after entering service than those with CAA primary certification.

The CFM 56, being a Franco-American co-operative venture, was originally approved, by the FAA and DGAC jointly, as being in compliance with both FARs and JARs. When validation of the type approval was sought from the CAA, for administrative reasons, they wished to deal with only one nominated primary certificating authority. An agreement was reached whereby the primary certificating authority for the CFM 56-3 variants was the FAA. Thus the CFM 56-3-B1 and subsequent -3B-2 and -3C-1 developments were viewed as FAA approved engines and, by means of a 'limited audit', granted CAA validation. This agreement, however, did not inhibit the CAA from unilaterally withdrawing the type approval of the CFM 56-3C after the two later fan blade failures which occurred on British registered aircraft.

---

[10] Joint Airworthiness Requirements (JARs) are the successors to BCARs for current CAA approvals. They are also used by the Directorate Generale d' Aviation Civile (DGAC) of France in common with the Authorities of other JAA member countries.

1.17.6.3   Fan and compressor airflow, stalling and recovery

The purpose of the compressor in a gas turbine engine is to drive a mass of air from a region of relatively low pressure, at the intake, to one of higher pressure in the combustion chamber. In an axial flow compressor the air passes through a series of stages of aerofoil blades arranged in annuli on a rotating spool with annuli of static aerofoil vanes (stators) between each stage. Each rotating stage accepts air from the preceding stators, compresses and delivers it to the following stators which produce the intake conditions for the next stage. The relationship between the stage inlet and outlet pressures is known as the stage pressure ratio which is related to the rotational speed of the engine. It is, by design, less than the maximum that it would be possible to develop under any prevailing conditions so that there is a margin for airflow fluctuations to occur without causing the stage to stall. It is, however, desirable to keep this margin as small as possible for the best overall powerplant efficiency. This concept of a stall margin can be applied to a complete multi-stage compressor as well as to a single stage.

The condition of aerodynamic stalling occurs when the airflow round an aerofoil separates from the suction surface. When this occurs, the ability of the aerofoil to fulfill its function is greatly reduced until the conditions of the airflow approaching it are altered so that the flow reattaches itself.

Compressor blade aerofoils work by drawing air from the stage inlet by creating a suction. In order to obtain the maximum stage pressure rise at the existing rotor speed, this suction is, by design, close to the maximum that it is possible to develop and, consequently, to the stalling point. Thus if the inlet or outlet conditions alter over part or all of a stage annulus, the airflow may separate from the blades, leaving all or part of the stage stalled. If a stage stalls, the airflow through it breaks down and it will no longer be able to deliver the pressure or the airflow that the succeeding stage needs at its inlet in order to deliver what its successor needs in turn. As a result, this next stage attempts to achieve a pressure ratio of which it is incapable and stalls in turn. In a similar way, the preceding stage is prevented from delivering the airflow that it should and also attempts to achieve a higher stage pressure ratio than its capability and stalls. This process will cascade rapidly in both directions through the compressor and results in a loss of pressure and airflow delivery to the combustion chamber. As a result, the high pressure hot gas in the combustion chamber will flow forwards through the compressor until the pressure within it falls enough to equal what the compressor is able to deliver. In the meantime the compressor speed will decay as a result of the high drag caused by the separated airflow and a reduction in the driving force from the turbine caused by the loss of combustion chamber pressure and gas flow. At the same time the combustion chamber temperature will also start to rise, because the airflow will be less than is required for the existing fuel flow. When the combustion chamber pressure has reduced sufficiently, the compressor will attempt to re-establish the airflow and pressure deliveries which are consistent with the speed to which it has decayed.

Thus, a compressor stall is initiated by at least one stage attempting to achieve a pressure ratio of which it is incapable under existing conditions. In a turbofan engine, the fan itself may be regarded as a single stage compressor in so far as the by-pass stream is concerned, but the central portion of the fan also creates the inlet conditions for the booster. Thus a fan stall can affect the airflow through the booster and core sufficiently to cause compressor stalls in either or both. In general, however, fans are less prone to stalling than other compression stages.

In order to control the airflow in each stage at engine speeds other than that for which the design is optimised, there are devices to restrict and adjust the direction of the airflow (variable stator vanes) or to bleed off excess air (variable bleed valves) at various stages. The pressure ratio that the complete compressor is required to achieve at any time is determined by the gas temperature and pressure which is necessary to drive the turbine, which powers the compressor and delivers the required gas flow for propulsion.

There are three basic causes of compressor stall:-

(i) Overfuelling, which raises the combustion chamber pressure to a value which the compressor is unable to deliver at the existing engine speed and intake conditions. This may be the result of a fuel system malfunction or the inability of the fuel system to reduce fuel flow sufficiently whilst the engine is attempting to recover from a previous stall.

(ii) Malfunction of the compressor airflow control system such that an individual stage becomes incapable of producing the pressure ratio demanded of it.

(iii) The inability of a stage to produce the pressure ratio and airflow demanded of it, either as a result of a sudden change of intake conditions, or loss of efficiency due to damage or occlusion. The damage to which blades are most sensitive is usually twisting, as is often caused by bird ingestion, or severe hard object damage to a significant proportion of the blades of one stage. The sensitivity of a compressor to these effects is increased by normal deterioration in use, like tip wear or blade erosion.

When the cause of a compressor stall is not a hard failure of the fuel or airflow control systems, the engine will usually attempt to recover by itself. It does this as a result of the fuel and airflow controller sensors detecting the changes that have occurred to the engine operating parameters and making adjustments to make the fuel and air flows more suited to the condition in which the engine finds itself. The most important change that these systems make to aid recovery is a reduction of fuel flow and thus a reduction of throttle demand will always assist the engine in its efforts to recover, and may be essential. If the compressor stall occurs at a high power setting, the recovery is particularly sensitive to demand and a very slight reduction or increase of demand may influence whether or not the compressor can recover. This is especially the case when an engine has sustained compressor and/or turbine damage, and consequently has a reduced stall margin.

If the engine is fitted with an autothrottle and it is engaged, it may, by altering the throttle demand, affect the tendency for the engine to recover from stalls, or not. How the autothrottle varies throttle position in response to engine behaviour depends entirely on the particular autothrottle and the control mode logic in use at the time. (paragraph 1.17.6.4)

During the certification process, one of the requirements which an engine has to meet is to demonstrate that a complete blade, liberated from a disc whilst the engine is running at the maximum overspeed condition, does not penetrate the casing. Following the liberation of the blade it must also be demonstrated that the engine can be shut down by normal controls after 15 seconds of continued running. Whilst performing this test on the CFM 56 it was observed that, with the very high vibration levels which are a natural consequence of the loss of a complete fan blade, the engine stalled so completely that it effectively shut itself down. This behaviour is not inconsistent with the certification requirements.

It has been observed during tests to demonstrate compliance with various airworthiness requirements that the CFM 56, in common with other high by-pass engines, can suffer a persisting compressor stall as a result of very high vibration levels. In the sequence of the accident to ME, the No 1 engine continued to run in a stalled state after Event 2.

1.17.6.4   *Boeing 737-400 autothrottle characteristics in N1 mode.*

With the N1 mode engaged, the autothrottle is designed to input a throttle lever angle (TLA) to the MEC which in conjunction with the PMC (see paragraph 1.6.2), will maintain, on each engine independently, a target N1 speed which is dependent on the thrust mode set on the FMC.

Normally the MEC and PMC will maintain N1 with a constant TLA set by the autothrottle. If, however, N1 falls below target, the autothrottle will increase TLA and if N1 rises above target it will reduce it. The rate of TLA movement is normally restricted to a maximum of 3° per second.

TLA will also be reduced if N1 is seen to be accelerating very rapidly, from an underspeed, towards the target speed. This feature is intended to counteract the natural tendency for N1 to overswing the selected speed which, under some circumstances, might lead to a momentary overspeed.

There is a further feature, designed to prevent overboosting of unresponsive engines, which comes into operation only if the N1 speed is more than 10% below the target speed. Under these conditions, the autothrottle will set a TLA appropriate to a lower N1 than target until the engine has accelerated to this lower value. When the engine reaches this reduced N1 target, TLA will then be increased to the correct target N1 setting. When the conditions to activate this feature exist, rates of reduction of TLA greater than 3°/sec can occur.

When this feature is active, the throttle retard to counter N1 overswing may also be activated by the engine accelerating towards the reduced target N1, and result in a further reduction of TLA.

The value of TLA recorded on the FDR is that which is actually applied at the MEC, and is resolved to 0.35°. Since the autothrottle servos are physically about mid-way between the pilots thrust levers and the MEC, there can be some mechanical hysteresis and a time lag between the servo making a demand and the TLA at the MEC settling to that position.

1.17.7 *Subsequent fan blade fractures on Boeing 737-400 aircraft*

In June 1989 there were two further instances of fan blade fracture on CFM56–3C engines fitted to Boeing 737-400 series aircraft. Both of these occurred to aircraft belonging to UK operators and at similar flight conditions to those at the time of the first event in the ME accident.

1.17.7.1 *Incident to Dan Air Boeing 737-400, G-BNNL on 9 June 1989*

In this incident, the aircraft was climbing at –3C rated power through FL250 when the crew reported symptoms which were initially identical to those reported by the crew of ME, including the almost immediate presence of smoke in the cockpit, but subsequently with a much higher continuing vibration level which persisted even whilst the engine windmilled after shut down. The crew identified the failed No 1 engine correctly, by reference to the engine vibration indicators, and completed a full shut-down drill.

The FDR showed that the engine was unable to sustain power and ran down before the crew began the engine shut-down drill. Fuel flow began to reduce within 2 seconds of the onset of the vibration and reached zero within 9 seconds; the throttle was partially closed after 6 seconds and fully closed after 24.

Although the No 1 engine had quickly shut itself down, it appeared to the commander that, except for the No 1 engine vibration indicator, all the engine instruments looked alike and it took time for him to be certain that he had correctly identified the affected engine. When asked to explain his observations in greater detail he said that he had glanced repeatedly at the engine instruments and they appeared to be well-matched. He saw no tumbling digits and made his assessment solely on the basis of the high vibration shown on the No 1 engine vibration indicator. The first officer also observed no change on the engine instruments apart from the high reading on the No 1 engine vibration indicator. However, he later qualified this statement by saying that, having identified the No 1 engine as the source of the vibration, he could not recollect monitoring the No 1 engine instruments again. He added that, in conditions of high vibration, the small size of the EIS instruments and their manner of presenting information made them difficult to read. The aircraft landed without further incident.

Examination of the engine after landing showed that the fan had been massively damaged (Appendix 1, fig 4a), with severe damage to the leading edges of all blades. One blade had fractured close to the root and another just below the mid-span shroud, both entirely by overload rupture. There was a third blade fracture, however, just above the mid-span shroud which appeared to be very similar to that on blade No 17 from the No 1 engine of ME, in that it was very flat and consistent with fatigue over a large proportion of the blade cross-section, particularly the forward part. (see Appendix 1, figs 5 & 6)

Examination of the engine at the manufacturer's factory showed other similarities to the No 1 engine of ME. The fan abradable seal was entirely missing, although there was a trace of the blue abradable material residue and there was some evidence of rubbing on the fan casing surface within the abradable path. In addition, there were many impact dents on the casing due to impact of fan blade fragments, but no penetrations. The forward acoustic lining panels were also completely missing, the intermediate panels were badly torn over part of the periphery and some blade fragment damage had occurred to the rearmost panels.

Inspection of the security of component attachments on the auxiliary gearbox, and the pipework on the fan case, showed that several parts had become loose. The MEC to fuel pump attachment nuts had worked loose and one had broken. In addition, when the MEC was dismounted, the seal around the high pressure delivery port from the fuel pump was found to have torn outwards. It was also noted that the pipe unions to the VSV rod on the MEC, and the high pressure fuel line on the TC3[11] timer, had worked loose. Application of pressure to the fuel system in the 'as received' state demonstrated that all these joints (including the

---

[11] TC3 unit: Turbine tip clearance control timer schedules cooling air around turbine casing to control turbine blade tip clearance.

MEC to pump) leaked under pressure. Their degree of looseness was measured and experiments to determine the nature of these leaks under full system pressure were conducted in isolation. The mountings of the igniter boxes and the PMC, which are also mounted on the fan case, had 'overtravelled' and sustained damage.

1.17.7.2   *Incident to British Midland Boeing 737-400 G-OBMG on 11 June 1989*

In this incident, the aircraft was climbing at -3C rated power through FL290 when the crew reported that there was an onset of 'thumping' and severe vibration. Reference to the engine instruments revealed high indicated vibration with a low and fluctuating N1 on the No 2 engine. This engine was throttled back to idle power, reducing the vibration, and after some time the vibration indication decreased from the maximum (5 units) to about 3 units. A single engined approach and landing was made with the No 2 engine at idle power. No smoke was seen in the cockpit at any time, although a smell of burning was noticed. The cabin crew reported that there was considerable smoke in the aft cabin and that flames and sparks had been seen to come from the right engine. The cabin smoke was observed to clear quickly after the right engine had been reduced to idle. The aircraft landed without further incident.

Examination of the No 2 engine fan after shut down (Appendix 1, fig 4a) revealed that the outer panel of one fan blade had detached outboard of the mid-span shroud and become lodged in the space between the fan and fan outlet guide vanes. The fracture surface was almost identical to that which was recovered from the No 1 engine of NL (Appendix 1, figs 6 & 7). Some damage had occurred to the fan abradable liner and the forward acoustic panels, but apart from this there appeared to have been very little damage to the engine. It was also found that, in common with NL, there had been loosening of several pipe unions and of the MEC to fuel pump attachment nuts.

1.17.7.3   *FDR comparisons*

The flight data recorders from both aircraft were read out after the incidents. It was seen that, in both cases, the initial response of the affected engine was practically identical to that observed at the first event on ME. The fan speed dropped sharply from an initial setting of around 98% to about 85 % followed by a slight recovery. After this initial similarity the three patterns diverged as a result of the differences in damage and engine handling. (see Appendix 4, fig 10 for comparison of traces)

Vibration level information was not available on the recorder from NL, but information from the pilots indicated that the vibration gauges showed full scale deflection (5 units) on the No 1 engine at all engine speeds after the incident. By contrast, the vibration recorded on the No 2 engine of MG fell back into the indication range (< 5 units) after the power was reduced to idle and settled at a similar level to that recorded on ME in the period of reduced power flight after the first event.

1.17.7.4　*Metallurgical examination of the fractures*

The blades with fatigue-like fractures from these two aircraft were examined using optical, scanning and transmission electron microscopes which revealed that both fractures were characteristic of high cycle fatigue, and very similar. Both had a sub-surface fatigue origin on the concave (pressure) side of the blade, slightly above the leading edge of the mid-span shroud and just at the the inner extent of the shot peened layer (about 0.006/8 inch below the surface). There was no evidence of any pre-existing metallurgical defects at the origins from which both cracks had propagated. Both cracks had extended, between elliptical fronts, through the blade thickness and towards both the leading and trailing edges. There were detail differences between the two fractures (see Appendix 1, figs 6 & 7) one of which was the identification of what appeared to be two arrest marks on the Dan Air blade, but only one such mark on the British Midland blade. Examination of the fatigue striation spacing showed that, between the arrest marks, the spacing increased as the crack length extended. Final fracture of both blades was by tensile rupture of residual areas at both the LE and TE with shear lips on the convex (suction) side of the blade. No defects were found associated with the microstructure at or near the origins and the blade dimensions, geometry and material specification conformed to the manufacturer's drawings.

1.17.8　*Incidents involving fan blade damage from bird ingestion*

1.17.8.1　*Bird strike on Boeing 737-400 G-OBMF on 7 June 1989*

The No 2 engine ingested a bird on take-off just prior to rotation. The crew reported that during the initial climb a moderate vibration was felt through the airframe, like tyres running over rough concrete, but no abnormality appeared on any engine instrument. About 10 to 15 seconds later the reading on the No 2 engine vibration indicator rose to 1.8 units. At 3,000 feet, when power was reduced, the reading on the No 2 vibration indicator rose to 4.3 units. When the No 2 engine was throttled back to idle the reading on the vibration indicator fell to below 1 unit and the airframe vibration ceased. After landing it was found that one fan blade was severely bent and two others slightly bent.

1.17.8.2 *Bird strike on Boeing 737-300 G-OBMB on 6 January 1990*

Just after rotating for take-off the aircraft flew through a flock of birds. Vibration was felt, reportedly from an engine, but there were no instrument indications of abnormal operation. Both engine vibration indicators remained at low readings until the throttles were retarded to climb power at flap retraction height, when the No 2 engine vibration indicator reading rose to maximum. When the No 2 engine was throttled back to idle power, the reading on the vibration indicator fell to below 1 unit. After landing severe damage was found on 10 fan blades.

1.17 8 3 *AVM response to birdstrike damage*

During the course of certification testing of the modified fan blades conducted in early 1990 it was necessary to perform a birdstrike test on a complete CFM 56-3C-1 engine. The manufacturer, CFMI, was asked to pay particular attention to the vibration data arising from this test in the light of the reported behaviour of the AVM during the two incidents described.

A considerable amount of data was obtained but certain points were relevant :-

(i) The recorded vibration levels were low (within the measurable range of the AVM gauge) and imbalances were moderate and due to 'shingling' rather than material loss.

(ii) A pronounced 'dip' occurred in the vibration level at approximately 4500 RPM on the tested engine. This was a function of the response of the engine mass to the excitation and would be influenced by the way in which the engine was mounted. It was also established, from an examination of past test records, that the lowest point of this 'dip' in response occurred at different fan speeds on individual engines. The most common speeds for the minimum sensitivity of the engine were between 4750 to 4900 RPM, which is in the band of take-off fan speeds.

Either side of this dip, the response increased rapidly. There was, therefore, only a very narrow band of N1 speed where the reduced response occurred, and the gauge would register almost no reading whilst this speed was maintained, if the imbalance was relatively small.

(iii) Additional broad-band sensors (fitted for test purposes only) located close to the forward engine mount detected a noticeable series of shocks caused by an aerodynamic effect occurring once per fan revolution. Although they were therefore synchronous it was noted that they were not detectable by a tracking AVM system because they did not posess the characteristic sinusoidal waveform of a mechanical imbalance. They might well, however, be perceivable as a vibration through the airframe.

1.17.9 *Fatigue initiation and growth at stress levels close to the endurance limit*

The endurance limit of a material is defined as the combination of steady and cyclic stress levels which can be applied to it without causing significant fatigue damage. For each steady stress there is a maximum oscillatory stress which can be superimposed and a designer will refer to a Goodman Diagram for a specific material which will give this relationship. Whilst designing components for an infinite life, it must be ensured that this combination of steady and vibratory stress is never exceeded.

This limitation has to be imposed at the most critical point of a component which is subjected to a combination of steady and cyclic loading, and, in the case of damage tolerant design, a degree of damage must be assumed. Changes in cross section and intersections of planes on a component act as local stress raisers and the degree to which they do this is called the stress concentration factor, or k_t. Similarly, surface imperfections, inclusions in the material and extraneous damage act as stress raisers, the k_t for which become greater as the ratio of their depth to end radius increases. In general, the higher the value of k_t the more easily fatigue cracking will initiate because the concentration effect will raise the local stresses. When a crack is present it causes a stress intensification at its base and the intensity factor, K_1, is related to the crack depth, amongst other considerations. As the crack grows longer, its K_1, and consequently the rate of fatigue growth, usually increases. Ultimately the K_1 becomes so high that the local stresses at the crack end, due to the steady load alone, are sufficient to cause complete failure of the component through the remainder of the load-bearing section.

If an undamaged component is subjected to combined steady and cyclic stresses which are at, or only just above, the endurance limit at some position, it must be subjected to these stresses for a large number of cycles before sufficient fatigue damage has accumulated for a crack to initiate. After initiation has occurred, the presence of the crack will constitute a stress raiser, locally lifting the combined stresses well above the endurance limit and the crack growth will proceed at an accelerating rate. In this way, the crack growth period can be a very small proportion of the total time to complete fracture.

When considering the fan blades of the CFM 56–3C engine in the light of all three fatigue fractures, the manufacturer calculated that in order to make the leading edge area (at the level of the mid-span shroud) as sensitive to fatigue damage from this particular vibratory mode as the area at centre chord (above the shroud), a defect with a k_t of at least 2.5 was required. A defect of semi-circular cross section has a k_t of 3.0, so 2.5 implies a defect with a bottom radius greater than its depth (ie more shallow). The actual depth of the defect before crack initiation has very little influence on the stress raising properties of the defect unless it erodes a significant proportion of the cross sectional area.

1.17.10   *Cracked fan disc*

After the third fan blade fatigue fracture, the manufacturer issued an All Operator Wire, on 12 June 1989, advising of the situation and strongly recommending strict fan blade inspection and restriction of engines to -3B-2 ratings. Later the same day, the CAA issued an Emergency Airworthiness Directive which withdrew the Type Approval of UK registered Boeing 737-400 aircraft.

As a result of this, one operator, whilst removing the fan blades from a CFM 56–3C–1 engine, found that a fan disc post, which forms the side of the dovetail slot, had a crack at the base of the post head. This disc was returned to the manufacturer for examination where it was found that the crack was also the result of high cycle fatigue.

The following day the manufacturer sent another All Operator Wire informing of this further development, and on 15 June a further wire informed all operators of an FAA Telegraphic Airworthiness Directive which required the removal and replacement of all fan blades and discs which had been operated at -3C-1 thrust ratings in flight. Once these replacements had been effected the engines could be returned to service, but restricted to -3B-2 ratings.

1.17.11   *Changes in seat and cabin structural requirements*

1.17.11.1   *In the United States*

During the early 1980s the FAA undertook extensive studies concerning the possible upgrading of the Federal Aviation Requirements (FARs) affecting seats and structural load factors in crashes; these load factors had remained essentially unchanged since 1952. These studies covered a wide range of aircraft categories, including Transport Category types (FAR Part 25), and involved a number of agencies, including the National Aeronautics and Space Administration (NASA), the airframe and seat manufacturers and the Civil Aeromedical Institute (CAMI).

These studies culminated, for Transport Category aircraft, in the issue of a Notice of Proposed Rule Making (NPRM No 86-11) in July 1986. The NPRM proposed to upgrade the static load factors defined in the FARs and also proposed adoption of new dynamic test standards for seats. A cost-benefit analysis, using the proposed figures, was included within the NPRM.

Following a period of consultation, the FAA issued its revised FAR Part 25 rules in May 1988, effective from 16 June 1988 for new types of Transport Category aircraft (Amendment 25-64). The final rules closely matched the NPRM both in the upgrading of the static load factors and in the definition of two dynamic test requirements for seats:-

Static Load factors - The static load factors applied to seats and other items of mass in the cabin were upgraded to:

Upward	-	3.0g (previously 2.0g)
Sideward	-	3.0g–airframe, 4.0g–seats and attachments (previously 1.5g)
Downward	-	6.0g (previously 4.5g)
Rearward	-	1.5g (no previous requirement)
Forward	-	9.0g (previously 9.0g)

Dynamic Test Requirements - Two tests were defined, using instrumented 170 lbs anthropomorphic test dummies to simulate the occupants. Test 1 approximates to a near-vertical impact, with some forward speed, applying a minimum of 14g deceleration from a minimum velocity of 35 feet/second, canted aft 30° from the vertical axis of the seat. Test 2 approximates a horizontal impact with some yaw, applying a minimum of 16g deceleration from a minimum of 44 feet/second, the seat yawed 10° from the direction of deceleration. To simulate the effects of cabin floor deformation, the parallel floor rails or fittings in test 2 are misaligned by at least 10° in pitch 10° in roll before the dynamic test. The tests require that the seat remains attached, although it may yield, and the requirements include a set of pass/fail criteria limiting the pelvic load (1500 lbs), head deceleration (Head Injury Criterion of 1000 units) and axial femural load (2250 lbs).

Of these two tests, Test 2 (16g deceleration with 44 feet/second velocity change) is generally considered the more stringent. The peak deceleration value (16g) and the velocity change (44 feet/second) were chosen as the result of a study of crash dynamics and the levels were also considered to be compatible with existing floor strengths in the current fleet of transport category aeroplanes.

Although these rules took effect in June 1988 as Amendment 25-64 to FAR 25, they apply only to new transport category aircraft types and do not apply to existing aircraft types, or to their derivatives. A further NPRM (88-8) has been issued to cover the proposed installation of the upgraded seats in new aircraft of current type and within the existing fleet; all Part 25 (Transport Category) aircraft would be required to have seats installed meeting the new criteria by June 1995.

1.17.11.2   In the United Kingdom

In October 1989 the JAA issued Change 13 to JAR 25. In the case of the Emergency Landing Conditions (JAR 25.561 and .562) the new provisions were very similar to FAR Amendment 25-64, with identical static load factors and dynamic tests. The principal difference was that, in the JAR change, the dynamic test requirements were to apply only to passenger seating whereas in FAR Amendment 25-64 the dynamic test requirements applied both to passenger and to crew seating.

In common with FAR Amendment 25-64, the requirements of Change 13 would only apply to new aircraft types presented for certification and would not apply to existing aircraft types, or to their direct derivatives.

1.17.12   Crash dynamics research

During the past 15 years a considerable amount of research has been conducted to make quantitative assessments of the crash dynamics of transport-size aircraft. In the USA this programme has been primarily sponsored by the FAA and NASA. A principle objective has been to define a survivable impact envelope and to relate these impact conditions to the structural response of the airframe and the dynamic response of the passenger occupant. This has required the development of analytical tools, such as the computer program KRASH, and full-scale tests such as the Controlled Impact Demonstration of a Boeing 720 at Edwards Air Force Base.

One full-scale test particularly relevant to ME was the testing of a complete section of narrow-body jet transport (B707) in a longitudinal impact in 1988. The test section of fuselage was 10 feet long and was configured with three rows of two passenger triple seats secured to the floor with standard track fittings and occupied by 165 lb dummies. The aim was to perform longitudinal impacts of 9g and 14g; the actual results were 7.4g and 14.2g. The 14.2g test achieved a velocity change of 36.2 ft/sec. Although neither the seats nor the floor were identical to ME, it is significant that, at these acceleration levels, the floor and seat track did not fail or sustain permanent deformation.

1.17.13   Aft facing seats

For some 40 years there has been a continuing technical debate about the potential for reducing the severity of impact injuries in aircraft accidents by installing the passenger seats to face the rear of the aircraft. The distinct advantage of this configuration is that the impact loads are evenly distributed over the area of the seat-back, rather than being carried on the lap belt and by contact of unrestrained body segments with the seat in front.

In the 1950s research was conducted into rearward-facing seats, particularly in the United States, but this was without the use of sophisticated dynamic test facilities and did not result in any legislative change in either the USA or UK. The relevant sections of BCARs and JARs currently allow, but do not require, rearward-facing seats in transport aircraft, subject to the same loading criteria as forward-facing seats.

The principle of rearward-facing seats was accepted by the Royal Air Force in 1945 and a requirement was stated to the Air Ministry, who decided that future RAF transport aircraft would be fitted with 25g rearward-facing seats. This principle has generally been followed (*e.g* Hastings, Andover, VC 10) but not exclusively (Tristar). A study by the RAF Institute of Aviation Medicine in 1954, based on a number of accidents to RAF transport aircraft with a mix of forward-facing and rearward-facing seats, indicated that the rearward-facing seats were effective in reducing impact injuries. However, there have been no recent accidents to modern RAF transport aircraft on which to base further study.

Amongst the arguments raised against rearward-facing seats are that such seats would weigh considerably more than conventional seats and would impart unacceptably high loads to the cabin floor because of their higher effective moment arm. Although not part of a comprehensive research programme, dynamic tests performed at the FAA Civil Aeromedical Institute on purpose-built rearward-facing seats have indicated acceptable floor loads under 16g decelerations, at minimal extra weight.

Other arguments raised against rearward-facing seats are that they could be less effective in accidents in which the main decelerative force is not along the longitudinal axis of the aircraft; that they could expose occupants to the risk of injury from loose objects in an accident; that greater improvements have been made in the design and construction of forward-facing seats; that they may not be suitable for use in modern jet transports with their high climb-out angles; and that they could be psychologically less attractive to passengers.

1.17.14   *Child restraint systems*

In January 1989 Article 34 of the Air Navigation Order 1985 (now Article 37 of ANO 1989) was amended, requiring that, for take-off, landing, emergency conditions and flight in turbulence, 'all passengers under the age of two years are properly secured by means of a child restraint device'. This amendment became effective on 1 July 1989, with a partial exemption until 31 October 1989. In the absence of a UK standard specifying the requirements for child restraint systems for use in aircraft, this amendment was generally interpreted within the airline industry as requiring the use of the supplementary 'loop-type' belts, using similar webbing and buckles to the standard belts.

There has been a paucity of research to determine the effectiveness of the supplementary belt device in survivable decelerations. The CAA has recently funded a test programme to research this and study alternatives such as the use of conventional car child-seats in aircraft. The studies which have been done previously indicate that the main asset of the supplementary belt in a severe deceleration is to prevent the infant from becoming a free projectile within the aircraft cabin. The advantages for the infant are more questionable as the supplementary belt appears to apply high loads to the infant's abdomen and, in addition, analysis of test film shows damaging interactions between the infant and supporting adult during test decelerations.

In the USA, the FAA does not require, but does encourage, the use of approved child/infant seats aboard aircraft. This originated from the need for child seats in general aviation aircraft and in May 1982 the FAA issued TSO-100, setting out the requirements for child restraint systems in aircraft. In February 1985 this was changed to TSO-100a, adopting the requirements of Federal Motor Vehicle Safety Standard No 213 and thus consolidating the automotive and aviation requirements into a single standard. However, the FAA does not require the airline to provide the child seat or to make available an aircraft seat to which to attach the child seat. Thus the onus of provision is placed entirely on the accompanying adult passenger, although changes in the Federal regulations are pending following the accident to the United Airlines DC-10-10 at Sioux City, Iowa on 19 July 1989.

There is no CAA standard or code of requirements for child seats in aircraft. Within the EEC the current standard for child seats in motor vehicles is EC Regulation 44, containing most of the requirements of British Standard 3254 and, like FMVSS 213, both BS 3254 and EC Regulation 44 include the requirement for dynamic testing. In EC Regulation 44 this dynamic testing is to a peak value of at least 20g of longitudinal deceleration; the requirement of FMVSS 213 is comparable, requiring a 30 mph (44fps) deceleration within 80 milliseconds. There are two important distinctions between the two sets of standards, however: FMVSS 213 is devised around simple lap belt attachments whereas EC Regulation 44 has to cater for a wide diversity of attachments, and neither BS 3254 nor EC Regulation 44 contains provisions concerning flammability.

CAA 'Notice to AOC holders'

In March 1990 the CAA issued a 'Notice to Air Operator's Certificate (AOC) Holders' entitled 'Optional use of car-type seats for the restraint of infants under the age of 2 years'. This Notice informed operators of public transport aircraft that the use of certain car-type child seats would be allowed from a specified date; the approved seats were those labelled as complying with FAA TSO-100/100a or FMVSS 213 together with an initial list of 4 types of child seat readily available within the UK (2 by Britax, 2 by Mothercare).

The Notice also contained the requirements dealing with the location, installation and use of the child seats. As in the USA, the onus to provide the child seat remained entirely on the accompanying adult and the Notice did not require the airline to make a passenger seat available, nor did it require that the airline permit the passenger to use a child seat.

1.17.15   Loading of overhead stowage bins

To determine the probable loads imposed on the overhead stowage bins during the impact, it was necessary to estimate the average mass in a bin. A CAA study at Heathrow Airport in 1981-82 determined a mean carry-on baggage mass of 5.5 kg for adult passengers on domestic scheduled flights but did not include coats, cameras or handbags. For estimates of loading, therefore, a sum of 6.0 kg per passenger is assumed for G-OBME. Over the 26 full-length (60 inch) bins this gives 59.6 lbs per bin, approximately 33% of the placarded mass.

1.17.16   Requirements for fuel tank protection

BCAR chapter D3-8 (Emergency alighting) has specific requirements (9g forward and 4.5g downward) concerning the minimum design loads to prevent an engine becoming detached and rupturing a fuel tank in a crash. In the case of wing fuel tanks this is appropriate to engines mounted above or behind the wing.

Chapter D5-2 (Fuel systems) of BCAR Section D states:

'2.8   Crash Protection

2.8.1   Fuel tanks shall, so far as is practicable, be designed, located and installed so as to render the liberation of fuel in or near the fuselage or near the engines unlikely in otherwise survivable crash conditions.

(a)   In particular, it is desirable that:-

(i)   Fuel tank installations should be such that the tanks will not be ruptured by the aeroplane sliding with its landing gear retracted, nor by a landing gear nor an engine mounting tearing away.
(ii)   Fuel tanks inboard of the landing gear or inboard of, or adjacent to, the most outboard engine should have the strength to withstand fuel inertia loads appropriate to the emergency alighting conditions of D3–8.'

JAR 25.963 (Fuel tanks: general) requires that:

'(d)   Fuel tanks must, so far as is practicable, be designed, located and installed so that no fuel is released in or near the engines in quantities sufficient to start a fire in otherwise survivable crash conditions.'

and that:

> 'fuel tank installations should be such that tanks will not be ruptured by the aeroplane sliding with its landing gear retracted, nor by a landing gear, nor an engine mounting tearing away.'

JAR 25.721 (Landing gear) requires that:

> 'a) The main landing gear system must be designed so that if it fails due to overloads during take-off and landing (assuming the overloads to act in the upward and aft directions), the failure mode is not likely to cause - *(for this class of aircraft)* -.the spillage of enough fuel from any part of the fuel system to constitute a fire hazard.'

1.17.17   Other survivable accidents

A study was made of the detailed reports from a number of accidents which had occurred to narrow-body jet transport aircraft in the USA and Canada between 1972 and 1988. The 13 accidents selected all involved narrow-body aircraft and at least a partially survivable impact; 5 occurred during the take-off phase, 6 during the approach and landing phase and 2 were power-off forced landings (Appendix 3, fig 24).

On comparing these accidents with ME, it was apparent that the structural disruption to ME was characteristic of other off-airfield accidents which had involved landing undershoots, failed go-arounds and power-off forced landings. Accidents involving rejected take-offs and landing over-runs were generally less severe. Two recurrent features of these accidents were the major disruption which had been caused by an impact after the initial ground impact, and the occurrence of 2 major fuselage failures, one forward and one aft of the wing.

Another recurrent feature was the incidence of passengers who had been sufficiently incapacitated by the impact that they either died from the effects of fire, or would have died had a fire developed. These instances of incapacitation appeared generally to have been due either to passenger collision with neighbouring seats or failure of the seats to remain attached to viable structure.

Accident to Eastern Airlines L-1011 Tristar in the Everglades on 29 December 1972

This accident was not part of the study as the crash dynamics of wide-body transport aircraft are not identical to those of narrow-body aircraft. However, the significance of the Everglades accident was that, despite a 3000 feet/minute rate of descent and an airspeed of over 190 kts at the impact into flat marshland, 67 of the 161 passengers survived. The National Transportation Safety Board (NTSB) report (AAR-73-14) stated 'No complete circumferential cross-section remained of the passenger compartment of the fuselage, which was broken into four main sections and numerous small pieces'. The NTSB did not place this accident in the survivable category.

The NTSB concluded that a major factor in the passenger survival rate was the design of the passenger seats, which incorporated energy absorbers in the support structure and which were bolted to a series of platforms which, in turn, were fitted to the aircraft seat tracks. It was noted that many of the seat units remained attached to these platforms and that failures occurred because the basic aircraft structure was compromised, rather than the platform attachments.

1.17.18 *Analysis of deceleration data*

In analysing the different deceleration data relating to this accident it became apparent that typical deceleration signals, both from tests and computer simulations, were considerably more complex than the theoretical triangular, trapezoidal and sinusoidal pulse models. The following paragraph from the FAA summary report on the Controlled Impact Demonstration (CID) reflected this, stating:

> 'When analyzing data of this nature, there is a tendency to condense it all into a single statistic - the peak value of acceleration. However, it must be realized when quoting so called 'peak g's' that the method of filtering and determination of those values are understood, as well as the implication these hold for the response of the system of interest. This pulse can be thought of as consisting of an underlying primary pulse upon which is superimposed a high frequency oscillation. Virtually all analysts agree that in many situations the high frequency content is of little relevance, but there is less agreement on the shape of the primary pulse. Various analysts see this underlying shape to be triangular, sinusoidal, or trapezoidal. In some situations, even the exact shape of the primary pulse is of secondary importance and any of the above shapes may be used as long as the corresponding velocity change is correct.'

The deceleration pulse values in this report correspond, therefore, to the fundamental 'underlying pulse' and not, unless specified, to the higher 'peak g' values

1.17.19 *Airborne closed circuit television monitoring*

With the advent of miniature television cameras and recording equipment it has become apparent that flight crews could be presented with external views of their aircraft during flight. A logical extension of this concept would be the monitoring of previous 'blind' areas such as cargo holds and closed wheel bays in addition to the recording of flight-deck activity and instrumentation for accident investigation purposes. AAIB became involved when the Robert Gordon Institute of Technology (RGIT) proposed a system based on the Panasonic miniature camera and invited AAIB comments. A meeting with the CAA confirmed their interest and it was proposed that a proof of concept trial would be mounted using the Panasonic camera on the RAE[12] BAC 1-11. Subsequent to this decision, other agencies declared an interest in the project and the CAA found it necessary to go

---

[12] RAE   Royal Aerospace Establishment at Farnborough

to competitive tendering for the proof of concept trial. During this investigation, AAIB have remained in close contact with RAE, RGIT, and CAA and have hosted several presentations by equipment manufacturers. A recommendation relating to the provision of flight deck crews with external views of their aircraft was made in the AAIB Report on the accident to Boeing 737 G-BGJL at Manchester International Airport on the 22 August 1985 (Report 8/88).

The aims of such an airborne closed circuit television monitoring system would be as follows:-

(i) To provide flight deck crew with an external view of the major areas of their aircraft in all weathers, both day and night.

(ii) To provide flight deck crews with a view of cargo bays to aid in decision making following an associated fire warning.

(iii) To provide a record of flight deck activity and flight instrumentation for the purposes of in flight post-incident recall by flight crews and accident investigation. This aspect would be of particular use in 'glass cockpits' and would provide a valuable supplement to the future provision of full digital recording of flight instrument parameters on the FDR.

(iv) To provide cabin crews with a view of areas of the cabin not currently manned by cabin staff. This system could also be used as a security system whilst the aircraft was on the ground.

(v) To provide a recording of all such information, that would be protected to the same standards as those specified for FDRs and CVRs.

1.17.19.1 *Cameras*

There are several suitable cameras available and some are already qualified for airborne use. They vary in size but none would appear to present any structural or aerodynamic problems when mounted on an aircraft. Transmission of data from the camera head to the monitor and recorder would appear to present few problems in aircraft up to the size of the Boeing 747. Cameras can function in a wide range of light conditions, but may require supplementary lighting in full dark conditions. There are various options available to protect the lens from contamination by dirt or ice.

1.17.19.2 *Monitors*

No problems are envisaged with the technology of monitors, but their siting on aircraft will need careful consideration.

1.17.19.3   Recorders

The available technology for recorders may require further development. It is claimed that recorders based on current commercial equipment could provide up to 6 hours of video recording, together with 4 tracks of high quality audio, housed within a standard ½ ATR box. Recorders would be capable of recording the output of several cameras, but recording quality would fall in direct proportion to the number of outputs recorded.

1.17.19.4   Human Factors

The integration of video information into the routine and emergency procedures used by flight deck crews will need careful consideration. This aspect should be investigated in parallel with the equipment development, to ensure that the final system is compatible with the prescribed flight deck procedures.

1.17.19.5   Current status

A proof of concept trial of an airborne closed circuit television monitoring system is currently being sponsored by the CAA and it is understood that a basic system will be tested in 1991. RAE, in conjunction with private industry, has completed a proof of concept trial and is developing a production system. Two major airlines are currently studying such systems as private ventures.

1.17.20   AAIB Special Bulletin S2/89

This Special Bulletin was issued on 20 March 1989. It summarised the factual information then available from this investigation and listed 7 Safety Recommendations made to the CAA up to 23 February 1989. A copy of this Special Bulletin is included at Appendix 6.

1.18   New investigation techniques

The use of the KRASH computer program (paragraph 1.16.4) for the analysis of the aircraft impact sequence was the first time that this type of computer-based dynamics modelling had been used as part of an aircraft accident investigation. Previous uses had included the prediction of crash dynamics in controlled impact demonstrations. The simulation was conducted within a time-scale compatible with the accident investigation process and made a distinct contribution to the crashworthiness and survivability aspects of this investigation.

The occupant simulation study (paragraph 1.16.5) was computer-based and was undertaken by H W Structures Ltd, using the crash victim simulation program MADYMO. Although this type of occupant response simulation has been in use for some time in automotive safety engineering, this appears to have been its first use within the context of the investigation of a transport aircraft accident.

2. ANALYSIS

2.1 Crew actions

2.1.1 *The reaction of the flight crew to the engine problem*

2.1.1.1 *Fault diagnosis*

After an uneventful take-off and climb the crew suddenly heard an unusual noise, accompanied by vibration, as the aircraft passed through FL 283. The noise was heard in the cabin as a series of thuds and the FDR indicated that it was directly associated with the stalling of the fan and/or the LP compressor with attendant surging of the No 1 engine. In addition to the noise and vibration, the lateral and longitudinal accelerations recorded on the FDR were consistent with the reported lower frequency shuddering that was sufficiently marked to shake the walls of the forward galley. Very soon after the onset of these symptoms there was a smell of fire and possibly some visible smoke in the cockpit. This combination was interpreted by the pilots as evidence of a serious engine malfunction, with an associated fire, and appears to have driven them to act very quickly to contain this perceived condition.

Neither pilot appears to have assimilated from the engine instruments any positive indication of malfunction, but subsequent tests showed the engine instrument system to have been serviceable and there was no evidence to indicate that it did not display the large engine parameter variations that occurred when the compressor surged. The FDR showed four distinct excursions in N1 on the No 1 engine, with a 6 second period of relative stability between the second and the third.

Throughout the period of compressor surging, the No 2 engine showed no parameter variations but because the first officer was unable to recall what he saw on the instruments, it has not been possible to determine why he made the mistake of believing that the fault lay with the No 2 engine. When asked which engine was at fault he half-formed the word 'left' before saying 'right'. His hesitation may have arisen from genuine difficulty in interpreting the readings on the engine instruments, or it may have been that he observed the instruments only during the 6 second period of relative stability between the second and third surges. However, any uncertainty that he may initially have experienced appears to have been quickly resolved because, when the commander ordered him to 'THROTTLE IT BACK', without specifying which engine was to be throttled back, the first officer closed the No 2 throttle.

The commander said that he gained from the engine instruments no clear indication of where the trouble lay. He had, however, disengaged the autopilot 8 seconds after the first compressor surge and most of his attention thereafter would probably have been on the handling of the aircraft and the flight instruments. The fact that when the aircraft rolled to the left he made no corrective movements with the flying controls appeared to indicate that he did not detect from the behaviour of the aircraft any loss of thrust from the No 1 engine. After the accident, he stated that he had judged the No 2 engine to be at fault from his knowledge of the aircraft air conditioning system. His reasoning was that he thought the smoke and fumes were coming forward from the passenger cabin; the air for the cabin came mostly from the No 2 engine; therefore the trouble lay in that engine. Whilst this reasoning might have applied fairly well to other aircraft he had flown, it was flawed in this case because some of the conditioning air for the passenger cabin of the Boeing 737-400 comes from the No 1 engine. In any case, his assessment was not supported by the evidence because the fumes had been perceived in the cockpit, and it was not for some time that he was able to confirm from the flight service manager that there had also been smoke in the passenger cabin. It seems unlikely that in the short time before he took action his thoughts about the air conditioning system could have had much influence on his decision. It is considered to be more likely that, believing the first officer had seen positive indications on the engine instruments, he provisionally accepted the first officer's assessment.

The speed with which the pilots acted was contrary to both their training and the instructions in the Operations Manual. If they had taken more time to study the engine instruments it should have been apparent that the No 2 engine indications were normal and that the No 1 engine was behaving erratically. The commander himself might have had a better chance to observe these abnormal indications if he had not disengaged the autopilot, but this action by itself should not have prevented him from taking whatever time was necessary to assimilate the readings on all the engine instruments. In the event, both pilots reacted to the emergency before they had any positive evidence of which engine was operating abnormally. Their incorrect diagnosis of the problem must, therefore, be attributed to their too rapid reaction and not to any failure of the engine instrument system to display the correct indications.

Therefore, in view of the possibility of future occurrences of severe engine out-of-balance conditions and concern regarding the possible reactions of flight crews involved, it was recommended that the CAA should take action to advise pilots of Boeing 737-300/400 aircraft, and of other types with engines which have similar characteristics, that where instances of engine-induced high vibration occur, they may be accompanied by associated smoke and /or smells of burning entering the flight deck and/or cabin through the air-conditioning system, due merely to blade tip contact between fan/compressor rotating assemblies and the associated abradable seals. (Made 23 February 1989).

2.1.1.2 *The recovery of the No 1 engine*

There then occurred an event that led both pilots into the fatal misconception that the action they had taken in haste had in fact been the correct action. As soon as the No 2 engine throttle was retarded, the symptoms they described as 'vibration' appeared to cease. The No 1 engine compressor surges and the associated noise and shuddering certainly ceased at this time, most probably because the autothrottle was disconnected (see paragraph 2.2.2.2), but the FDR showed that the high vibration level did not. However, although this vibration continued to show on the FDR and was felt by many of the passengers, it appears to have been no longer perceived by the pilots, and the smell of burning seems not to have intensified. Thus, having failed to note the continuing maximum reading on the No 1 engine vibration indicator or the fluctuating fuel flow and being apparently unaware of the continuing vibration, both pilots were convinced that closing the No 2 throttle had stopped not only the noise and the shuddering but also the vibration, as was shown by the commander's comment some 50 seconds later when he said 'SEEMS TO BE RUNNING ALRIGHT NOW'.

From subsequent tests it is apparent that the No 1 engine vibration indicator was at the top of its scale within 2 seconds of the onset of vibration and remained there for about 3 minutes, until after that engine was throttled back for the descent. Yet it appears that the reading on this indicator was not noticed by either pilot, and this indicates a weakness in training philosophy. The commander seems to have been aware of the less than satisfactory performance of the earlier types of vibration monitor, probably from his past experience on the McDonnell Douglas DC9. His subsequent training by Boeing on the 737 did not draw his attention to the much improved performance of the newer AVM system, and he had not practised an emergency in which the AVM indications were used as a visual cue to assist him in fault diagnosis. Similarly the first officer, who had no previous experience on turbojet or turbofan powered aircraft, had not had his attention drawn to the AVM indicators in this context during his training. Both pilots, however, should have been aware of the Operations Manual Bulletin issued by Boeing in March 1988, which introduced the procedure to be followed in the event of high engine vibration. This bulletin implicitly drew attention to the vibration indicators. It was therefore recommended that the CAA should review the current attitude of pilots to the engine vibration indicators on Boeing 737-300/400 aircraft, and other applicable types with turbofan engines, with a view towards providing flight crews with an indication of the pertinence of such vibration instruments when engine malfunctions or failures occur (Made 23 February 1989). In addition, it is further recommended that the CAA should require that pilot training associated with aircraft which are equipped with modern vibration systems, and particularly those aircraft which are fitted with high by-pass turbofan engines[13], should include specific instruction on the potential value of engine vibration indicators in assisting the identification of an engine which has suffered a failure associated with its rotating assemblies (Made 30 March 1990).

2.1.1.3 *The engine instrument system*

The failure to detect, or at least to identify correctly, disparities in the readings of the engine instruments is perhaps most important with regard to the vibration indicators. Unlike the transient fluctuations that would have appeared on the primary engine instruments, the reading on the No 1 engine vibration indicator rose to maximum and remained there for about 3 minutes. On the EIS, however, not only is the pointer of this vibration indicator much less conspicuous than a mechanical pointer (Appendix 2, figs 1 & 2) but, when at maximum deflection, it may be rendered even less conspicuous by the close proximity of the No 1 engine oil quantity digital display, which is the same colour as the pointer and is the dominant symbology in that region of the display (Appendix 2, fig 3). In view of the limited attention both pilots appear to have given to the vibration indicators, it is a matter for conjecture whether or not they would have failed to notice such a maximum reading on the mechanical pointer of a hybrid display, clearly separate from any other distracting indication, but there can be little doubt that it would have been easier to see.

The informal survey of pilot opinion of the EIS (paragraph 1.17.3) showed that 64% preferred engine instruments with full length mechanical pointers. This finding was almost certainly influenced by lack of familiarity since the survey was conducted when the EIS was relatively new in service, and it is not surprising that at that time most pilots should have expressed a preference for the older type of display, with which they were familiar. The result of the survey was also influenced by the replies of the BMA pilots, which were more critical of the EIS than those of other airlines. Also, because of a natural resistance to change, the fitness of new equipment for its purpose may not be judged on pilot preference alone, although this must be an important factor. With these reservations, the least favourable interpretation of the results was that the EIS displayed engine parameters clearly, but its ability to attract attention to rapidly changing readings was less satisfactory. The latter aspect, however, was less important in the case of this accident because the crew were alerted to abnormal operation by other signs and had time, or should have taken time, to study the engine instrument readings.

---

[13] Excluding those aircraft fitted with a computerised engine warning system which includes engine vibration as an alerting parameter.

One finding of the pilot survey, that the LED pointers of the EIS are less conspicuous than the mechanical pointers on the hybrid displays, is however a cause for concern. In this respect, whilst the introduction of the EIS may represent progress in terms of improved reliability and maintainability, it may be a retrograde step in terms of presentation of information. Moreover, although it was type-certified as fit for its purpose by both the FAA and the CAA during October 1988, it appears to have been introduced without any thorough evaluation of its efficiency in imparting information to line pilots. Now that the system has been in use for some time and EIS-equipped flight simulators are available, the reduced conspicuity of the pointers may assume less importance and it may be too late for a new evaluation of the system to be worthwhile. Nevertheless, this change in presentation indicates how important it is for all new developments in aircraft indicating systems to be subjected to comprehensive evaluation of their effect on line pilot performance before being introduced to service. It is therefore recommended that the regulatory requirements concerning the certification of new instrument presentations should be amended to include a standardized method of assessing the effectiveness of such displays in transmitting the associated information to flight crew, under normal and abnormal parameter conditions. In addition, line pilots should be used in such evaluations (Made 30 March 1990).

The layout and methods of displaying information on engine instruments are considered in Appendix 2.7, which concludes that although the EIS provides accurate and reliable information to the crew, the overall layout of the displays and the detailed implications of small LED pointers, rather than larger mechanical ones, and of edge-lit rather than reflective symbology, require further consideration. Neither pilot noticed the maximum reading on the No 1 engine vibration indicator and at least one of them gained the impression from the engine instruments, or from some other cue, that the No 2 rather than the No 1 engine was failing. If they gained this impression from the engine instruments then there is a possibility that the methods of displaying information on these instruments may have contributed to the error.

The error would probably not have been made if the vibration indicators had included a visual warning of which engine was affected by excessive vibration. It may be seen from the preamble to the FAA requirement for a vibration monitoring system (paragraph 1.17.4) that it was intended to provide the flight crew with a vibration warning, and later aircraft powered by certain high-bypass turbofan engines, such as Boeing 757 aircraft and the Airbus series, do include high engine vibration in their crew alerting systems. It is therefore recommended that the CAA should require that the engine instrument system on the Boeing 737-400 aircraft type, and other applicable public transport aircraft, be modified to include an attention-getting facility to draw attention to each vibration indicator when it indicates maximum vibration (Made 30 March 1990).

2.1.1.4   The shut-down of the No 2 engine

Although the initial misidentification of the damaged engine may be seen as the start of the accident sequence, the commander's decision to throttle back the No 2 engine did not, by itself, lead directly to the accident. In fact this decision would have been entirely appropriate in the absence of any positive indication on the engine instruments; he would then have reduced power on each engine in turn in order to identify the one that was causing the vibration. It is likely that, if the No 1 engine had not ceased to surge at the same time that the No 2 throttle was closed, an effect considered to be connected with the disconnection of the autothrottle (paragraph 2.2.2.2), the accident would not have occurred.

It is also likely that, if the No 2 engine had not been shut down, the accident would not have happened, and some explanation must be sought for the commander's decision to shut it down. It is now known that the engine was operating normally but, because the decision to shut it down was made after its throttle had been closed, having failed to recognise its normal operating parameters before closing the throttle, the crew could no longer confirm its normal operation by comparison with the No 1 engine instruments. There is, however, no evidence from the CVR that the crew consulted the engine instruments or attempted any other analysis of their situation before shutting down the No 2 engine. Indeed, it appears that they were so sure that they had contained the situation that the commander engaged in lengthy communications with BMA Operations just after the No 2 throttle had been closed.

It may be indicative of what was in their minds that, when the first officer notified the emergency to London Airways, he said '...AT THE MOMENT IT'S LOOKING LIKE AN ENGINE FIRE....', and it may be that the commander's further action was taken in the belief that the engine was on fire. If this was the case, then he should not have accepted the first officer's selection of the 'Engine Failure and Shutdown' checklist, when the 'Engine Fire, Severe Damage or Separation' checklist would have been more appropriate. Once the No 2 engine had been shut down, it would appear that the apparent absence of any manifestation of abnormality other than the No 1 engine vibration indication, which they did not notice, persuaded both pilots that, in the commander's own words, '.... the emergency had been successfully concluded and the left engine was operating normally.' Moreover, as the commander also said later, the clearance from the flight deck of the smell of fire powerfully reinforced their conviction that they had taken the correct action.

In the aircraft 'non-normal' checklist severe vibration does not necessitate an engine shut-down, provided it is not accompanied by abnormal engine indications, nor does the presence of smoke or fumes in the cockpit. The crew, therefore, did not comply with the checklist in shutting down the engine since they did not see any abnormal engine indications. Nor did they follow the more general instructions in the Operations Manual or their training, both of which required them to evaluate all the evidence available before taking this action. However, the Operations Manual contained no guidance on the action to be taken in the event that vibration and smoke/fumes occurred together. Because severe fan shaft vibration can cause damage to the fan and/or the LP compressor abradable seals, and fumes can enter the aircraft from these sources, it would have been prudent for the aircraft manufacturer to have included an appropriate warning and a suitable procedure for such a contingency in the aircraft Flight Manual. It was therefore recommended that the CAA should request the Boeing Commercial Airplane Company to produce amendments to the existing aircraft Flight Manual to indicate what actions should be taken when engine-induced high vibration occurs, accompanied by smoke and/or the smell of burning entering the flight deck and/or cabin (Made 23 February 1989).

2.1.1.5 *Subsequent actions of the operating crew.*

Having shut down the No 2 engine, the commander decided to land at the nearest suitable airfield. Although it is possible that he was influenced by the fact that East Midlands Airport (EMA) was his company's main operating base, it is more likely that he was influenced by the urgency which he felt when he first smelt 'fire'. He initiated a flight pattern that would enable him to land the aircraft with the minimum delay, but which left him little time to reconsider the nature of the emergency or the actions that had been taken. Whilst the decision to land without delay was correct, the shortness of the flight time between Event 1 and the approach to land at EMA may have influenced the outcome of the emergency.

From the start of the descent the cockpit workload was high as the pilots received and acknowledged ATC directions, notified their situation to the operating company, broadcast to the passengers on the cabin address system and completed the descent and approach checklists for a single-engined landing. Some time was lost as the first officer attempted unsuccessfully to programme the flight management system (FMS) to produce the correct flight instrument display for landing at EMA. Such reprogramming of the FMS for landing at a hitherto unspecified diversion airfield is unusual and rarely if ever practised. From the CVR it may be inferred that he possibly attempted to enter EMA as the next en route point without first selecting the route page and entering it as an arrival airfield. It is therefore recommended that the CAA should ensure that flight crew currency training in simulators includes practice reprogramming of flight management systems, or any other such systems which control key approach and landing display format, during unplanned diversions so that they remain practised in the expeditious use of such systems (Made 30 March 1990).

More time was spent when the commander accepted a request from EMA to make a call to the fire vehicles. Nevertheless, it must have seemed to the commander that his plan allowed all necessary tasks to be completed in time, for he made no attempt to slow down the rate of activity or to re-engage the autopilot to reduce his own workload, and he did not ask ATC for a quiet radio frequency. When, some 7 minutes after the engine was shut-down, the commander began to review what had occurred, the reading on the No 1 engine vibration indicator had reduced and there was no other indication on the engine instruments of the damage to that engine. When his review of events was interrupted by an ATC transmission, he did not resume it, and this seems to indicate that he remained confident of the safety of the aircraft. There can be little doubt, however, that the high workload in the cockpit contributed to the failure of the crew to notice the abnormally high reading on the No 1 engine vibration indicator that was evident for nearly four minutes after the initial vibration. It is therefore recommended that the CAA should review the current guidance to air traffic controllers on the subject of offering a discrete RT frequency to the commander of a public transport aircraft in an emergency situation, with a view towards assessing the merits of positively offering this important option (Made 30 March 1990).

Even at that stage of the approach to land when there was still time to restart the No 2 engine, the commander obtained a required increase in power from the No 1 engine, which must again have confirmed to him that his previous actions had been correct. The engine, however, again produced high vibration, which elicited no comment by either pilot and appears not to have been perceived against the background of cockpit activity at the time. 4 minutes later the No 1 engine lost power and the accident became inevitable. Although the commander instructed the first officer to restart the No 2 engine some 50 seconds before the crash, and the CVR recorded that the first officer attempted to comply, the No 2 engine fan shaft showed no significant rotation at impact.

At this time flight conditions were outside the envelope for a 'windmill' start. Starter assistance would have been needed to rotate the engine, requiring the No 2 engine start switch to be selected to the 'GRD' position. Because this switch would have moved automatically to 'OFF' as soon as electrical power was lost, there was no evidence to show whether or not a starter assisted start was attempted.

However, the normal starter assist procedure would perhaps not have been effective for there would probably have been insufficient bleed air pressure from the failing No 1 engine to rotate the No 2 engine, and without rotation there would have been no fuel flow to the engine. It is likely, therefore, that the only procedure that would have restarted the engine was that appropriate to a restart from a condition of double engine failure, which would have required both air conditioning packs to have been switched off and pressure air from the APU to have been connected to the bleed air manifold. The checklist in the Quick Reference Handbook gave a procedure suitable only for the restart of the No 1 engine and an attempt to start the No 2 would have required improvisation. This checklist has since been amended to cover the restart of either engine. After the accident the positions of the switches on the bleed air control panel showed that no double engine failure restart drill had been attempted. The first officer, however, had comparatively little experience of the aircraft and could not have been expected to recognize the need for, improvise and accomplish an unlisted procedure in the time between the final loss of thrust on the No 1 engine and the impact with the ground. Even if he had devised and followed a suitable procedure, it is doubtful if the engine could have been started and brought up to idle speed in the short time available.

2.1.2   *Crew cooperation*

2.1.2.1   *Flight crew coordination*

Among the important factors that affect the ways in which individual crew members relate to one another are their personalities, relative ranks, roles (*ie* handling, non-handling) and relative levels of competence. The commander, although he had no management or training responsibilities, had been a captain with the operating company for 14 years, whereas the first officer had flown jet transport aircraft for only 6 months. Nevertheless, this wide difference in rank and their limited previous association appear not to have influenced coordination adversely. The CVR did not suggest any undue deference from the first officer to the commander, and the atmosphere appeared relaxed in the early part of the flight with both pilots addressing each other by their first names.

Although the first officer was the handling pilot when the emergency occurred, the commander then disengaged the autopilot and, although no words were said, it was apparent to the first officer that the commander had taken control of the aircraft. This change in handling may have had an effect on the first officer's ability to interpret the engine instrumentation. Since he was likely to have been more concerned with handling the aircraft than with monitoring these instruments during the early part of the flight, he was not, perhaps, as acutely associated with interpreting them as he would have been as the non-handling pilot, and this rapid change of perceptual 'set' could have contributed to his identification of the wrong engine.

The relative and absolute levels of competence of the crew members are difficult to gauge. Both pilots had met company requirements during conversion training and subsequent base and line checks, and their training records reflect no difficulty in comprehension, or lack of competence. There is, therefore, no suggestion that any large ability mismatch on the flight deck affected coordination. Indeed, the CVR suggests that the pilots worked together as a team throughout the flight, and that the decisions made on the flight deck were all accepted jointly.

2.1.2.2 *Coordination between the flight deck and the cabin*

It was extremely unfortunate that the information evident to many of the passengers of fire associated with the left engine did not find its way to the flight deck even though, when the commander made his cabin address broadcast, he stated that he had shut down the 'right' engine. The factor of the role commonly adopted by passengers probably influenced this lack of communication. Lay passengers generally accept that the pilot is provided with full information on the state of the aircraft and they will regard it as unlikely that they have much to contribute to his knowledge. Even those passengers who noticed the commander's reference to the right engine may well have assumed that the commander had made a slip of the tongue, or that the problems they had seen with the left engine were in some way consequential to an important problem with the right engine that the commander had dealt with. It cannot therefore be regarded as surprising that information from the passengers was not made available to the pilots.

The same information was available to the 3 cabin crew in the rear of the aircraft but they, like the passengers, would have had no reason to suppose that the evidence of malfunction they saw on the left engine was not equally apparent to the flight crew from the engine instruments. In addition, it would appear that there was not the same awareness of possible error, since these cabin crew members stated that they had not heard the commander's reference to the right engine. This may have been because the cabin crew, engaged on their own duties, were not aware of any more than the general sense of the broadcast. In addition, cabin crew are generally aware that any intrusion into the flight deck during busy phases of flight may be distracting, and this is particularly true if the flight crew are known to be dealing with an emergency. There can thus be at these times a firm division between flight deck and cabin, and it is notable in this context that in this accident the flight service manager made no initial attempt to approach the flight deck until he was called. However, it must be stated that had some initiative been taken by one or more of the cabin crew who had seen the distress of the left engine, this accident could have been prevented. It must be emphasised, nonetheless, that present patterns of airline training do not provide specifically for the exercise of coordination between cabin and flight crew in such circumstances.

2.1.3   *The influence of stress*

One aspect of flying that is extremely difficult to address in training is the stress presented by an emergency. Although all pilots are aware of the general requirement to avoid making hasty decisions in the air, it is much easier to advocate such a policy on the ground than it is to execute it in the air when presented with an unusual emergency. The response of any individual to a given emergency will be affected by three factors - the perceived severity of the problem, the personalities of the individuals concerned and the training they have received.

The noise and smell which suddenly alerted this crew to the emergency quickly led them to believe that they were experiencing a severe problem, and it may reasonably be assumed that this would have had a marked effect on their affective states. No formal assessment of the personalities of the pilots has been undertaken, but there was nothing in their records to suggest that they were likely to differ significantly from most other pilots in their response to stressful stimuli.

It is notable from many accidents that crews are more likely to remain calm during hazardous events if they understand the situation and have an appropriate drill to implement. In this accident the combination of initial symptoms was outside their experience and training, and there was no specific drill for such a combination. Thus the combination of severity and novelty must have acted to increase their arousal. Under such circumstances it is understandable that their first desire was to identify the problem. Although this is obviously a first requirement in order that action may be taken, uncertainty reduction also has considerable psychological importance in that it is much more comfortable and reassuring to be able to impose structure on a situation and deal with a known rather than an unknown problem. Two effects of increased arousal on the desire to reduce uncertainty may be contemplated. The first is unnecessary haste in making a decision about the nature of the problem and the second is failure to question that decision, once it has been made.

Although there is evidence in this accident that both these factors may have prevailed to some extent, there is no evidence that this crew was abnormally affected by stress, or that they responded to the situation in a uniquely unexpected manner. In particular it should be noted that the second of these effects - the reduction in likelihood that they might question the accuracy of their decision - would have been heavily influenced by the fact that the reduction in No 2 engine power had apparently stopped the shuddering. There is considerable research on the topic of 'causality' from which it is clear that in this situation it would have required an exceptional crew to question the association between their action and its apparently obvious, and highly desirable, consequence. The commander attempted, during a period of slightly lower workload, to review the events that had passed. It was unfortunate that further events intervened to curtail this review since it is possible that he may have realised, given more time, that there was a risk that they might have shut down the wrong engine.

A last factor which may have influenced this crew's behaviour, given the stressful nature of the events, is the flight simulator training which they would have experienced. In the simulator virtually all engine problems result in an engine shutdown. Since this crew would have been under both practical and psychological pressure to come up with a programme of action, it cannot be regarded as surprising that the actions they embarked upon were those that they had practised in the flight simulator.

2.1.4   *Flight crew training*

The performance of flight crew in emergency situations may be regarded as a product of their natural ability and their training. It is possible to identify three aspects of the circumstances of this accident where a different pattern of training could have favourably influenced the outcome. The ability of the pilots to extract information from the EIS must be questioned, and so must the apparent lack of coordination between the flight deck and the cabin crew. The most important issue, however, concerns the preparation of pilots generally to cope with unforeseen situations which are not covered in their emergency checklists.

2.1.4.1   *Training on the EIS*

When the operating company took delivery of their first EIS equipped aircraft, training on the EIS was included in a one day course on the differences between the Series 300 and Series 400 aircraft (paragraphs 1.5.1 and 1.5.2). No EIS equipped flight simulator was available at that stage and so the first few flights of pilots who were new to the EIS system were supervised under normal line checking procedures. The result of this pattern of training was that the first time that a pilot was likely to see abnormal indications on the EIS was in-flight in an aircraft with a failing engine. This could be regarded as undesirable on at least two counts. The first is that if the crew encountered any problem with display interpretation under normal line conditions, there would invariably be spare capacity in the system to enable them to spend a little extra time checking the readings on the display. In the circumstances of this emergency, they may not have perceived that such time was available, and were thus in a situation where they had to interpret novel readings (*ie* acquire a new skill) under the worst possible conditions. The second reason is that it is possible that new forms of engine instrumentation are, subjectively, more different from the old instrumentation when presenting abnormal readings than when presenting normal states, and that the slightly different techniques required to interrogate these instruments under abnormal conditions may not have been acquired by this crew.

For both of these reasons it would appear evident that crews should be provided with EIS display familiarisation in the simulator. During such training they would be able to witness a full range of failures, enabling them to acquire the necessary visual and interpretive skills, before being presented with associated problems on an aircraft in flight. It is therefore recommended that the CAA should review current airline transport pilot training requirements to ensure that pilots, who lack experience of electronic flight displays, are provided with familiarisation of such displays in a flight simulator, before flying public transport aircraft that are so equipped (Made 30 March 1990).

2.1.4.2   *Training for flight crew/cabin crew coordination*

It could be argued that the pilots of this aircraft did not make effective use of the cabin crew as an additional source of information. Such co-operation could be encouraged by joint training exercises between flight and cabin crews. In addition, it should be possible to provide simulator exercises in which it would be appropriate for pilots to ask for cabin crew to give a briefing on events in the cabin and for the role of the cabin crew to be taken, in such exercises, by the simulator instructor. Such training would serve to provide pilots with the knowledge that cabin crew are a source of information that should be considered in certain emergencies. Equally, cabin crew could be trained to appreciate that one factor which they should consider during any emergency is the provision to the pilots, in a timely way, of a summary of the sights and sounds witnessed in the cabin. It is therefore recommended that training exercises for pilots and cabin crew should be introduced to improve co-ordination between technical and cabin crews in response to an emergency (Made 30 March 1990).

2.1.4.3   *Pilot training*

2.1.4.3.1   *Technical training*

With the increased complexity of modern aircraft systems it has become generally accepted that pilots cannot be expected to have an in-depth technical knowledge of all the systems on their aircraft. In addition, technical development has produced systems with much improved fail-safe characteristics which can give the flight crew continued system performance following anticipated discrete failures within such systems. Because of this technical progress, associated pilot training has become increasingly based on the 'need to know' principle. This approach has its limitations and largely rests on the assumption that all technical failures with which a flight crew may be confronted can be anticipated. This is an unsafe assumption.

In this accident, the pilots were suddenly presented with an unforeseen combination of symptoms that was outside their training or experience. It may be contended that fan/compressor blade contact with the surrounding abradable seals during conditions of severe out-of-balance running could not have been anticipated technically. Even if this is accepted, this effect has now been demonstrated.

It is also apparent that this flight crew did not assimilate the readings on both engine vibration indicators. The reaction of pilots to indications on the flight deck is modified by their general experience and many pilots of earlier gas turbine aircraft have become dismissive of engine vibration indicators due to the inferior performance of such systems. Such views are liable to prevail on modern aircraft unless the technical knowledge of pilots is effectively revised.

The prime factor which appeared to confirm to this crew that the No 2 engine was at fault was the sudden reduction in noise and shuddering which occurred when the No 2 engine was throttled back. It is considered (paragraph 2.2.2.2) that this effect was due to the No 1 engine recovering from a series of compressor stalls, due to the autothrottle disconnection which preceded throttling of the No 2 engine. This is yet another technical systems finding which should be covered in pilot training since it may have implications for engine failure discrimination where the affected engine is experiencing compressor stalls, with autothrottles engaged.

Such findings raise questions concerning the level of technical training available to pilots of modern aircraft. In addition they illustrate the point that such training should also include an appreciation of systems response under abnormal conditions, particularly where the associated symptoms have the potential to mislead flight crews in an emergency situation.

2.1.4.3.2 *Decision training*

Training of flight crew can be classified under three broad headings. There is training designed to provide the pilot with specific handling or psychomotor skills; that designed to ensure that pilots are familiar with procedures (*eg* the pattern of behaviour required to deal with an engine fire); and that designed to provide the pilot with general techniques for dealing with unexpected and possibly poorly defined problems.

Flying training and checking has traditionally concentrated on the first two types of training, and this accident provides evidence of the efficiency of that training. The aircraft was controlled satisfactorily by the captain, and the engine shut down procedure was carried out with accuracy. Any errors made on the flight deck in this accident were at the highest decision making level. The crew was not presented with a clear cut fire warning, with which they would undoubtedly have dealt satisfactorily, but with a noise, shuddering and the smell of burning. Nowhere in their previous experience would they have been presented with this particular situation, and it was therefore up to them, or at least up to the commander, to formulate a plan for dealing with it.

Because it is not possible to anticipate every emergency or combination of circumstances and reduce such situations to a level at which pilots may be trained to deal with them procedurally, it may be argued that it is the essence of the pilot's task to bring his flexibility and decision making potential to bear on those situations that cannot be anticipated. Such considerations have led to the development of 'Line Oriented Flying Training', 'Cockpit Resource Management', 'Flight Deck Management' and other training concepts designed to provide pilots with experience of evaluating unusual situations, albeit in the flight simulator, in the belief that such practice in making high-level decisions will transfer positively to the real flight deck. Such courses are not presently required for British airline transport pilots, and hence their training tends to contain a heavy procedural bias. This accident emphasises the fact that occasions arise when it is important for pilots to have the ability to evaluate novel situations correctly, and consideration should thus be given to requiring that evidence evaluation and decision training, as well as procedural training, should be included in company training and checking procedures.

It is therefore recommended that the CAA should review current airline transport pilot training requirements with a view towards considering the need to restore the balance in flight crew technical appreciation of aircraft systems, including systems response under abnormal conditions, and to evaluate the potential of additional simulator training in flight deck decision making (Made 30 March 1990).

2.2   Engine failure analysis

2.2.1   *General*

From the engine investigation standpoint, the pre-accident sequence fell into three distinct phases; the initial problem when there was a sudden onset of heavy vibration, shuddering and compressor stalling which ceased after about 20 seconds, referred to as Event 1; an intermediate period during the descent at low power which lasted up to the second sudden onset of severe vibration during a power increase on approach, followed by a sudden thrust loss on the No 1 (left) engine about 50 seconds before impact, referred to as Event 2. During both these events there were reports of flames and sparks emanating from the No 1 engine.

Examination of the engine parameters recorded on the FDR over the previous 25 hours did not reveal any evidence of a significant change in either engine's characteristics. Up to the instant of Event 1, both engines had been performing entirely normally, neither showing any evidence of abnormal vibration levels nor of changes in the N1/N2/EGT relationships. At Event 1, the FDR record showed changes occurring to the No 1 engine parameters only. No changes occurred to the No 2 engine parameters at this time and it was retarded and subsequently shut down, having displayed normal indications at all times.

After the initial period of heavy vibration and stalling on the No 1 engine, the FDR record showed that, when this engine had restabilised there was only a small change in engine thrust. There was, however, a marked increase in vibration level on the No 1 engine, saturating the indication system at high fan speed, but reducing to fall within the measurable range (less than 5 units) after the fan speed was reduced to 33% during the descent. These levels were consistent with those produced by an engine with a fan which had one blade outer panel missing when compared with the data derived from engine testing (see paragraph 1.16.1) and that later available from the FDR record from the blade failure on G-OBMG (paragraph 1.17.7.3). There had also been a loss of overall engine efficiency, indicated by a higher EGT/N1 ratio compared with that required before Event 1. The vibration levels induced by the imbalance caused by the loss of a fan blade outer panel on the No 1 engine would have resulted in tip rubbing of blades throughout the compressor at the high N1 (97%) recorded immediately after Event 1. This would have led to a loss of compressor efficiency, which would have required the combustion temperature to have risen in order to supply sufficient energy to the LP turbines to drive the fan.

Between the time that the No 1 engine stabilised and Event 2, this engine responded, apparently normally, to the applied throttle demands. It continued, however, to exhibit abnormally high vibration levels for the power settings used and these levels were considerably above those exhibited at any power setting before Event 1 (see Appendix 4, fig 4). It also continued to operate with a raised EGT/N1 ratio although, without the indications of a similar undamaged engine for comparison, these changes would not have been obvious.

Just before Event 2, the No 1 engine initially responded to an increased throttle demand by increasing its fan speed to 70%. Rapid changes in engine parameters then occurred, after which N1 and N2 decayed, the exhaust gas temperature

(EGT) increased slowly and the engine ceased to respond to the throttle. The engine then remained, seemingly locked, in this condition until the end of the FDR record (see Appendix 4, fig 3).

Strip examination of the No 2 engine (paragraph 1.12.2.1.1), including the MEC, revealed only damage which was consistent with the effects of ground impact, with the engine either stopped or windmilling very slowly. No evidence was found of any pre-existing imbalance, nor of any fire. This accorded with the FDR record which showed that the engine had been first retarded, and subsequently shut down, without any performance or vibration excursion having occurred.

By contrast, the strip examination of the No 1 engine (paragraph 1.12.2.1.2) showed that, although the damage resulting from ground impact was very similar to that observed on the No 2 engine, there were marked differences in its condition. The fan and fan case showed evidence of fan break-up at high energy and there were two areas of fire damage. There was also a great deal of rubbing damage to the rotating seals and blade tips of all compressor stages, consistent with this engine having run at considerable power, with a very high level of vibration. No evidence was found of imbalance due to whole or part blade loss in any rotating stage apart from the fan, nor was there any bearing distress to account for the vibration levels recorded. There was evidence of hard object ingestion throughout the compressors and of wood ingestion through to the turbine section, where it had been charred. This wood ingestion showed that the engine had been running right up to the time of impact, with combustion still being sustained.

2.2.2   *No 1 engine failure sequence*

2.2.2.1   *Fan failure sequence*

On reconstruction of the No 1 engine fan, it was established that, although all fan blades were found to have fractures or damage of some type, only the fracture of blade No 17 exhibited the characteristics of fatigue. If this fracture had occurred first, the initiation of Event 1 would have been the sudden separation of a single fan blade outer panel. This would have induced a localised disturbance in the fan airflow, coupled with severe imbalance, both of which can cause the onset of a fan stall, and subsequently a booster and core stall. (see paragraph 1.17.6.3). The severe imbalance would also have caused blade tip and air-seal rubbing throughout the engine, with a consequent degradation of the engine stall margin. The rubbing of the fan and booster blades on the abradable tip path seals would have generated a considerable amount of acrid smelling products. These would have been entrained into the core engine and thence, through the bleed air system, into the air conditioning. The reported smells of 'rubber' and 'hot metal' would have been consistent with such effects.

Appendix 4, fig 10 shows that the initial reaction of the No 1 engine of ME to the first event was almost identical to that of the No 2 engine of MG, which is known to have suffered a fan blade outer panel separation, with very little subsequent damage. It can be seen that the No 1 engine of ME almost restabilised during Event 1 about 6 seconds after the onset of compressor stalling, but it appears that the power set at that time was greater than the engine, with its then degraded stall margin, could sustain and it entered a series of stalls which lasted about 20 seconds. The autothrottle was disconnected about 20 seconds after the onset of Event 1 and at a moment when it had set a slightly lower throttle angle than that which had been required for the rated power climb. This reduction in power demand appears to have enabled the No 1 engine to recover from its compressor stalling. The stall sequence and the recovery from it are examined in detail in paragraph 2.2.2.2. Subsequently, the vibration levels on the No 1 engine of ME at reduced thrust were comparable to those experienced on the No 2 engine of MG under similar conditions. These similarities indicate that, after Event 1, the No 1 engine fan of ME was in a comparable state to that of the No 2 engine of MG. The continued operation of the No 1 engine of ME, after such a fan blade failure, may be understood when compared with the result of the test on an engine which had one fan blade outer panel missing (paragraph 1.16.1) which showed that there was no detectable loss of performance or efficiency in this condition.

Thus all the No 1 engine symptoms at Event 1 were consistent with the instantaneous loss of the outer panel from one fan blade and the presence of a fatigue fracture on blade No 17 alone indicated that this was the first event. The comparability of the vibration levels with those of MG and the maintenance of power after Event 1 suggested that the No 1 engine fan had suffered very little damage apart from the loss of one outer panel at that time. This implied that the separated panel had either passed through the fan, like that on MG, or had become embedded in the acoustic liners of the fan case, or intake duct forward of the fan.

Between the end of Event 1 and the occurrence of Event 2 there was no evidence of any significant change in the condition of the No 1 engine. Since this engine was being operated at reduced RPM during the descent, compared with that at the time of Event 1, it was unlikely that the rotor blade tips, or the rotating seals, would have rubbed further than they had during the first event. This also implied that the fan had suffered no significant additional damage between the two events. At Event 2, the condition of the No 1 engine clearly deteriorated abruptly. Since the strip examination of this engine did not reveal any catastrophic failures in the booster, core engine or LP turbines, nor any malfunction of the fuel control system, this change would appear to have been the result of additional fan damage. The finding, on the ground below where Event 2 took place, of fragments of at least three fan blades, including parts of blade No 17, together with parts of acoustic liner and their attachments, also indicated that the cause of this deterioration was additional fan damage.

Since blade No 17 was the only fan blade to have suffered a fatigue failure, it was concluded that the initiating occurrence for Event 2 must have been the ingestion by the fan of a foreign object. The finding of parts of blade No 17 outer panel under that part of the final approach path where Event 2 occurred suggested that the release of this outer panel from a place of entrapment was the most likely cause of the additional fan damage. This view was supported by the condition of the fan on the Dan Air engine (NL incident) in which outer panel separation caused immediate massive fan damage, albeit at a higher power setting than that applicable to Event 2. The behaviour of the Dan Air engine after the blade outer panel separation suggested that the resulting airflow with such fan damage is likely to induce a 'locked compressor stall' unless engine power is retarded, and even then it might not be possible to re-establish any significant power.

The exact sequence of the fan failure at Event 2 was difficult to analyse in the light of the additional damage suffered by the fan during impact with the motorway. The presence of fragments of blades 4 and 5 at the location of Event 2, combined with the severe overheating observed on the blade 6 outer panel suggested that blade 6 outer panel detached at this juncture and became trapped between the fan blade tips and the abradable liner. This was the most likely origin of the 'fire' in the intake reported by many witnesses and the associated sparks would also have constituted a potential source of ignition for both fire zones by penetration of the intake duct into the fan case cowl and by passage down the fan exhaust to ignite fuel and oil atomising from the trailing edge of the bypass duct.

2.2.2.2   *Recovery of the No 1 engine from the series of stalls at Event 1*

The timing of the recovery of the No 1 engine from its series of stalls was clearly crucial to the crew's understanding of their situation. The influence of throttle lever angle (TLA) on the ability of the engine to recover and how the autothrottle affected the throttle position has thus to be considered.

Appendix 4, fig 11 shows the relative variation of a number of parameters over a period of 35 seconds, starting 4 seconds before Event 1. The parameter traces shown are as recorded, without offsets for mechanical or electronic delays. There is approximately a 0.5 second delay in N1, but autothrottle position lag is not readily estimated, as it is mainly a mechanical hysteresis dependent on the movement demanded. However, all the parameters shown were sampled at a rate of 1/sec. and as a result, the actual peak and trough values may not have been recorded. This is particularly true of N1 and, to a lesser extent, throttle position (TLA recorded at the MEC input lever) on the No 1 engine which was changing, in both value and sense, very rapidly. Therefore, to give some idea of what the extreme values of N1 might have been, the slopes have been extended (in broken lines) where the peaks and troughs obviously have been truncated.

Examination of these parameters and relating them to the autothrottle logic in use at the time (paragraph 1.17.6.4) has shown that, after making due allowance for the various lags, the autothrottle has reacted correctly to the N1 excursions, in accordance with its design. The loss of the actual maxima and minima, and the hysteresis lag, of TLA is demonstrated by the apparent reduction and subsequent increase of TLA after the autothrottle was disconnected and just before the engine settled at the reduced N1. It is possible that TLA reduced to an angle of as much as 1° below that recorded in response to the combination of N1>10% below target but increasing towards the reduced N1 target very rapidly. Whilst at this condition, the 4th stall occurred and the autothrottle was then returning TLA to the position of the reduced target N1, since N1 was no longer increasing.

This resulted in the throttle lever coming to rest, with the autothrottle disengaged, at the reduced target N1 appropriate to the logic law which prevents overboosting of an unresponsive engine. With the gas path degradation caused by the fan damage, the engine would have had reduced responsiveness. This reduced TLA position therefore most probably prevented a large N1 overswing and permitted the engine to recover and stabilise.

It can be seen at Appendix 4, fig 11 that the closing of the No 2 engine throttle coincided almost exactly with the start of the final stall recovery acceleration of the No 1 engine, which would have become smooth running (apart from the imbalance vibration) at that instant.

The evidence thus indicated that it was the disengagement of the autothrottle at a time when it had, whilst operating correctly, demanded a reduced TLA which permitted the stable stall recovery of the No 1 engine. This caused the closure of the No 2 engine throttle lever to appear to coincide with the cessation of the shuddering from the No 1 engine.

2.2.3   *Cause of fatigue initiation in fan blade No 17*

The metallurgical examination of this blade established that the fracture had propagated initially by fatigue, the origin of which appeared to be on the pressure face of the blade about 1.25mm aft of the true leading edge. The transference of the original leading edge and pressure face surfaces to the adjacent blades, as a result of inter-blade clashing, made it impossible to identify any surface feature which may have led to fatigue initiation. However, the depth of the material removed from the pressure face indicated that if there had been an anomaly at the origin of the fracture it must have been only very small (see Appendix 1, fig 3).

During the initial part of the investigation, the manufacturers were convinced, by the work that they had done during the engine type certification, that there were no severe blade vibration modes anywhere in the operating envelope of the fan in the absence of serious blade distortion. The possibility that bird or other foreign object damage might have caused sufficient blade damage and distortion to account for fatigue initiation and growth to critical length between Events 1 and 2 was explored, but engine testing with damaged and distorted blades did not reveal sufficient vibratory excitation at the powers used during the flight. It was also concluded that such damage would have had to be so gross that it could not have been present on the blade before Event 1 without revealing itself as loss of fan efficiency and/or engine vibration or, if it had been present before take-off, being visible during the normal pre-flight inspection. Thus the initial conclusions reached were that the pressure face had suffered a small but particularly sharp surface damage feature with a large k_t, that there was insufficient information available from the fracture surface to indicate how long such a feature had existed and that it was an isolated failure.

However, after metallurgical examination of the two fan blade fractures suffered by G-BNNL and G-OBMG had revealed a number of features common to each other and to that from ME, it became clear that there was a generic problem affecting the −3C-1 variant of the CFM 56. Both of the later fractures had originated at the base of the shot-peened layer on the blade pressure face, close to the mid-chord position and just above the leading edge of the mid-span shroud. There was no detectable evidence of any surface damage nor of any metallurgical or microstructural deficiencies in either blade. The examination also revealed that once the fatigue had initiated, it had progressed to its critical length and final rupture extremely rapidly, taking three flights to complete separation in the case of the NL, and only two in that of MG.

The position of the fatigue origins was in the region of the blade where the highest vibratory stresses were expected for one particular vibratory mode but, on the basis of the data collected during the certification testing, these had been shown to be well below the manufacturer's reduced endurance limit. Initiation of fatigue at the base of the compressive layer below shot peening is typical of the result of cyclic loading at stress levels above the endurance limit and the very high initiation/propagation time ratio indicated that this level was only just above the endurance limit. This implied that the fan blades had been subjected to an hitherto unsuspected blade vibration.

Comparison of the two later fractures with that from ME showed that although the fatigue origin on the ME blade was near the leading edge, the planes of all three fractures ran very close together. (See Appendix 1, fig 8) This suggested that all three failures were the result of the same problem. Examination of the blade vibration modes established during certification revealed that the nodal line indicated by the planes of the three fractures matched, amongst others, that to be expected from a second order system vibration mode[14]. Furthermore, a comparison of the stress levels induced by this mode in the leading edge zone, relative to those at mid-chord, indicated that a defect with a k_t of as little as 2.5 could render the leading edge as sensitive to fatigue nucleation as the mid-chord zone. Thus, since a score with a semi-circular cross section which ran chordwise across the blade surface would have had a k_t of 3, a relatively minor defect resulting from FOD would be sufficient to move the natural initiation zone from the mid-chord to the leading edge when the fan was subjected to this mode.

2.2.4 *Source of vibratory stresses*

At the time that the CFM 56–3C-1 came into service, the manufacturers had satisfied themselves and the certificating authorities that the type met all the airworthiness requirements, amongst which was the requirement to ensure that all blade stages were free from 'unacceptable vibratory stresses'. (See Appendix 1, extract 1) This had been demonstrated by reference to all the past testing of blades and test bed running of strain-gauged engines. This latter testing, even when done with –3B variants, had required the engines to be run at physical speeds considerably above those which were permitted in flight, even for the –3C–1. These tests had demonstrated that throughout the engine speed range there were only synchronous responses and these produced acceptable vibratory stresses. However, in order to reach the very high fan speeds required for certification whilst testing at sea level, it was necessary to use a variable fan nozzle to avoid driving the core engine beyond its limits. By doing this, the airflow through the fan becomes unrepresentative of that which actually occurs at high altitude as the fan is working on a different operating line. It was believed, however, that any instability features which existed would show up, albeit at reduced levels, and if they did so, then a more representative test would have to be undertaken to establish the actual stresses created. Not having observed a

---

[14] Blades and disc vibrating as an entity

tendency to produce any instabilities at sea level, the manufacturers and certificating authorities were satisfied, and no tests were performed on a strain-gauged engine in an altitude test cell, or in flight.

After the two later fan blade fatigue fractures, it became suspected that the fan was being subjected to higher vibratory stresses than were thought to exist. The fact that all three fan blade fatigue fractures had occurred across the same blade section, at similar flight conditions of engine speed and altitude and that all three engines had completed a similar number of flight cycles (although significantly higher running hours in the case of the Dan Air engine), indicated that there was an unique vibratory mode involved which was excited regularly. On comparing the operating conditions to which the –3C-1 was exposed with those of the –3B–2, there were only two areas of significant difference; the take-off thrust and the rated power climb thrust. Since take-off thrust is only used at relatively low altitudes, it was believed that test bed running accurately reflected true operating conditions. It appeared more likely, therefore, that the excitation occurred during rated power climb at a considerable altitude, a regime in which the true airflow conditions were known to be different from those tested up to that time.

In order to achieve the high physical fan speeds necessary on a test bed to simulate more accurately the high corrected fan speeds at altitude, it was necessary to run the core engine to speeds and temperatures which considerably shortened its life. The initial test bed running directed at exposing any unknown vibrations revealed some non-synchronous vibratory excitation of the fan. A review of the vibration survey made during the modified splitter tests, conducted after the accident to ME and unrelated to the investigation, then also revealed what, in retrospect, was a small indication that the problem existed.

Following the test bed research, the strain-gauged blade tests conducted on a flight test engine confirmed the presence and mode of the vibratory response and showed that it could produce stress levels approaching the endurance limit.

2.2.5 *Failure of the certification process to reveal vibration*

The CFM 56 was originally certificated jointly by FAA and DGAC as being in compliance with the requirements of FARs and JARs. With regard to the requirement to demonstrate freedom from damaging vibration, CFMI had adopted the normal US manufacturers' approach and had tested a strain-gauged engine in a sea level test cell. As this test had not revealed the presence of any such vibrations, the FAA and DGAC accepted that the engine had been demonstrated to have met the requirements of both FARs and JARs. Because of their reciprocal validation agreement with the FAA, the CAA also accepted the type certification of the CFM 56-3C

The tests performed, after the two later incidents, on strain-gauged engines in the flying test bed showed that the previously undetected system mode vibration of the fan was consistently excited when using -3C rated climb power above 10,000 ft. Although none of the measured vibratory stresses on the fan blades resulting from this excitation were above the endurance limit, they were sufficiently large to suggest that, with the anticipated variation of excitation of individual blades within a fan, some blades might experience stresses at, or above, this limit.

Had a similar flight test been performed during the certification testing, the manufacturer and certificating authorities would have become aware of the vibration mode and the engine could not have been considered acceptable for introduction into service before the characteristic had been eliminated.

Previous certification history, on other engine types, had suggested that such characteristics would reveal themselves, to a degree, during sea level testing. It appears, however, from the experience of this accident, and the two subsequent incidents, that this was not a safe assumption since the level of blade excitation was so low as to be masked by the background signal 'noise'. Although it will continue to be necessary to attempt to identify potentially hazardous modes using refined procedures on heavily instrumented ground test engines, only by test in the real operating environment can the actual excitation levels be reliably ascertained.

It is therefore recommended that the type certification requirements for gas turbine engines should be amended so that it is mandatory to perform instrumented flight tests to demonstrate freedom from damaging vibratory stresses at all altitude conditions and powers which an engine will encounter in service (Made 30 March 1990).

2.3 Fire

2.3.1 *Source of fire*

The first indication of fire in the No 1 engine nacelle occurred shortly after Event 2 in the fan failure sequence when there was evidence from both the FDR and CVR that a fire warning had been triggered. Although the fire warning was not related to the No 1 engine by the FDR evidence, it was by the subsequent conversation between the commander and first officer recorded on the CVR.

The examination of wreckage on the accident site indicated that only the No 1 engine and nacelle had evidence of fire damage and the more detailed examination revealed that there was no evidence of fire elsewhere on the aircraft. Examination of the No 1 engine and nacelle revealed that there were three separate and distinct fires which had occurred on this power plant. Of these, two were in zones monitored by fire detection loops, one on the outboard side of the fan case and the other on the underside of the combustion case. Neither had evidence of the presence of any forcing air draught to show that they had been burning in flight. The third fire had been on the outside of the nacelle, on the outboard side of the reverser duct, remote from any detectors. This fire showed the characteristics of having been slipstream driven and must have been burning whilst the aircraft was in flight.

Since the fire on the outboard side of the reverser duct was in an unmonitored zone, it is highly unlikely that it could have triggered the warning. Thus, since the warning had been triggered in flight, there must have been fire or very hot gases present in one of the other two zones. The fire on the underside of the combustion case, although in a monitored zone, had been very minor and showed the characteristics of a restricted fuel ground fire. It was also seen that this fire centred on a fractured fuel nozzle fitting which had clear evidence of having been damaged during the ground impact sequence, indicating that this fire was entirely post impact. Thus the fire warning must have been triggered by the fan case detectors.

The fan cowling itself is a nominally enclosed space, the only venting being via the cowl drain at the bottom, just ahead of the cowling firewall. Thus, even if the intake duct were breached by fan debris, it is unlikely that there was a fast airstream through the fan cowl in flight. The ground fire which had affected the fan case after the aircraft had come to rest had consumed a large proportion of the forward cowling and had overlaid any evidence, on the outside of the fan case, of any fire which might have occurred in flight. The reconstruction of the cowling, however, showed that some areas of the forward cowl which had broken free at impact had not been involved in the ground fire. By positioning these pieces it was possible to show that a fire had been present in the fan cowl before it had been broken up by impact and that fire appeared to have been present on the outboard side of the fan case and above the level of the MEC.

The investigation of the two other engines involved in fan blade fatigue failures showed that fuel pipe unions and the seal between the HP fuel pump and the MEC were susceptible to being loosened to the point of leaking if subjected to severe vibration. Furthermore, the trials performed to try to establish the characteristics of such leaks showed that atomised fuel spraying could occur as the result of unions being loosened to the extent found with the fuel pressures to be expected whilst the engine was running.

The exposure to vibration of the 3 engines which suffered fan blade fractures was compared. It was observed that the No 2 engine from MG had suffered a brief initial period of very high vibration at a high power setting, under similar conditions to that seen on the No 1 engine of ME but of about half the duration. Thereafter the engine was throttled back to a flight idle setting for a similar duration to that experienced by the ME engine during the descent. During the approach to East Midlands, the ME engine experienced two exposures to higher vibration levels as a result of engine power being increased. Thus the No 1 engine of ME had experienced greater exposure to vibration than the No 2 engine of MG and was likely to have at least as much loosening of pipe unions. Consequently, since the fuel unions found on the MG engine were sufficiently loose to produce atomising spray leaks, it is probable that immediately before Event 2, at the time of the second power increase, atomised fuel sprays were present in the fan cowl of the ME engine.

If such leaks were present with no ignition source, the free fuel would have run to the base of the cowling and escaped through the vent and drain apertures. The airstream around the outside of the nacelle flows upwards and outboard, the upwards component increasing with angle of attack. The evidence of fluid streaking running in this direction showed that a significant quantity of fuel and oil, which could also have been liberated by a similar union loosening process, had been present in flight. When the fluid on the outside of the nacelle reached the trailing edge of the cowling, it would have been drawn off as a highly combustible atomised mist by the slipstream.

The source of ignition for the fluid mist from the trailing edge could have come from either the flames resulting from compressor stalling passing down the fan stream or incandescent fan blade particles generated by the fan break-up at Event 2. The same potential sources could also have ignited fuel sprays within the fan cowl if the inlet duct had been breached. Although no evidence remained to demonstrate that it had been, the likelihood of a breach being made by fan break-up fragments is reasonably high, and no evidence was found of an alternative ignition source within the cowl.

2.3.2   *Potential effects of fire*

Although the effects of the fire were restricted to the No 1 engine and nacelle, this was principally due to the fact that the airfield fire service was able to attack it with appropriate extinguishants before it had time to spread. Had it been a significantly longer time before fire fighting was possible, although there was very little fuel spillage from the aircraft, it is probable that a much greater loss of life would have resulted.

The likelihood of a post crash ground fire will be much greater if there has been fire on an aircraft in flight. Fuel or oil leakage from loose pipe unions is an ever-present hazard and will always increase the possibility of a fire in flight.

It must be accepted that the vibration levels experienced on the No 1 engine of ME were orders of magnitude greater than those normally present and, therefore, more likely to cause loosening of pipe unions. However, it is under such conditions that there is likely to be an increased risk of accident. Although the fitting of locking wire to pipe unions would not entirely prevent loosening of these unions, it would limit the degree of looseness and, consequently, the likelihood of an atomised spray with a higher susceptibility to ignition. The fuel and oil pipe unions on the fan case of the CFM 56, in line with current practice, are not generally wirelocked; the control air pipes are the only ones, in this zone, wirelocked as a matter of course.

Although wirelocking of pipe unions will not prevent leakage of combustible fluids completely, its benefits and shortcomings should be reviewed in relation to the potential reduction of fire hazards in vulnerable zones. It is therefore recommended that the potential for fuel and oil system leakage within the fan case area of high by-pass turbofan engines, during conditions of excessive vibration, should be reviewed by the engine manufacturers and the CAA with a view towards modifying such systems to minimise such leakage and the associated fire risk (Made 30 March 1990).

2.3.3 *Fuel tank integrity*

The other major factor which affected the post-crash fire was the lack of a major release of fuel in the impact. This was partly due to good fortune, in that the centre section fuel tank, which was ruptured, did not contain fuel for this flight and that the damage to the left wing-tip occurred outboard of that fuel tank. It was, however, more largely due to the continuing integrity of the wing fuel tanks further inboard, which did not rupture despite the separation of both main landing gear (MLG) legs and the almost complete separation of both engines.

The wreckage showed that both MLG legs separated entirely consistently with the crashworthiness features of their design, failing the fuse-pin bolts and leaving the rear wing spars intact. In the case of the engines, the structural failures occurred within the pylons themselves, leaving the fuse-pin bolts in place; the separations were, in this instance, benign and the forward wing spars were not disrupted.

The excerpts in paragraph 1.17.16 are from the applicable airworthiness code (BCAR Section D) and the current code (JAR-25). They concern fuel tank penetration and address the MLG failure mode case (JAR-25.721) and the rear-mounted engine case. However, they do not address, other than in very general terms, the case for wing-mounted podded engines such as on the Boeing 737-400 and similarly configured transport aircraft. It is recommended, therefore, that the CAA should review the existing Joint Airworthiness Requirements concerning fuel tank protection from the effects of main landing gear and engine detachment during ground impact and include specific design requirements to protect the fuel tank integrity of those designs of aircraft with wing-mounted engines. (Made 30 March 1990)

2.4 Aircraft systems.

2.4.1. *Aircraft systems-general.*

Evidence from both the FDR and the flight crew did not indicate that there were any abnormalities connected with the flying controls, fuel or hydraulic systems which could have contributed to this accident. Accordingly, the systems examination was largely confined to those areas which could have had a bearing on the crew's perception of the failure in the No 1 engine.

In addition to the integrity and function checks of the EIS and associated wiring, the fire/overheat detection system and the vibration monitoring system, some tests were also performed on the air conditioning system.

2.4.2 *Air conditioning system.*

As referred to in paragraph 2.1.1.1, the commander stated that his knowledge of the air conditioning system had led him to believe that the problem lay in the No 2 engine. Thus, although it has since been established both by analysis and by the study of similar incidents of severe fan imbalance that smoke and/or fumes may be expected to be emitted from the abradable engine seals, it was considered prudent to ascertain that the air conditioning system itself had not generated smoke. Although smoke or smells of burning perceived in the aircraft could have come from a number of sources, the sudden perception of such indications, coupled with vibration might have indicated a problem in one of the rotating components in the air conditioning system and it was for this reason that the air cycle machines and the circulation fans were selected for examination. No evidence of pre-impact failure was found.

2.4.3. *Engine fire and overheat detection system.*

The discovery, during testing, that the fire detection module exhibited the 'latch-up' phenomenon (paragraph 1.12.2.3) raised the question as to whether the system may have been dormant during a period in which a fire had occurred in No 1 engine and thereby denied or delayed a fire warning to the crew. This was not considered likely for two reasons. Firstly, the evidence of airborne fire on the No 1 engine was consistent with it being of short duration, compatible with the period of time that elapsed between the fire bell being heard on the CVR and impact with the ground. Secondly, had the fire been burning at an earlier stage with the detection system latched-up then it would not have provided a fire warning at all once the system became unlatched.

Apart from this discrepancy, no other faults were found in the fire and overheat detection system. The wiring associated with the system was also found to be connected in the correct left/right sense.

2.4.4 *Performance of the AVM system.*

The AVM was designed to detect radial accelerations at a frequency corresponding to the speeds of the rotating engine assemblies. It will not detect vibration which is outside a narrow band of N1 or N2 speeds such as, for example, that induced by engine stalls or aerodynamic effects on individual blades. This was necessary to achieve the freedom from spurious alerts which were a feature of the older generation of vibration warning systems and which contributed to a loss of confidence in such systems.

The various tests which were carried out on the equipment fitted to ME (paragraph 1.16.3) were performed to establish not only that it was serviceable according to its specification, but also that it was, by design, capable of providing information to the crew of the accident aircraft during the critical early phase following the fan blade failure in the No 1 engine.

The conclusion of the tests was that the AVM system was serviceable and should have been indicating a full-scale reading on the No 1 engine vibration gauge within about 2 seconds of the fan blade outer panel separation occurring. Subsequent incidents of fan blade separation (see paragraph 1.17.7) confirmed this behaviour. However, in the two incidents which involved fan/compressor damage caused by bird ingestion (paragraphs 1.17.8.1 & 1.17.8.2) the crews reported significant delays in presentation of associated readings on the vibration gauges, even though vibration was obvious to the crews.

The reasons for such occurrences were not clear and, if it were to be argued that birdstrike damage is analogous to the blade separation case, then it would appear to have pointed to some unexplained deficiency in the AVM system performance. Further consideration, however, indicated that the two situations are not directly comparable as birdstrike damage seldom involves significant loss of mass of the rotating assemblies, although it may distort the fan/compressor blades.

The birdstrike tests conducted on a CFM 56-3C-1 engine during the course of the certification testing of the modified fan blades confirmed the non-linear response of the engine to an imbalance with variation of fan speed.

The recorded vibration levels resulting from a birdstrike were low (within the measurable range of the AVM gauge) showing that the actual imbalances were small. With the 'dip' in the engine sensitivity to imbalances which occurs at around the take-off RPM range, some engines might have virtually no response to these small imbalances. Since, however, the engine sensitivity to imbalance rises rapidly with reducing fan speed, the vibration and its indication would rise as the engine thrust was reduced. For the much higher imbalances encountered with a fan blade outer panel separation it is considered that the response, even at the minimum of the dip, would still produce close to maximum reading on the vibration gauge. The once per revolution impulses, detected during the tests, could well give rise to perceptible vibrations, although they would not be indicated.

2.4.5. *Engine instrument system.*

The series of tests of the primary EIS conducted or supervised by AAIB showed beyond any reasonable doubt that, not only was the unit serviceable, but the data recorded on the FDR was a subset of the information displayed to the crew. This confirmed that the data points on the FDR were displayed on the EIS but, because of the limitations of the FDR sample rate, extra points also existed which could not be recalled.

Establishing actual values or precise behaviour of the instruments during the critical early stages of the first event are of little importance beyond showing that significant fluctuations of the primary indications, particularly N1, did occur during this period. This was demonstrated.

The performance of the EIS during the blade separation incident to G-BNNL (paragraph 1.17.7.1), in which the commander reported that his primary engine instruments apparently showed no abnormalities despite the fact that the FDR recording indicated rapidly decaying primary parameters as the engine ran down, remains unexplained. A theoretical analysis could find no failure case in which data recorded on the FDR could differ significantly from that displayed on the EIS, and testing of the units from ME revealed no such behaviour. It should also be borne in mind that each primary parameter is served by its own microprocessor and circuitry and any suggestion that some obscure fault could have affected all four parameters thus appears highly improbable.

The only secondary parameter of importance to this investigation, namely vibration, is discussed in paragraph 2.4.4. There was no evidence that the technical performance of the secondary EIS unit affected the flow of information available to the crew of ME.

Checks on the wiring to and from both EIS units found no signs of incorrect connection with regard to left/right sense.

2.4.6 *Airborne closed circuit television monitoring*

The accident would probably have been averted if the pilots had been able to observe the pulsating flames and blue sparks which emanated from the No 1 engine after the primary fan blade failure and which were clearly apparent to many in the passenger cabin.

The technology is currently available to provide flight crews with an external view of major areas of their aircraft by means of closed circuit television. Internal zones such as cargo bays and areas of the passenger cabin can also be covered. Such a facility would enable the flight crew to assess various types of external problem such as fire, landing gear status, airframe damage, icing etc. Internal coverage would provide an additional means of assessment of cargo bay problems and cabin status, in addition to ground security monitoring.

This accident has also highlighted another area in which the availability of television monitoring could have benefit. With the increasing use of electronic 'glass-cockpit' display technology the facility to process information, prior to its display, has been greatly enhanced. This can improve the presentation of information to a crew and, importantly, can also be used to greatly assist their decision-making by giving them computer-assisted diagnosis. With such improved information techniques however it becomes increasingly vital to be able to demonstrate, during any post incident/accident investigation, the displayed information with close fidelity. This may present problems depending upon the type of signal processing employed, and particularly where the sensors have been attempting to 'track' an abnormal situation. In short, the question which arises concerns whether the information displayed to a crew may always be faithfully replicated after an incident. It is therefore considered that it would greatly benefit future crews and associated investigations if all such displayed information were recorded by means of television monitoring coverage of the flight deck. If, in addition, a playback facility were included, pilots could recall instrument display information after acting to contain an in-flight emergency.

It is therefore recommended that the CAA should expedite current research into methods of providing flight deck crews of public transport aircraft with visual information on the status of their aircraft by means of external and internal closed circuit television monitoring and the recording/recall of such monitoring, including that associated with flight deck presentations, with a view towards producing a requirement for all UK public transport aircraft to be so equipped (Made 30 March 1990).

2.5 Flight recorder design requirements

The system of recording using temporary buffer storage as employed by the UFDR can mean that at impact, if the contents of the buffers have not been transferred onto the recording medium, then that information will be lost. In the UFDR this can be up to 1.2 seconds of data. In this instance a knowledge of the impact parameters was important to the survivability investigation. The loss of the last moments of data meant that the impact parameters had to be estimated. The lost data in the buffer may have yielded more accurate information. If a recorder has to employ a temporary buffer storage, that storage medium should be made non-volatile (*i.e.* recoverable after power off) and contained within the armour protected enclosure.

The European Organisation for Civil Aviation Electronics (EUROCAE) are at present formulating new standards[15] for future generation flight data recorders; these standards will permit delays between parameter input and recording of up to 0.5 seconds. These standards may be adopted worldwide and do form the basis of the new CAA specifications for flight data recorders. It is therefore recommended that the manufacturers of existing flight data recorders which use buffering techniques should give consideration to making the buffers non-volatile and hence recoverable after loss of power, and EUROCAE and the CAA should reconsider the concept of allowing volatile memory buffering in flight data recorders (Made 30 March 1990 and also included in AAIB Report No 2/90).

Because of the length of time (64 seconds) between successive samples of the engine vibration, it was not possible to be precise about when vibration levels increased or decreased. Whilst this is not a parameter that the CAA specifications require to be recorded, it is recommended that, where engine vibration is an available parameter for flight data recording, the CAA should consider making a requirement for it to be recorded at a sampling rate of once per second (Made 30 March 1990).

---

[15] Minimum Operational Performance Requirement for Flight Data Recorder Systems   Ref:- ED55

2.6 Survival aspects

It was apparent from an early stage of the investigation that the first impact of ME, at the top of the motorway eastern embankment, caused much less damage to the airframe than the second impact, at the edge of the western carriageway. This was confirmed by the ground impact marks, by the KRASH analysis and by the items of wreckage which became detached before the second impact. It was thus the second impact which caused both of the major fuselage failures and the separation of the engines.

The lack of any indication of the velocity between the impacts from either the FDR or the cockpit instrumentation prevented an accurate determination of this velocity, but analysis of the trajectory gave a velocity of between 80 and 100 kts at the second, and major, impact (paragraph 1.12.1.1).

2.6.1 *Injuries*

The initial injuries that occurred were caused by the impact of a seat occupant into the back of the seat in front. In those areas where the floor structure, and hence the seat attachment, failed the initial injury mechanism was compounded by secondary impacts of the seat occupant with loose seats and passengers, and other parts of damaged aircraft structure.

The injuries suffered by the passengers sitting in seat rows 10-17 and 25-27 (paragraph 1.13) clearly show both the advantages of being retained in a fixed seat and the limitations of sitting in a forward facing seat restrained only by a lap belt. Virtually all the passengers suffered from severe bruising under the lap belt and five passengers sustained iliac fractures as a direct result of lap belt loading.

In addition to the results of direct loading of the pelvis by the lap belt the following generalised injury mechanism occurred. As the seat occupant moved forward, the knees contacted the back of the seat in front, loading the knee and the upper leg. This transmitted load back into the pelvis causing a variety of injury, including dislocation of the hip, fracture of the hip joint and fracture of the pelvis. Fractures of the femur occurred as a result of the combination of axial and bending loads induced by the front cross bar of the seat as well as contact with the back of the seat in front. Depending upon the position of the lower leg, damage was caused to the knee as the upper leg moved forwards in relation to the lower leg. In a similar manner, where the foot was fixed by contact with aircraft or seat structure, the foot and ankle also sustained injury as the lower leg moved forward in relation to the foot and ankle, causing a combination of torsional and posterior dislocation injuries.

Gross lower leg fractures occurred where the seats failed and the lower legs were trapped and subjected to secondary impacts.

The overall mechanism is illustrated in Appendix 5, fig 4 (computer simulation of occupant response).

Head and chest injury occurred even where passengers had adopted the crash position and some passengers who rested their heads on their forearms prior to the impact fractured their forearms as a consequence. Some other passengers braced themselves by placing their extended arms onto the back of the seat in front and some of them suffered fractured upper arms and shoulder joints in consequence.

The child seated on his mother's lap in seat 3F sustained major head and limb injuries as a result of the accident and the mother sustained major injuries, some of which were suggestive of having been caused by forcible flexion of the mother over the child during the impact.

It has not been possible to determine the role of the overhead bins in the causation of head injury. The majority of the bins were necessarily removed by the rescuers and there was no evidence to show whether or not either the bins or their contents had been in forcible contact with any of the aircraft occupants.

2.6.2   *Occupant simulation*

The simulation (paragraph 1.16.5) offered additional insights into the injury mechanisms. Measurements of the seat belt webbing stiffness showed a mean elongation of 14% ±4% at 11 kN load. This variation was greater than that permitted in automobile applications and can have a significant effect on occupant kinematics and femoral axial load.

A further point noted was the effect of the tubular spar across the front of the seat as a source of loading of the femur in bending. The new FAA and JAA regulations (paragraph 1.17.11) concentrate on femoral axial loads induced when knee contact occurs with the seat in front, but the simulation showed that femoral bending loads were significant and were considerably affected by occupant position (paragraph 1.16.5):

Upright occupant:	femoral axial	3.4 kN
	femoral bending	1.3 kN
Braced occupant:	femoral axial	2.3 kN
	femoral bending	2.7 kN

The greater vertical femoral load results from the shift of body mass in the seat caused by the adoption of the brace position.

The computer graphics showed that the unrestrained head and torso were free to pivot around the lap strap and impact the back of the seat in front, giving rise to chest, upper limb and head injury. The simulation indicated that Head Injury Criterion (HIC) values of 278 for the braced individual compared with 974 for the unbraced passenger. This value of 974 is just below the HIC 1000 value which is used in US Federal Safety Standards as the limiting value for head impact acceptability.

The computer analysis also showed that seat back breakover stiffness is critical in the control of occupant kinematics and should be controlled within close limits. This control should be part of a larger process to engineer seats to be more impact friendly in terms of both kinematics and attenuation, whilst avoiding sharp edges and protuberances.

2.6.3   Assessment of deceleration

There were 4 principal means of assessing the deceleration pulse transmitted, in the second impact, to the cabin floor around the centre-section. These were:

(i)   KRASH simulation results
(ii)   basic kinematics calculation
(iii) passenger and pilot seat damage related to dynamic testing
(iv)   comparison with previous calibrated airframe tests.

It became evident during the survivability investigation that the major factor in determining the magnitude of the deceleration pulse in the second impact was the resultant (horizontal and vertical combined) velocity at this impact. The estimates basically covered the range of 77 knots to 99 knots: the highest probability was in the range of 85 to 95 knots.

On the balance of evidence, therefore, the KRASH simulation which best represented the velocity conditions at the second impact was Run 2 (Appendix 3, fig 22), which gave mid-fuselage longitudinal decelerations (mass 2) of 26.1 g (peak) and 17.8g (fundamental). Of these two values, the fundamental signal represented the plastic deformation signal transmitted to the seats and should be used for comparison purposes. The pulse shapes (appendix 3 fig 22) indicated that the initial impulse in the second impact was primarily longitudinal followed by a vertical pulse when the engine nacelles and the fuselage centre section contacted the carriageway. The corresponding value for the vertical deceleration was 23g (peak).

A basic kinematics calculation of the deceleration along the direction of motion, based on the measured crush distance and assuming a 25% velocity change in the second impact, gave a mean deceleration of about 22g.

The previous dynamic testing of Model 4001 passenger seats had shown deformation of the forward leg 'U-straps' in 16g longitudinal decelerations conducted with 170 lb dummies. (paragraph 1.6.8.3) The occurrence in ME of similar damage in centre-section seats with lighter occupant loadings indicated a resultant deceleration level in excess of this 16g level.

The 1988 FAA full-scale test of a complete section of B707 fuselage achieved a 14.2g longitudinal deceleration through a velocity change of 36.2 ft/sec with 6 triple-seats loaded, in each case, with three 165 lb dummies. The lack of failure or permanent deformation of the floor or of the seat tracks in that test indicated a longitudinal deceleration for ME well in excess of this 14.2g level.

In summary, these results indicated a resultant deceleration, in the second impact, within the centre section, with a peak value of between approximately 22 and 28g. The geometry of the impact showed that the initial pulse was primarily longitudinal, followed by a lower, vertical, pulse when the nacelles and centre section contacted the carriageway. The lack of damage in the tail section indicated a value there closer to, but still above, 14g. Previous, instrumented, impacts have indicated that the peak deceleration levels in the forward nose section would probably have been slightly higher than in the centre section.

2.6.4   *Seating*

From the analysis of the major deceleration impulse (paragraphs 1.16.4.2 & 2.6.3) it was apparent that the forces encountered in the second impact were considerably greater than those for which the airframe and the furnishings were designed and certificated. It is in this context that the discussion around the seat performance in ME takes place. Although the analysis of seat damage was complicated by the differing occupant weights and seat occupancy, a number of distinctive patterns emerged.

2.6.4.1   *Crew seating*

The injury scores of the cabin crew on the forward flight attendant seats were considerably lower than the passengers in the first rows of seats and this appears to have been due both to the fact that the attendant seats were rearward-facing and that the seats, although suffering some structural damage, remained in position. The advantages of the seating remaining in position and the provision of upper torso restraint are reinforced by the fact that the pilots, although seated in the area of highest deceleration, did not suffer injuries with scoring greater than the passengers in rows 1-5 (Area I in Appendix 3 fig 7). Both pilots' seats and the forward attendant seat suffered some structural damage. It is, however, not possible to tell whether this alleviated the impact loading or added to the occupant injuries.

The movement of the aft double attendant seat (paragraph 1.12.2.5) while still attached to its supporting bulkhead highlights the fact that a crew or passenger seat can only be as strong as the structure to which it is attached. Similarly, the injuries caused to the stewardess on this seat by a food service cart were due to the release of the cart by the upward structural separation of the counter-top on which the cart 'quarter-turn' latches were mounted and not by any seat failure.

2.6.4.2 *Passenger seating*

A distinctive feature of the reconstructed seats throughout the passenger cabin was that the rear attachments were generally still engaged with the seat track and that, where the seat and track had separated from each other, the absence of damage on the seat rear attachment fitting showed that it was the seat track which had failed. It appeared that the lack of structural failure in this area of the seats was at least partially due to the articulated joint built into the rear attachment (paragraph 1.6.8.3), an innovation largely stemming from the FAA dynamic test requirements (paragraph 1.17.11).

The front legs in this design of seat are not positively locked into the seat tracks and had thus become detached from the track lips in all areas where the continuity of the seat tracks was disrupted. In the centre and rear sections (Areas II and IV), where the seat track remained continuous, the front legs remained engaged and the number of 'U'-strap collapses was distinctly higher in the centre section (Area II) than in the areas forward and aft of the wing (Areas I and III). This confirmed that the disruption in the cabin floor in Areas I and III was largely due to the seat inertial loads passing through the front legs.

The examination of previous accidents (paragraph 1.17.17), the early dynamic testing of seats designed to the previous ('9g') static criteria and the dynamic testing of this model of passenger seat (paragraph 1.6.8.3) together indicated that fewer injuries occurred in ME than would probably have been the case with passenger seats of an earlier generation. However, some structural failures of the seats did occur, such as the front spar failures in the overwing section of the fuselage, and consideration should be given as to whether the new requirements of FAR Amendment 25-64 (paragraph 1.17.11), and hence JAR 25 Change 13, are sufficient in the long term.

The deceleration levels specified in the dynamic test requirements of FAR Amendment 25-64 (paragraph 1.17.11) were based on an FAA study of crash dynamics and were, to some extent, constrained by the need to be compatible with the existing floor strengths of current aircraft types and the existence of suitable test facilities. While the performance of the seats in ME indicates that seats designed to these dynamic requirements will certainly increase survivability in aircraft impacts, they do not necessarily represent an optimum for the long term. This is particularly true if matched with cabin floors of improved strength and toughness.

Another potential area for improvement is in the criteria applied to the loads experienced by the anthropomorphic dummy. For instance, the FAR Amendment 25-64 test measures femoral axial load without addressing the significant femoral bending loads.

It is recommended, therefore, that the CAA should actively seek further improvement in the standards of JAR 25.561 and .562 and the level of such standards should not be constrained by the current FAA requirements (Made 30 March 1990).

The provisions of Change 13 to JAR 25.561 and .562 are only applicable to new certifications and not to existing aircraft types nor their direct derivatives. Thus the fitting of the improved type of seats into ME was not a legal requirement. The performance of the passenger seats in ME, however, strongly supports the case for fitting the improved seats into the current fleet and into new aircraft of existing type. In the USA, for instance, NPRM 88-8 covers the proposed installation of the improved seats within the existing fleet by June 1995 (ie within about one 7-year replacement cycle).

It is recommended, therefore, that the CAA should require that, for aircraft passenger seats, the current loading and dynamic testing requirements of JAR 25.561 and .562 be applied to newly manufactured aircraft coming onto the UK register and, with the minimum of delay, to aircraft already on the UK register (Made 30 March 1990).

2.6.4.3 *Detail design of passenger seating*

Although few fatalities occurred in the centre and rear sections of the fuselage, the detailed injuries (paragraph 2.6.1) demonstrated the limitations of current seat designs. The high incidence of femoral and pelvic injuries coincided with the deformations of the horizontal spars and lower seat backs of the seats. Although these lower injuries were not fatal, they were generally serious and immobilizing and would have materially altered the outcome had there been a major ground fire.

The mechanisms of head and lower limb injuries identified by the medical investigation (paragraph 1.13) were consistent with the occupant simulation (paragraph 2.6.2).

The principle that careful detail design of the seats considerably affects the injury outcome of an accident also applies in the case of the injuries caused by passenger impacts with items such as seat-back tray tables and arm rests. The current airworthiness requirement addressing seat design, JAR 25.785, requires the 'elimination of any injurious object within the striking radius of the head' but does not apply any criteria defining sharpness or deformation under load and makes no requirements for parts of the body other than the head. It also does not specify parameters such as seat back stiffness, which the occupant simulation identifies as being critical in the control of the kinematics of the occupant, or seatbelt webbing stiffness which can also greatly affect the kinematics. It is recommended, therefore, that in addition to the dynamic test requirements, the CAA should seek to modify the JARs associated with detailed seat design to ensure that such seats are safety-engineered to minimise occupant injury in an impact (Made 30 March 1990).

2.6.5 *Alternative seating configurations*

Throughout the development of public transport aircraft there have been a number of alternative seating configurations proposed, including energy-absorbing 'stroking' seats, three point harnesses and rearward facing seats. Each offers some advantage in passenger impact protection but also presents technical problems which need to be addressed. In the case of the energy-absorbing seat, for instance, the inertial loads on the passenger and the supporting structure would be relieved. A potential disadvantage would be the trapping of the legs of passengers in the adjacent row.

The attachment of a three point harness with lap and diagonal straps, such as commonly seen in automobiles, would require either a redesign of the seat back so that shoulder harness loads could be reacted, or that the shoulder harness be attached to the fuselage itself. This latter proposition is probably only applicable to commuter type aircraft. The harness would need to be on an inertial reel to avoid problems of harness entanglement on escape. Such a harness would produce a reduction in the degree of head and chest injury and would also have a significant effect on leg and pelvic injury because of improved kinematics and better load distribution. Appendix 5, fig 5 shows a further MADYMO graphic using the Cranfield Impact Centre KRASH data. A three point harness with the upper attachment made to the fuselage is shown. Comparison with Appendix 5, fig 4 shows the considerable improvement in occupant kinematics that is achieved.

An objection to using the three point harness is the effect that it would have on movement over the seats as an alternative form of exit in an emergency. Clearly, if the harness were to be attached to the top of the seat, the seat back would have to be made rigid and it would no longer be possible to collapse the seat back forward. Where a shoulder harness was attached to the airframe the option would still be lost, since a considerable potential for entanglement would exist.

An alternative to the three point harness is the rearward facing seat. Such a seat would be specifically designed for this configuration and the impact loads, instead of being carried on the lap belt and by contact of unrestrained body segments with the seat in front, would be evenly distributed across the seat back. The result, in this accident, given similarly strong seats that remained attached to the floor, would have been a considerable reduction in the severity of impact injury. Use of the rearward facing seat would be open to a number of practical difficulties. Static calculation indicates that the loads that such a seat would impart to the cabin floor, on impact, would be greater than with a forward facing seat. This is because the rearward facing seat back generates a greater moment-arm on the floor than is the case for the forward facing seat. Advice from the seat manufacturers and the Civil Aeromedical Institute of the FAA (paragraph 1.17.13) indicated that the difference dynamically is not as great as the static calculation suggests. This observation was born out by the MADYMO load simulations (see Appendix 5, fig 6). In this simulation the simulated seat has been stiffened and the pulse reversed. The seat back height has not been increased, which would be required to protect the neck. The incorporation of a limited amount of energy attenuation in the seat struts could reduce the loads into the cabin floor to those of standard forward facing seats.

A further objection raised against rearward facing seats is that the seat occupant would be exposed to facial impact from loose objects liberated during the impact. This is theoretically true but the solution seems to lie with achieving retention of overhead bins and their contents rather than avoiding the use of rearward seats. It is also likely that the incorporation of a three point harness on a forward facing seat would expose the occupant to a greater risk of head impact from behind for the same reasons, as the head would be maintained in a more erect posture. Clearly the solution to this problem must lie in the avoidance of free flying objects, rather than the rejection of improved occupant restraint.

Common to all the alternative seating configurations proposed is that they have complex implications and implementation would have to be founded on a firm basis of research and development. This would have to include such questions as the compatibility with the rest of the cabin, the level of passenger acceptability and the ability of the configuration to provide protection in a wide range of impact conditions. Up to now little of this research has taken place and the limited use of rearward facing seats in military transport aircraft has not answered these questions. It is, therefore, recommended that the CAA should initiate and expedite a structured programme of research, in conjunction with the European airworthiness authorities, into passenger seat design, with particular emphasis on:

    (i)   Effective upper torso restraint.

    (ii)   Aft-facing passenger seats   (Made 30 March 1990).

2.6.6   *Cabin floor structure*

The study of a sample of narrow-body jet transport accidents (paragraph 1.17.17) showed that the impact and structural disruption to ME was reasonably characteristic of off-airfield accidents involving landing undershoots, failed go-arounds and power-off forced landings, because although the geometry of the major impact was severe, it occurred at a speed below the stalling speed of the aircraft. The deceleration impulses (paragraph 2.6.3) were within the tolerance of a typical passenger when properly restrained. The preceding analysis of the seating in ME illustrates that the passenger seats remained in position in the areas in which the floor structure had survived intact. It was in the areas in which the floor had disintegrated that the most severe injuries occurred (paragraph 2.6.1).

A distinctive pattern of failure emerged from the examination of the floor structure (paragraph 1.12.2.7). The initial failure was of the longitudinal seat tracks under the vertical and longitudinal impact loading of the passenger triple-seats. The resulting displacement of the seat track members from the floor panels prevented those floor panels from reacting the longitudinal crash loads. The transverse floor beams then failed under the longitudinal and torsional crash loads, for which they were not designed, as well as from the vertical crash loads.

The floor structure in ME was typical of this class of aircraft. The certification data for this aircraft showed that the floor structure met the airworthiness strength requirements both of the USA and the UK. The impact of ME clearly exceeded these requirements (paragraphs 1.16.4.2 & 2.6.3). These requirements were current at the time of the granting of the type certificate to the Boeing 737-100 in 1967. They were for static strength only and did not require the manufacturer to demonstrate crashworthiness characteristics, beyond those static strength requirements.

A part of the rationale for the dynamic test requirements, such as the 16g/44fps longitudinal deceleration, selected by the FAA in the FAR Part 25 rule change (Amendment 25-64) was that these requirements were compatible with existing cabin floor strengths (paragraph 1.17.11). This has been largely supported by crash dynamics research, including large-scale dynamic testing (paragraph 1.17.12). However, the overall pattern of failure in ME, particularly regarding the lack of plastic deformation, showed that relatively minor engineering changes could significantly improve the resilience and toughness of cabin floors in this category of aircraft and take fuller advantage of the improved passenger seats. In particular, there would appear to be benefit in improved tolerance to out-of-plane loading and the provision of multiple load paths.

Although it may be questionable whether the cost and benefit balance would favour modification of existing airframes, future designs should certainly take account of dynamic loading criteria. This principle should also apply to future production of existing designs of transport aircraft. It is recommended, therefore, that the certification requirements for cabin floors for new aircraft types should be modified to require that dynamic impulse and distortion be taken into account and these criteria should be applied to future production of existing designs (Made 30 March 1990).

2.6.7 *Future floor requirements*

Looking towards future designs of cabin floor, it should be considered whether a substantial increase in decelerative loading could be accomplished, so as to take advantage both of seats designed to meet the current dynamic test requirements and future seats with enhanced capabilities.

The customary argument against large increases in cabin furnishing strength has been that such increases would require uneconomic weight increases in the fuselage to maintain the protection of the fuselage shell. However, the case of the L-1011 Tristar accident in the Everglades (paragraph 1.17.17) suggests that, even with very extensive fuselage disruption, a reduced number of fatalities and serious injuries will result from retaining the passenger seats on areas of toughened flooring so that, even after detachment from the fuselage shell, the seats will remain attached and retain their relative position on the flooring. It is recommended, therefore, that the CAA should initiate research, in conjunction with the European airworthiness authorities, into the feasibility of a significant increase in cabin floor toughness beyond the level of the current JAR/FAR seat requirements (Made 30 March 1990).

2.6.8 *Infant and child restraint systems*

The argument for child seats in cars has been well-established for over a decade. That an equivalent argument for placing infants and young children in child seats in aircraft has not emerged is at least partly due to the statistically small population of infants travelling by air and the failure of airline passenger statistics to reflect their presence.

It is clear from paragraph 1.17.14 that the supplementary loop-type belt provides some advantages over simple lap-holding of infants. It cannot provide, however, an equivalent level of survivability to that provided for the adult passenger in a conventional seat, or the greater level of survivability provided by a '16g' type passenger seat. It is recommended therefore that the CAA implement a programme to require that all infants and young children, who would not be safely restrained by supplementary or standard lap belts, be placed in child seats for take-off, landing and flight in turbulence (Made 30 March 1990).

In this light, the CAA Notice (paragraph 1.17.14) allowing the use of specific types of child seat should be welcomed. In general, the provisions of the notice align it with current FAA practice. This FAA practice reflects its origins in US general aviation and has clear limitations as a means of bringing about the universal use of child seats in transport aircraft. For instance, a passenger may unintentionally provide a non-approved child seat, or one incompatible with that airline's seat width and, even if the child seat is suitable, there is no compulsion on the airline to allow its use.

As a means of bringing about the universal use of child seats, therefore, it is logical that the onus of provision should be placed on the airline operator. There are clear advantages for an airline in only having to train its cabin staff to deal with the use of one type of child seat, optimised for the airline operation, and there are clear advantages for the passenger in not having to provide such a seat.

In the meantime, to promote the effective use of child seats and to put operators in a position to provide child seats themselves, a UK or JAA standard should be rapidly established for child seats for use in aircraft. It is therefore recommended that the CAA expedite the publication of a specification for child seat designs (Made 30 March 1990).

2.6.9   *Overhead stowage bins*

A notable feature of the aircraft wreckage was that all but one of the overhead stowage bins had become detached in the impact and that they had done so in a very similar manner (paragraph 1.12.2.8). In this mode of failure the first stage was the separation of the diagonal tie fitting from the upper surface of the stowage bin under the influence of the predominantly longitudinal inertial loads in the second impact. This was followed by the failure of the remaining lateral and vertical ties when the bins moved forward (Appendix 3, fig 21).

Confirmation of this failure mode was that the only bin not to have separated entirely from its fuselage attachments was 1R, the only bin at which forward motion was restricted by the presence of a substantial cabin bulkhead.

Although it was not possible to determine the actual mass or distribution of passenger belongings in the overhead bins, the results of the 1981-82 CAA survey (paragraph 1.17.15) indicated that the manufacturer's design and certification figure (3 lbs per inch of bin length) was generously conservative. In normal operation, it is unlikely that a set of bins would be overloaded.

As Flight BD092 was normally a routine and conventional operation, the assumed mass of passenger belongings (33% of placarded mass - paragraph 1.17.15) is probably reasonably accurate and there is no reason to believe that the static load testing performed for the FAA, and the static load analysis calculated for the CAA's more stringent requirements, were flawed. It is not, therefore, obvious why the bin attachments failed so consistently.

One possibility considered was that the product of the bin masses and their deceleration was sufficient to induce higher loads than the design and certification limitations of the attachments. Depending upon the exact figures used, this argument can be supported for the nose and centre sections of the fuselage, but the deceleration pulse in the tail section indicated by the KRASH analysis, by the seat and track damage and by the occupant injuries, was probably too low in the tail section for the impact loads to have been the only cause of the attachment failures.

This leads to the conclusion that the design of the overhead stowage bins installed in ME was not sufficiently robust to withstand the deformation of the attachment structure combined with the dynamic loading of the second impact. This dynamic loading ensured that, as well as the geometry of the fuselage attachments being deformed, the failure of one bin's longitudinal restraint would have resulted in additional loading on the ties of neighbouring bins, resulting in a cascading sequential failure.

Although the injury evidence (paragraph 1.13) did not indicate the degree of injury attributable to the bins, it is evident that they can cause additional injuries as well as hampering escape and rescue. In this accident, the almost complete detachment of the bins slowed down the rescue process and, had the ground fire spread, the result would have been more serious.

The current design load requirements for 'items of mass' in the cabin (paragraph 1.17.11) were derived from loadings under which the fuselage would remain structurally intact. Whatever the historical justification for this, ME and other accidents to modern narrow-body jet transports (paragraph 1.17.17) indicate that there is considerable benefit in retaining these items of mass in position despite the deformation of the fuselage attachment structure and even after some disruption of the fuselage. Such items of mass include cabin equipment (eg food service carts) as well as fixed items such as overhead bins and toilet modules. This improvement in retention would require both a substantial increase in the appropriate design load factors and design features (such as the incorporation of flexible mountings) to ensure that the items of mass would be restrained against the <u>dynamic</u> application of the crash pulses which generate these load factors.

It is recommended, therefore, that the certification requirements for cabin stowage bins, and other cabin items of mass, should be modified to ensure the retention of these items to fuselage structure when subjected to dynamic crash pulses substantially beyond the static load factors currently required (Made 30 March 1990).

There was also evidence that some of the bin doors opened during the last moments of flight, before the first impact (paragraph 1.15.1). The inadvertent opening of overhead stowage bins has long been a problem, especially in turbulence, and some airlines now fit bins which incorporate some form of secondary latching. It is recommended, therefore, that the CAA consider improving the airworthiness requirements for public transport aircraft to require some form of improved latching to be fitted to overhead stowage bins and this should also apply to new stowage bins fitted to existing aircraft (Made 30 March 1990).

3. CONCLUSIONS

(a) Findings

The aircraft

1. The aircraft had a valid certificate of airworthiness in the transport category (passenger) and had been maintained in accordance with an approved schedule.

The flight deck crew

2. The flight deck crew were properly licensed and rested to undertake the flight.

3. The flight deck crew experienced moderate to severe engine induced vibration and shuddering, accompanied by smoke and/or smell of fire, as the aircraft climbed through FL283. This combination of symptoms was outside their training or experience and they responded urgently by disengaging the autothrottles and throttling-back the No 2 engine, which was running satisfactorily.

4. After the autothrottle was disengaged, and whilst the No 2 engine was running down, the No 1 engine recovered from the compressor stalls and began to settle at a slightly lower fan speed. This reduced the shuddering apparent on the flight deck, convincing the commander that they had correctly identified the No 2 engine as the source of the problem.

5. The first officer reported the emergency to ATC, indicating that they had an engine fire and intended to shut an engine down, although there had been no fire warning from the engine fire detection system.

6. Whilst the commander's decision to divert to East Midlands Airport to land with the minimum of delay was correct, he thereby incurred a high cockpit workload which precluded any effective review of the emergency or the actions he had taken.

7. The flight crew did not assimilate the readings on the engine instruments before they decided to throttle-back the No 2 engine. After throttling back the No 2 engine, they did not assimilate the maximum vibration indication apparent on the No 1 engine before they shut down the No 2 engine 2 minutes 7 seconds after the onset of vibration, and 5 nm south of EMA. The aircraft checklist gave separate drills for high vibration and for smoke, but contained no drill for a combination of both.

8. The commander remained unaware of the blue sparks and flames which had issued from the No 1 engine during the period of heavy vibration and which had been observed by many passengers and the three aft cabin crew.

9. During the descent, the No 1 engine continued to run apparently normally, although with higher than normal levels of vibration.

10. Flight crew workload during the descent remained high as they informed their company at EMA of their problem and intentions, responded to ATC height and heading instructions, obtained weather information for EMA and the first officer attempted to re-programme the flight management system to display the landing pattern for EMA. Some 7½ minutes after the initial problem, the commander attempted to review the initial engine symptoms, but this was cut short by further ATC heading and descent information and instructions to change to the EMA ATC radio frequency.

11. Fifteen minutes after the engine problem occurred and some 4 minutes 40 seconds before ground impact, the commander increased power on the No 1 engine as the aircraft descended towards 3000 feet amsl and closed with the centreline of the instrument landing system. At this point, the indicated vibration on the No 1 engine again rose to its maximum value of 5 units but did not attract the attention of either pilot.

12. Fifty three seconds before ground impact, when the aircraft was 900 feet agl and 2.4 nm from the runway with landing gear down and 15° flaps selected, there was an abrupt decrease in power from the No 1 engine.

13. The commander immediately called for the first officer to relight the No 2 engine. The attempted restart was not successful, probably because there was insufficient bleed air pressure from the No 1 engine, pressure air from the APU was not connected and the bleed air crossfeed valve was closed. Even if pressure air had been available it is unlikely that power could have been obtained from the No 2 engine before the aircraft hit the ground.

14. The training of the pilots met CAA requirements. However, no flight simulator training had been given, or had been required, on the recognition of engine failure on the electronic engine instrument system or on decision-making techniques in the event of failures not covered by standard procedures.

15. The change from hybrid electro-mechanical instruments to LED displays for engine indications has reduced conspicuity, particularly in respect of the engine vibration indicators. No additional vibration alerting system was fitted that could have highlighted to the pilots which of the two engines was vibrating excessively.

The Cabin Crew

16. All members of the cabin crew were properly trained to undertake the flight.

17. Although the cabin crew immediately became aware of heavy vibration at the onset of the emergency and three aft cabin crew saw flames emanating from the No 1 engine, this information was not communicated to the pilots.

18. During the descent, the cabin crew carried out their emergency drills, checking that all passengers had their lap belts fastened and stowing all loose carry-on luggage in the overhead bins.

No 1 (Left) Engine

19. The No 1 engine suffered fatigue of one of its fan blades which caused detachment of the blade outer panel. This led to a series of compressor stalls, over a period of 22 seconds, until the engine autothrottle was disengaged.

20 The severe mechanical imbalance which arose because of the outer panel separation led to blade tip rubbing, particularly on the fan and booster sections abradable seals, which caused smoke and the smell of burning to be passed into the air conditioning system.

21. About 3 seconds after the autothrottle was disengaged, and whilst the No 2 engine was running down, the No 1 engine began to stabilise. However, its indicated vibration remained at maximum for at least 3 minutes until this engine was throttled back for the descent.

22. The evidence indicated that the timing of the sudden recovery of the No 1 engine from the compressor stalling was related to the autothrottle disengagement at a point when it had demanded a lower throttle lever angle than that required for rated climb, thereby allowing this engine to achieve stabilised running at a slightly lower speed.

23. During the descent, the No 1 engine responded apparently normally at the idle/low throttle settings used, although its indicated vibration remained higher than normal.

24. Fifty three seconds before ground impact, the No 1 engine abruptly lost thrust as a result of extensive secondary fan damage. This was accompanied by compressor stalling, heavy buffetting and the emission of pulsating flames. This damage was probably initiated by fan ingestion of the blade section released by the initial failure, which was considered to have partially penetrated, and temporarily lodged within, the acoustic lining panels of the intake casing before having been shaken-free during the period of high vibration following the increase in power on the final approach to land. Sections of fan blades were found below this point of the final approach, including two small fragments which were determined to be remnants of the blade section which detached initially.

25. The No 1 engine fire warning, which occurred on the flight deck 36 seconds before ground impact, was initiated by a secondary fire which occurred on the outboard exterior of the engine fan casing. It was concluded that the prolonged period of running under

conditions of excessive vibration had loosened fuel/oil system unions and seals on the exterior of the fan casing and that the inlet duct had probably been damaged sufficiently, by fan blade debris, to allow ignition of atomised fuel/oil sprays by titanium 'sparks' and/or intake flame.

26. This short duration in-flight fire on the No 1 engine was followed by a localised ground fire associated with this engine, which was successfully extinguished by the East Midland Airport Fire Service.

27. The fan blade fatigue fracture initiated as a result of exposure of the blade to a vibratory stress level greater than that for which it was designed, due to the existence of a fan system vibratory mode, induced under conditions of high corrected fan speed at altitude, which was not detected by engine certification testing.

No 2 (right) engine

28. The No 2 engine was running normally when it was throttled back to flight idle, and then shut down.

29. This engine showed no evidence of power at impact, consistent with the evidence from the flight data recorder.

30. Detailed strip inspection of this engine showed it to have been fully serviceable before ground impact.

Systems

31. The No 2 (right) engine vibration reports which appeared in the aircraft Technical Log during December 1988 but had been correctly addressed by ground technicians.

32. There were no malfunctions of the major airframe systems which contributed to this accident.

33. No evidence was found of any cross-connection or similar obvious wiring errors associated with either the engine instrument system (EIS) or the fire detection system.

34. The EIS fitted to the aircraft was serviceable at impact and tests indicated that it should have displayed those primary engine parameters recorded on the FDR, with close fidelity.

35. The airborne vibration monitoring system (AVM) was serviceable at impact. Tests showed that the system was capable of tracking vibration caused by the massive fan imbalance and of outputting its maximum value approximately 2 seconds after the start of the vibration.

36. Flight crew reports concerning the response of the AVM system during the two other cases of fan blade fracture on CFM56-3C engines which occurred subsequent to this accident supported the behaviour described above. Two cases of bird impact which resulted in fan damage generated crew reports of late indication on vibration gauges, although vibration was clearly felt by the flight crew. This was the result of the non-linear sensitivity of this engine type to small imbalances with changes of fan speed in the take-off and climb thrust range.

37. The engine fire and overheat detection system contained a fault which could have rendered it incapable of providing warning of a fire in either engine. However, the CVR evidence indicated that it did, in fact, provide a warning of the fire in the No 1 engine 36 seconds before impact.

Impact with the ground

38. The aircraft suffered two distinct impacts with the ground, the first just before the eastern embankment of the M1 motorway and the second on the western edge of the northbound M1 carriageway, at the base of the western embankment.

39. The first impact was at an airspeed of 113 knots CAS, with a rate of descent of between 8.5 feet/sec and 16 feet/sec. The pitch attitude was 13° nose up.

40. The second and major impact occurred at a speed of between 80 and 100 knots, at an angle of approximately 16° below the horizontal and with the aircraft at a pitch attitude of between 9° and 14° nose down. The associated peak deceleration was of the order of 22 to 28g, predominantly longitudinal.

41. In the second impact the forward fuselage separated from the overwing section of fuselage and the tail section buckled over, and to the right of, that section of fuselage just aft of the wing.

42. The incidence of passenger fatality was highest where the floor had collapsed in the forward section of the passenger cabin and in the area just aft of the wing. The cabin floor and the passenger seating remained almost entirely intact within the overwing and tail sections.

43. There was no major post impact fire, largely because the main landing gear legs and the engines separated from the wing without rupturing the wing fuel tanks. The separation of the landing gear legs was in accordance with their design. In the case of the engines, however, the separations occurred within the engine pylons themselves, leaving the fuse-pin bolts intact

Survivability

44. Of the 8 crew and 118 passengers on board, all crew members survived but 39 passengers died from impact injuries at the scene and a further 8 passengers died later in hospital. A further 74 occupants were seriously injured.

45. The decelerations generated in the second impact were greater than those specified in the Airworthiness Requirements to which the airframe and furnishings were designed and certificated. They were, however, within the physiological tolerance of a typical passenger.

46. Passenger survivability was improved due to the passenger seats being of a design with impact tolerance in advance of the current regulatory requirements. This was most evident in the overwing and tail sections of the cabin, where the floor had remained intact.

47. There is considerable potential for improving the survivability of passengers in this type of impact by improving the structural integrity of the cabin floor so as to retain the seats in their relative positions and by detail design improvements to the seats themselves.

48. There is a need for a structured programme of research into alternative seating configurations, with particular emphasis on the provision of effective upper torso restraint or aft-facing seats.

49. The injuries to the mother and child in seat 3F highlighted the advantages of infants being placed in child seats rather than in a loop-type supplementary belt.

50. Although the overhead stowage bins met the appropriate Airworthiness Requirements for static loading, all but one of the 30 bins fell from their attachments, which did not withstand the dynamic loading conditions in this accident.

51. Some of the doors on the overhead stowage bins opened during the last seconds of flight, demonstrating the need for some form of improved latching of the doors.

(b) Cause

The cause of the accident was that the operating crew shut down the No 2 engine after a fan blade had fractured in the No 1 engine. This engine subsequently suffered a major thrust loss due to secondary fan damage after power had been increased during the final approach to land.

The following factors contributed to the incorrect response of the flight crew:

1. The combination of heavy engine vibration, noise, shuddering and an associated smell of fire were outside their training and experience.

2. They reacted to the initial engine problem prematurely and in a way that was contrary to their training.

3. They did not assimilate the indications on the engine instrument display before they throttled back the No 2 engine.

4. As the No 2 engine was throttled back, the noise and shuddering associated with the surging of the No 1 engine ceased, persuading them that they had correctly identified the defective engine.

5. They were not informed of the flames which had emanated from the No 1 engine and which had been observed by many on board, including 3 cabin attendants in the aft cabin.

4. Safety recommendations

The following safety recommendations were made during the course of the investigation.

4.1　That the CAA consider increasing the frequency of existing engine inspections and engine health monitoring on Boeing 737-300 and Boeing 737-400 aircraft until the causes of the engine failure(s) are established. (Precautionary Recommendation made 11 January 1989.)

4.2　That the CAA call for an examination of the Boeing 737-300 and Boeing 737-400 engine Fire/Overheat and Vibration monitoring circuitry for left/right engine sense. (Precautionary Recommendation made 11 January 1989.)

4.3　The Civil Aviation Authority, in conjunction with the engine manufacturer, consider instituting inspection procedures for the examination of the fan stage of CFM56 engines to ensure the early detection of damage that could lead to the failure of a blade. (Made 10 February 1989)

4.4　The Civil Aviation Authority review the advice given in the Boeing 737-400 Maintenance Manual concerning the excessive generation of heat during blending operations with power grinding and blending tools. (Made 10 February 1989)

4.5　The CAA should take action to advise pilots of Boeing 737-300/400 aircraft, and of other types with engines which have similar characteristics, that where instances of engine-induced high vibration occur, they may be accompanied by associated smoke and /or smells of burning entering the flight deck and/or cabin through the air-conditioning system, due merely to blade tip contact between fan/compressor rotating assemblies and the associated abradable seals. (Made 23 February 1989)

4.6　The CAA should review the current attitude of pilots to the engine vibration indicators on Boeing 737-300/400 aircraft, and other applicable types with turbofan engines, with a view towards providing flight crews with an indication of the pertinence of such vibration instruments when engine malfunctions or failures occur. (Made 23 February 1989)

4.7　The CAA should require that pilot training associated with aircraft which are equipped with modern vibration systems[16], and particularly those aircraft which are fitted with high by-pass turbofan engines, should include specific instruction on the potential value of engine vibration indicators in assisting the identification of an engine which has suffered a failure associated with its rotating assemblies. (Made 30 March 1990)

---

[16] Excluding those aircraft fitted with a computerised engine warning system which includes engine vibration as an alerting parameter.

4.8 The regulatory requirements concerning the certification of new instrument presentations should be amended to include a standardized method of assessing the effectiveness of such displays in transmitting the associated information to flight crew, under normal and abnormal parameter conditions. In addition, line pilots should be used in such evaluations. (Made 30 March 1990)

4.9 The CAA should require that the engine instrument system on the Boeing 737-400, and other applicable public transport aircraft, be modified to include an attention-getting facility to draw attention to each vibration indicator when it indicates maximum vibration. (Made 30 March 1990)

4.10 The CAA should request the Boeing Commercial Airplane Company to produce amendments to the existing aircraft Flight Manuals to indicate what actions should be taken when engine-induced high vibration occurs, accompanied by smoke and/or the smell of burning entering the flight deck and/or cabin. (Made 23 February 1989)

4.11 The CAA should ensure that flight crew currency training in simulators includes practice reprogramming of flight management systems, or any other such systems which control key approach and landing display format, during unplanned diversions so that they remain practised in the expeditious use of such systems. (Made 30 March 1990).

4.12 The CAA should review the current guidance to air traffic controllers on the subject of offering a discrete RT frequency to the commander of a public transport aircraft in an emergency situation, with a view towards the merits of positively offering this important option. (Made 30 March 1990).

4.13 The CAA should review current airline transport pilot training requirements to ensure that pilots, who lack experience of electronic flight displays, are provided with familiarisation of such displays in a flight simulator, before flying public transport aircraft that are so equipped. (Made 30 March 1990).

4.14 Training exercises for pilots and cabin crew should be introduced to improve co-ordination between technical and cabin crews in response to an emergency. (Made 30 March 1990).

4.15 The CAA should review current airline transport pilot training requirements with a view towards considering the need to restore the balance in flight crew technical appreciation of aircraft systems, including systems response under abnormal conditions, and to evaluate the potential of additional simulator training in flight deck decision making. (Made 30 March 1990).

4.16 The type certification requirements for gas turbine engines should be amended so that it is mandatory to perform instrumented flight tests to demonstrate freedom from damaging vibratory stresses at all altitude conditions and powers which an engine will encounter in service (Made 30 March 1990).

4.17 The potential for fuel and oil system leakage within the fan case area of high by-pass turbofan engines, during conditions of excessive vibration, should be reviewed by the engine manufacturers and the CAA with a view towards modifying such systems to minimise such leakage, and the associated fire risk (Made 30 March 1990).

4.18 The CAA should review the existing Joint Airworthiness Requirements concerning fuel tank protection from the effects of main landing gear and engine detachment during ground impact and include specific design requirements to protect the fuel tank integrity of those designs of aircraft with wing-mounted engines (Made 30 March 1990).

4.19 The CAA should expedite current research into methods of providing flight deck crews of public transport aircraft with visual information on the status of their aircraft by means of external and internal closed circuit television monitoring and the recording/recall of such monitoring, including that associated with flight deck presentations, with a view towards producing a requirement for all UK public transport aircraft to be so equipped (Made 30 March 1990).

4.20 The manufacturers of existing flight data recorders which use buffering techniques should give consideration to making the buffers non-volatile and hence recoverable after loss of power, and EUROCAE and the CAA should reconsider the concept of allowing volatile memory buffering in flight data recorders (Made 30 March 1990).

4.21 Where engine vibration is an available parameter for flight data recording, the CAA should consider making a requirement for it to be recorded at a sampling rate of once every second (Made 30 March 1990).

4.22 The CAA should actively seek further improvement in the standards of JAR 25.561/.562 and the level of such standards should not be constrained by the current FAA requirements (Made 30 March 1990).

4.23 The CAA should require that, for aircraft passenger seats, the current loading and dynamic testing requirements of JAR 25.561 and .562 be applied to newly manufactured aircraft coming onto the UK register and, with the minimum of delay, to aircraft already on the UK register (Made 30 March 1990).

4.24 In addition to the dynamic test requirements, the CAA should seek to modify the JARs associated with detailed seat design to ensure that such seats are safety-engineered to minimise occupant injury in an impact (Made 30 March 1990).

4.25 The CAA should initiate and expedite a structured programme of research, in conjunction with the European airworthiness authorities, into passenger seat design, with particular emphasis on:
- (i) Effective upper torso restraint.
- (ii) Aft-facing passenger seats. (Made 30 March 1990)

4.26 The certification requirements for cabin floors of new aircraft types should be modified to require that dynamic impulse and distortion be taken into account and these criteria should be applied to future production of existing designs (Made 30 March 1990).

4.27 The CAA should initiate research, in conjunction with the European airworthiness authorities, into the feasibility of a significant increase in cabin floor toughness beyond the level of the current JAR/FAR seat requirements (Made 30 March 1990).

4.28 The CAA implement a programme to require that all infants and young children, who would not be safely restrained by supplementary or standard lap belts, be placed in child-seats for take-off, landing and flight in turbulence (Made 30 March 1990, amended 8 August 1990).

4.29 The CAA expedite the publication of a specification for child seat designs (Made 30 March 1990).

4.30 The certification requirements for cabin stowage bins, and other cabin items of mass, should be modified to ensure the retention of these items to fuselage structure when subjected to dynamic crash pulses substantially beyond the static load factors currently required (Made 30 March 1990).

4.31 The CAA consider improving the airworthiness requirements for public transport aircraft to require some form of improved latching to be fitted to overhead stowage bins and this should also apply to new stowage bins fitted to existing aircraft. (Made 30 March 1990)

E.J. TRIMBLE
Inspector of Air Accidents
Air Accidents Investigation Branch
Department of Transport

August 1990

CFM56-3

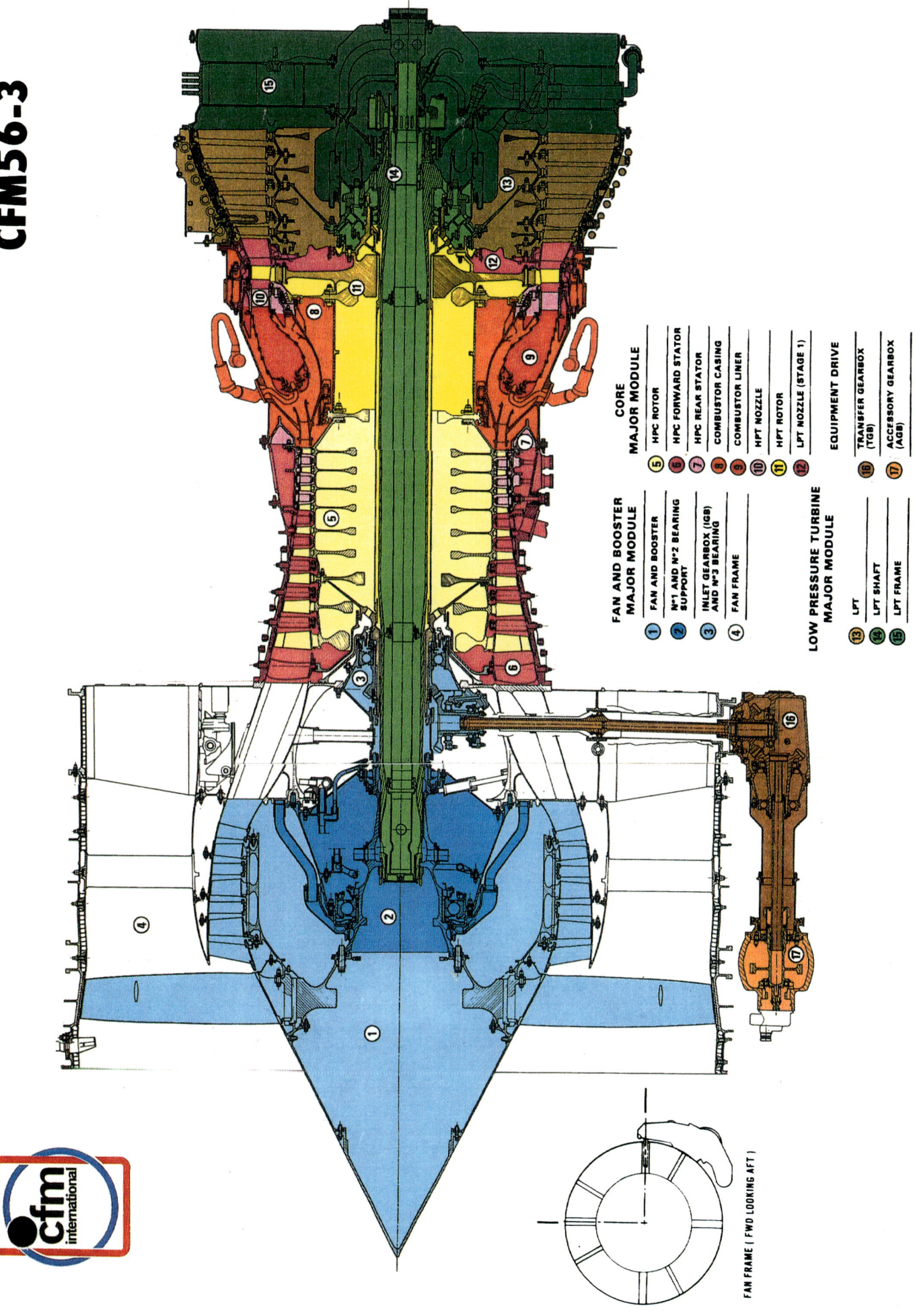

APPENDIX 1 FIG 1

FAN AND BOOSTER MAJOR MODULE
1. FAN AND BOOSTER
2. N°1 AND N°2 BEARING SUPPORT
3. INLET GEARBOX (IGB) AND N°3 BEARING
4. FAN FRAME

CORE MAJOR MODULE
5. HPC ROTOR
6. HPC FORWARD STATOR
7. HPC REAR STATOR
8. COMBUSTOR CASING
9. COMBUSTOR LINER
10. HPT NOZZLE
11. HPT ROTOR
12. LPT NOZZLE (STAGE 1)

LOW PRESSURE TURBINE MAJOR MODULE
13. LPT
14. LPT SHAFT
15. LPT FRAME

EQUIPMENT DRIVE
16. TRANSFER GEARBOX (TGB)
17. ACCESSORY GEARBOX (AGB)

FAN FRAME (FWD LOOKING AFT)

cfm international

Appendix 1
Figure 2

Fragmentation and other damage features of the fan of No.1 engine from G-OBME

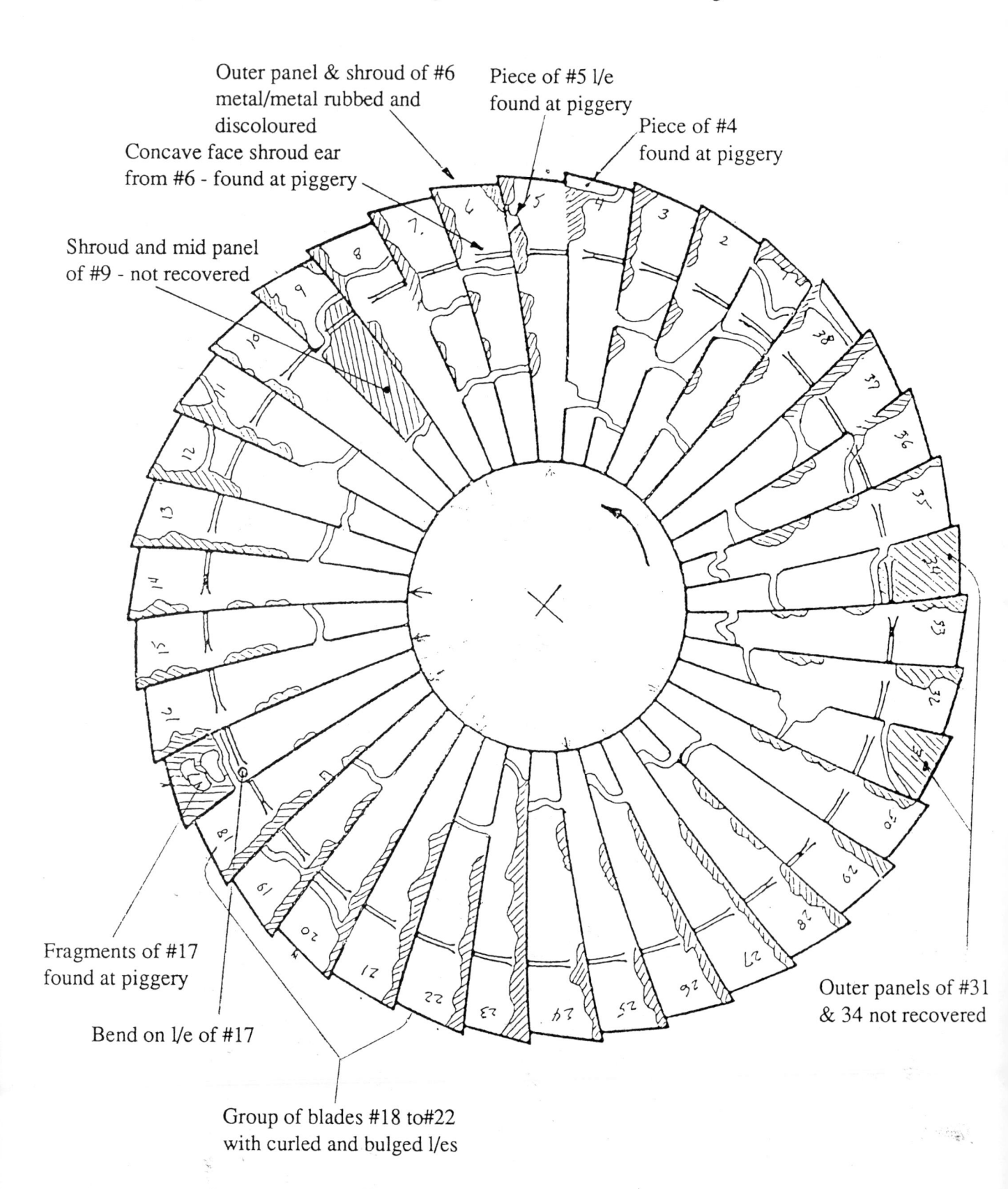

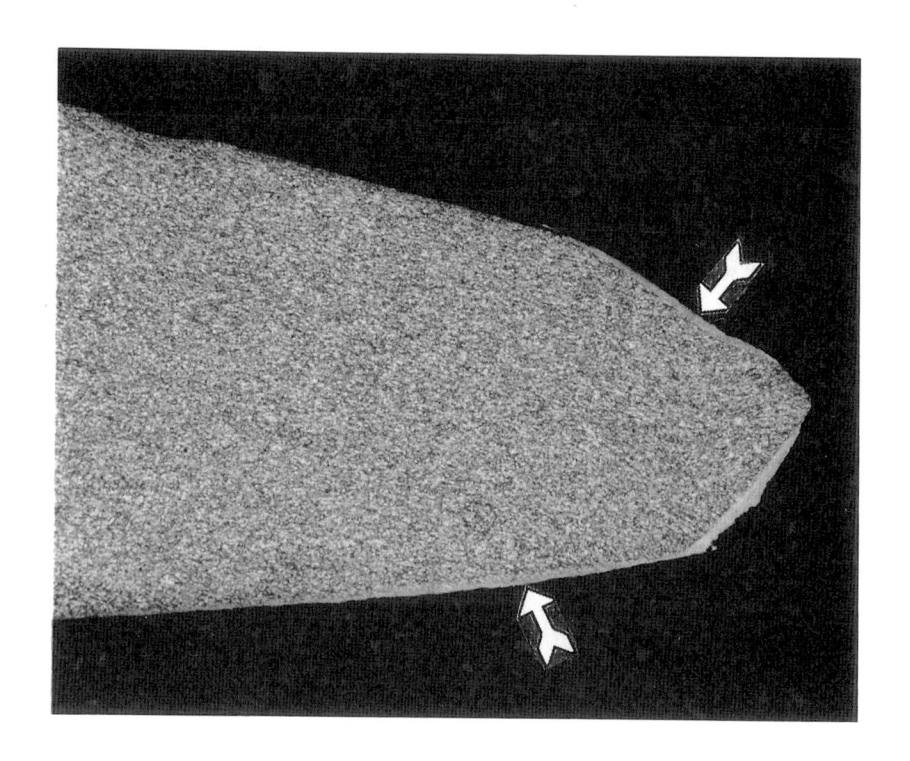

Figure 3

Microsection through the leading edge of blade 17 immediately below the plane of the fatigue crack.

This shows the even microstructure of the blade material as a whole and where the microstructure has been modified by high energy impacts.

The arrows point to the pressure (lower) and suction face impact facets where a shallow modified layer can be seen. The leading edge itself shows a much deeper bright modified layer.

Appendix 1
Extract 1

Extract from Joint Airworthiness Requirements   JAR E   ENGINES

JAR E   SUB-SECTION C3-TURBINE ENGINES FOR AEROPLANES
[CHAPTER C3-4 TYPE SUBSTANTIATION]

3   **VIBRATION SURVEYS**   Vibration surveys shall be made on the major rotating parts, compressor and turbine blading, and the Engine carcass.

3.1   General

3.1.1   Each survey shall cover all Engine conditions from Ground Idling to at least Maximum Engine Overspeed. Should there be any indication of a stress peak arising at high speed conditions, the survey shall be extended sufficiently to reveal the maximum stress values present, except that the survey need not extend beyond 105% of the maximum speed to be approved (other than Maximum Engine Overspeed) or 2% above Maximum Engine Overspeed, whichever is the higher.

3.1.2   Each survey shall enable an evaluation to be made of the effects, if appropriate to the particular part of the Engine being surveyed, of running with the most adverse compressor intake airflow distortion pattern declared by the constructor and the most adverse exhaust conditions, including the use of a thrust reverser.

3.1.3   The effects of likely fault conditions (such as out-of-balance, turbine entry blockage, fuel nozzle blockage, etc.) shall also be evaluated, if appropriate to the particular part of the Engine being surveyed.

3.1.4   For turbo-propeller Engines a representative flight propeller shall be fitted in cases where the results could be influenced by the presence of the Propeller.

3.2   Compressor and Turbine Rotors. It shall be shown by tests on an Engine or by other acceptable means that no dangerous vibratory stresses are likely to occur in compressor and turbine rotors (ie discs or drums) within the range of rpm covered by the survey.

NOTE: The evaluation of shafts is detailed in C3-4 App..12

3.3   Compressor and Turbine Blades

3.3.1   It shall be shown by strain gauging or other acceptable means that no unacceptable vibratory stresses are likely to occur in the compressor and turbine blading.

NOTES: (1) If, to avoid unacceptable blade vibratory stresses, the constructor declares prohibited speed ranges, these should be agreed by the Authority.
(2) The blade vibration survey and the variation of the incremental running referred to in 6.6.1 may be waived wholly or in part if the Authority is satisfied that the total hours run on the test bed or in flight, under representative conditions, prior to certification, is such as to demonstrate that the vibration stress levels are satisfactory. This may apply particularly in the case of small Engines if the dimensions of the blades make it difficult to complete a satisfactory vibration survey.

Appendix 1
Extract 1

3.3.2 The blade rows to be investigated and the number of blades in each row shall be agreed with the Authority. The blade rows will normally include:-

(a) the first compressor rotor blade row, all rows adjacent to variable incidence stator blades, and these stator blades if cantilevered, ie unshrouded,

(b) the last turbine blade row and the adjacent stator turbine blades if cantilevered,

(c) as many other rows of compressor and turbine rotor blades and the adjacent stator blades if they are cantilevered, as may be shown from the test results of (a) and (b) to be necessary.

NOTE: Should the investigation indicate resonances of large amplification factor in the above rows of blading, or should the investigation, development experience, calculation, etc., suggest that such resonances may be expected to occur in other rows of blading, the Authority reserves the right to require the vibration survey to be extended as necessary. In estimating from limited measurements the highest stresses likely to be experienced in the worst blade of any row, allowance should be made for the inevitable scatter in peak amplitudes which will occur when blades have the usual production tolerances on frequency.

3.4 **Engine Carcass.** Acceptable levels of Engine carcass vibrations shall be established from experience of development and type testing, and shall be declared for selected datum positions.

NOTE: These will be used in assessing the vibration characteristics of the Engine when installed in an aeroplane.

Extract from Joint Airworthiness Requirements JAR 25 LARGE AEROPLANES

JAR 25.939 Turbine engine operating characteristics

(a) Turbine engine operating characteristics must be investigated in flight to determine that no adverse characteristics (such as stall, surge, or flame-out) are present, to a hazardous degree, during normal and emergency operation within the range of operation limitations of the aeroplane and of the engine. (See ACJ 25.939(a).)

(b) Reserved.

(c) The turbine engine air inlet system may not, as a result of air flow distortion during normal operation, cause vibration harmful to the engine. (See ACJ 25.939 (c).)

(d) It must be established over the range of operating conditions for which certification is required that the powerplant installation does not induce engine carcase vibration in excess of the acceptable levels established during engine type certication under JAR-E, C3-4, paragraph 3.4. (See ACJ 25.939 (d).)

ACJ 25.939(a)
Turbine Engine Operating Characteristics (Interpretative Material)
See JAR 25.939(a)

1 The wording 'in flight' should be interpreted to cover all operating conditions from engine start until shut-down.

2 If the airflow conditions at the engine air intake can be affected by the operating conditions of an adjacent engine, the investigation should include an exploration of the effects of running the adjacent engine at the same and at different conditions over the whole range of engine operating conditions, including reverse thrust. An investigation of the effect of malfunctioning of an adjacent engine should also be included.

Appendix 1
Extract 1

ACJ 25.939(c)
Turbine Engine Operating Characteristics (Acceptable Means of Compliance and Interpretative Material)
See JAR 25.939(c)

1   The investigation should cover the complete range, for which certification is required, of aeroplane speeds attitudes, altitudes and engine operating conditions including reverse thrust, and of steady and transient conditions on the ground and in flight, including crosswinds, rotation, yaw and stall. Non-critical conditions of operation which need not be considered should be agreed with the Authority.

2   If the airflow conditions at the engine air intake can be affected by the operating conditions of an adjacent engine, the investigation should include an exploration of the effects of running the adjacent engine at the same and at different conditions over the whole range of engine operating conditions, including reverse thrust. An investigation of the effect of malfunctioning of an adjacent engine should also be included.

3   Compliance with the requirement may include any suitable one or combination of the following methods; as agreed with the Authority.

a.   Demonstration that the variations in engine inlet airflow distortion over the range defined in 1 are within the limits established for the particular engine type.

b.   An investigation of blade vibration characteristics by the method and of the scope indicated in JAR-E, C3-4 para 3.3 (except that Maximum Take-off rpm need not be exceeded) carried out on:-

i   a representative installation on the ground using test equipment where the actual conditions of operation in the aeroplane are reproduced, or

ii   a representative aeroplane on the ground and in flight as appropriate to the conditions being investigated.

c.   The completion of sufficient flying with representative installations prior to certification such as to demonstrate that the vibration levels are satisfactory.

d.   Any other method acceptable to the Authority.

ACJ 25.939(d)
Turbine Engine Operating Characteristics (Acceptable Means of Compliance)
See JAR 25.939(d)

Compliance with JAR 25.939(d) may consist of flight tests using vibration measuring equipment on which engine test bed vibration levels were established, or the equipment intended to be supplied on production engines provided the Authority considers the equipment sensitive enough for the purpose of showing compliance with the requirements.

Appendix 1
Extract 1

Extract from Federal Airworthiness Regulations   **FAR 25 ENGINES**

GENERAL

§25.901   **Installation**

(a)   For the purpose of this part, the airplane powerplant installation includes each component that -

      (1)   Is necessary for propulsion;
      (2)   Affects the control of the major propulsive units; or
      (3)   Affects the safety of the major propulsive units between normal inspections or overhauls.

(b)   For each powerplant -

      (1)   The engine installation must meet the applicable provisions of this subpart;
      (2)   The components of the installation must be constructed, arranged, and installed so as to ensure their continued safe operation between normal inspections and overhauls;

§25.903   **Engines**

(a)   *Engine type certification.* Each engine must be type certificated under Part 33.

§25.939   **Turbine engine operating characteristics**

(c)   The turbine engine air inlet system may not, as a result of air flow distortion during normal operation, cause vibration harmful to the engine.

Extract from Federal Airworthiness Regulations   **FAR 33 ENGINES**

§33.11   **Applicability**

This subpart prescribes the general design and construction requirements for reciprocating and turbine aircraft engines.

§33.19   **Durability**

Engine design and construction must minimize the development of an unsafe condition of the engine between overhaul periods. The design of the compressor and turbine rotor cases must provide for the containment of damage from rotor blade failure.

Appendix 1
Extract 1

§33.61 **Applicability**

This subpart prescribes additional design and construction requirements for turbine aircraft engines.

§33.62 **Stress analysis**

A stress analysis must be performed on each turbine engine showing the design safety margin of each turbine engine rotor, spacer, and rotor shaft.

§33.63 **Vibration**

Each engine must be designed and constructed to function throughout its normal operating range to rotational speeds and engine power without inducing excessive stress in any engine part because of vibration and without imparting excessive vibration forces to the aircraft structure.

§33.82 **General**

Before each endurance test required by this subpart, the adjustment setting and functioning characteristic of each component having an adjustment setting and a functioning characteristic that can be established independent of installation on the engine must be established and recorded.

§33.83 **Vibration test**

(a) Each engine must undergo a vibration survey to establish the vibration characteristics of the rotors, rotor shafts, and rotor and stator blades at the maximum inlet air distortion limit, over the range of rotor shaft speeds and engine power or thrust, under steady state and transient conditions, from idling speed to 103 percent of the maximum desired takeoff speed rating. The survey must be conducted using, for turbopropeller engines, the same configuration of the propeller type which is used for the endurance test, and using, for other engines, the same configuration of the loading device type which is used for the endurance test.

(b) The vibration stresses of the rotors, rotor shafts, and rotor and stator blades may not exceed the endurance limit stress of the materials from which these parts are made. If the maximum stress in the shaft cannot be shown to be below the endurance limit by measurement, the vibration frequency and amplitude must be measured. The peak amplitude must be shown to produce a stress below the endurance limit; if not, the engine must be run at the condition producing the peak amplitude until, for steel parts, 10 million stress reversals have been sustained without fatigue failure and, for other parts, until it is shown that fatigue failure will not occur within the endurance limit stress of the material.

(c) Each accessory drive and mounting attachment must be loaded, with the load imposed by each accessory used only for an aircraft service being the limit load specified by the applicant for the engine drive or attachment point.

Figure 4(a)

View on front of fan of G-BNNL after in-flight fan blade outer panel separation showing the very severe leading edge damage to all the remaining blades.

The blade which suffered outer panel separation is at the 4 o'clock position.

Note also, at the 12 o'clock position where a full blade and a half blade have been broken away.

Appendix 1

Figure 4(b)

View on front of fan of G-OBMG after in-flight fan blade outer panel separation showing the nearly total absence of leading edge damage on all the remaining blades.

The blade which suffered outer panel separation has been removed from the 12 o'clock position.

Appendix 1 Fig 5

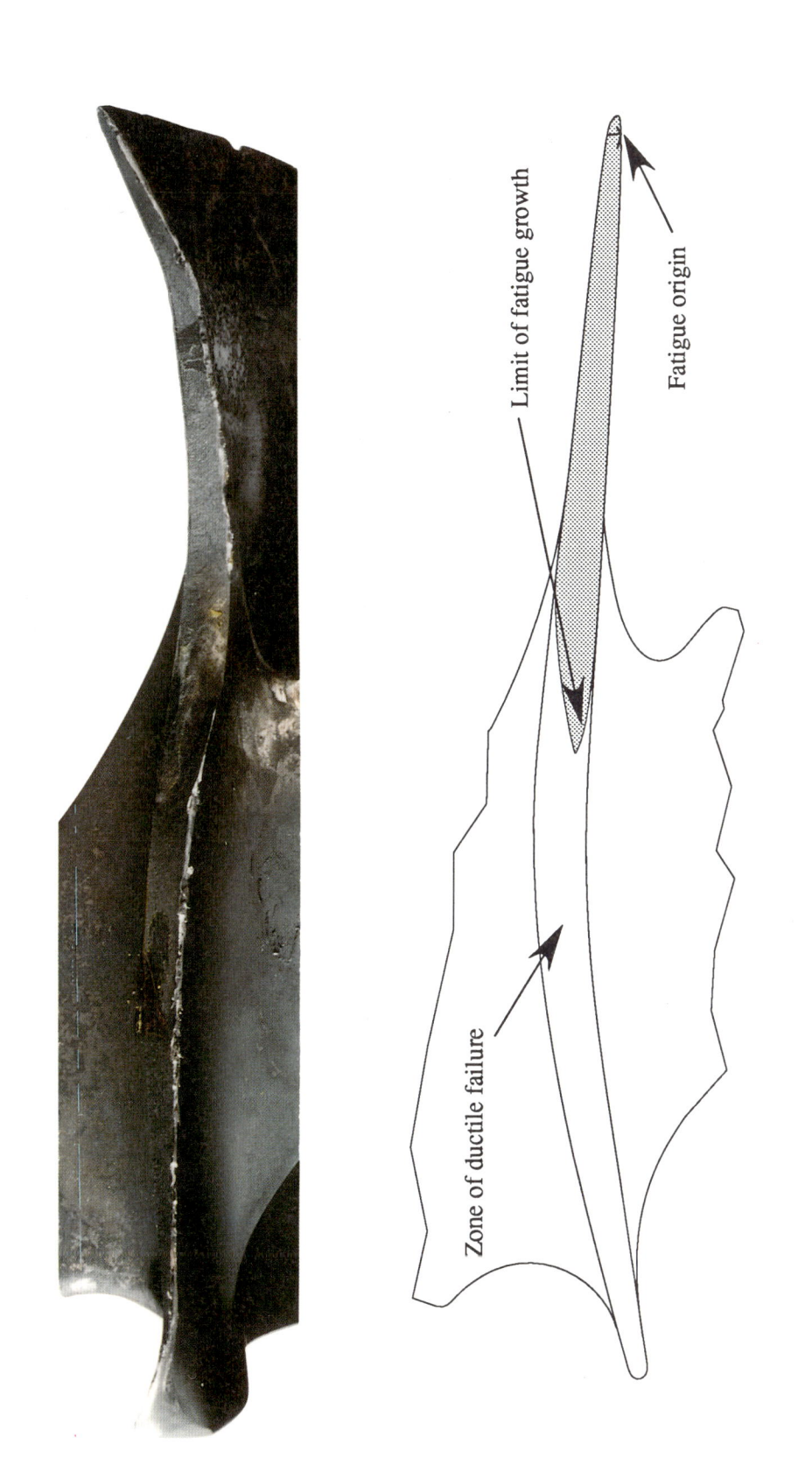

Features of fan blade fracture from G-OBME

- Fatigue origin
- Limit of fatigue growth
- Zone of ductile failure

Appendix 1 Fig 6

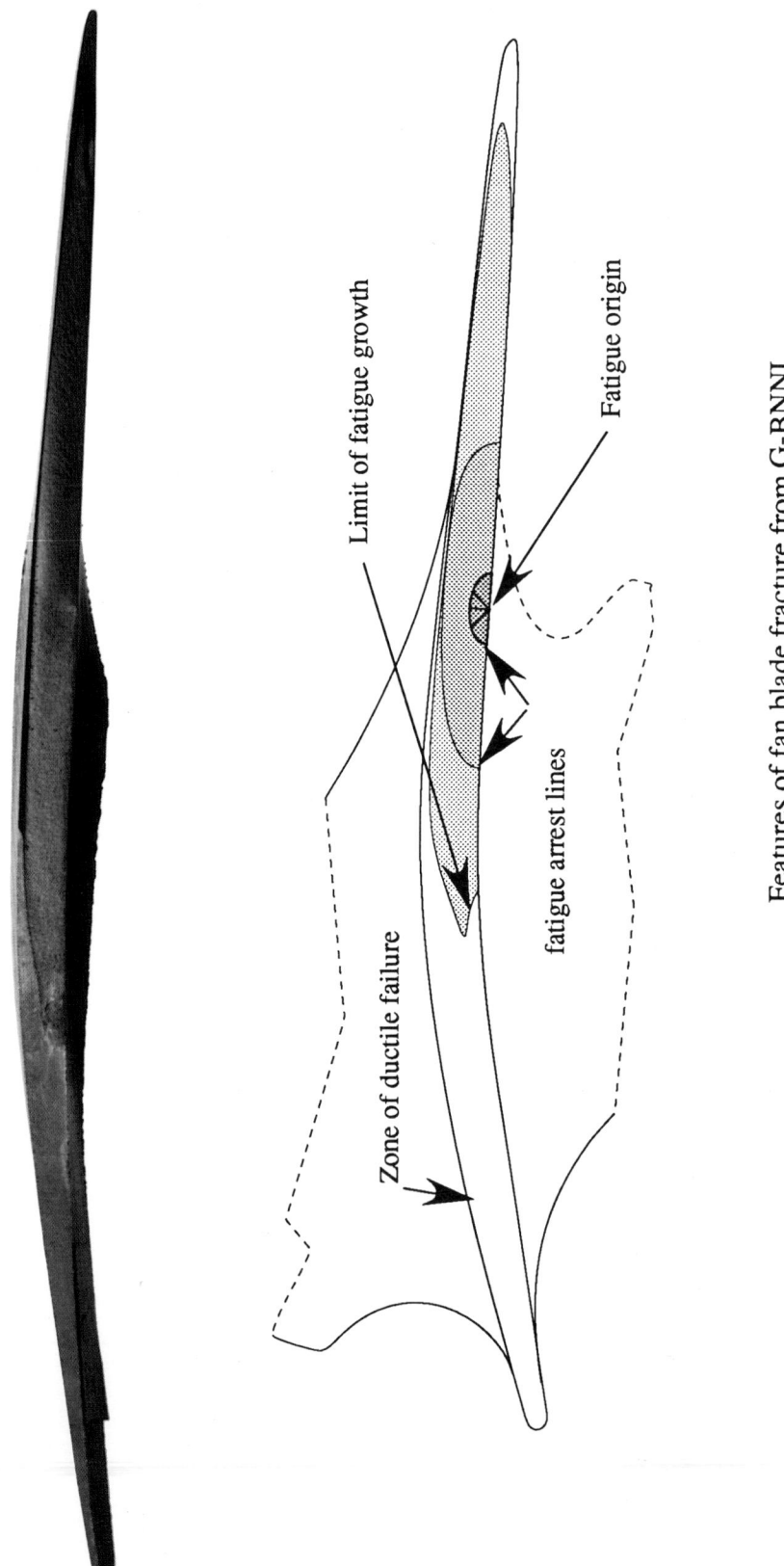

Features of fan blade fracture from G-BNNL

Appendix 1 Fig 7

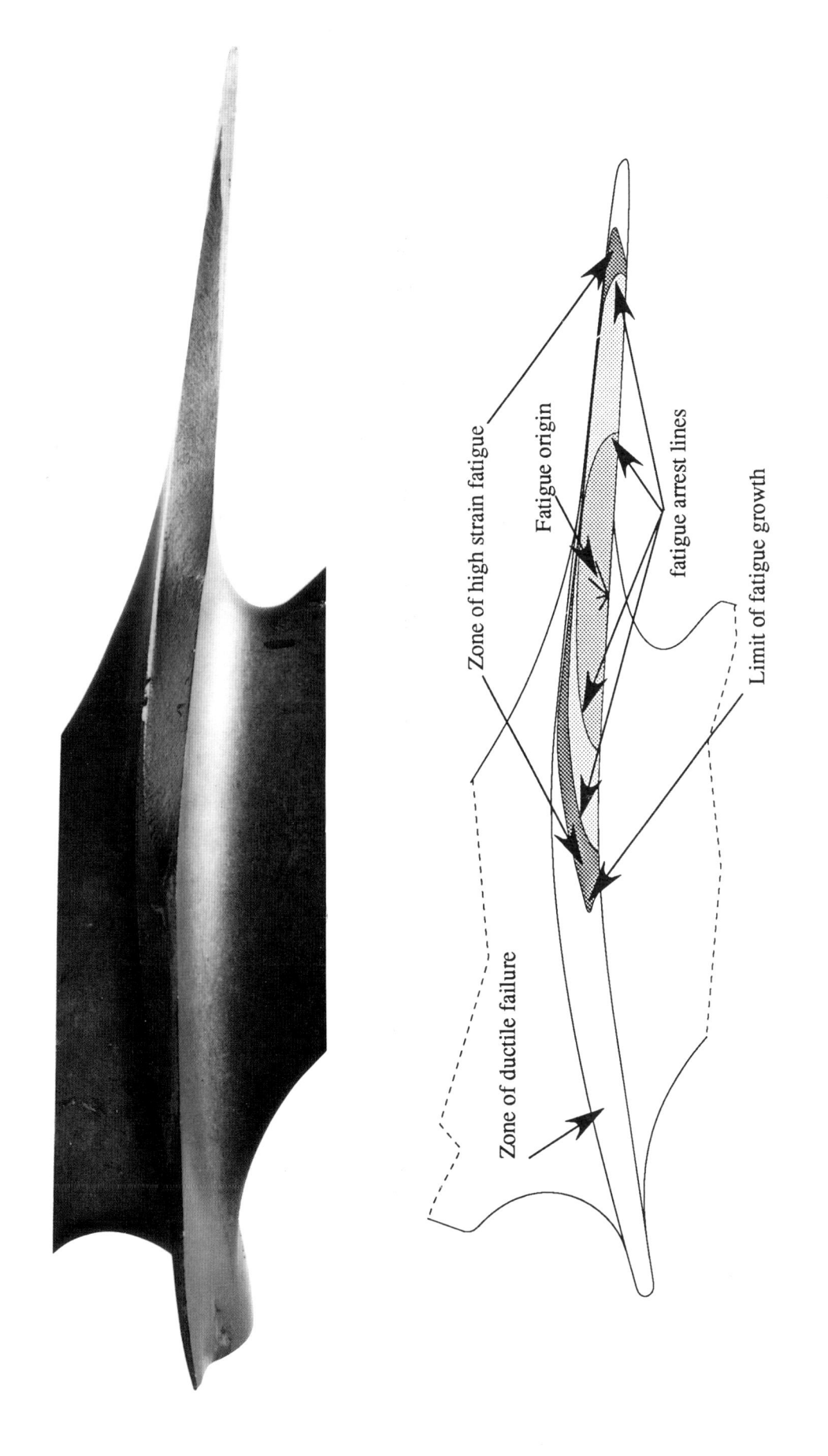

Features of fan blade fracture from G-OBMG

Appendix 1 Fig 8

From figure 5
Blade fracture from G-OBME
showing fatigue origin near leading edge

From figure 6
Blade fracture from G-BNNL
Progression of fatigue crack over 3 flights

From figure 7
Blade fracture from G-OBMG
Progression of fatigue crack over 2 flights

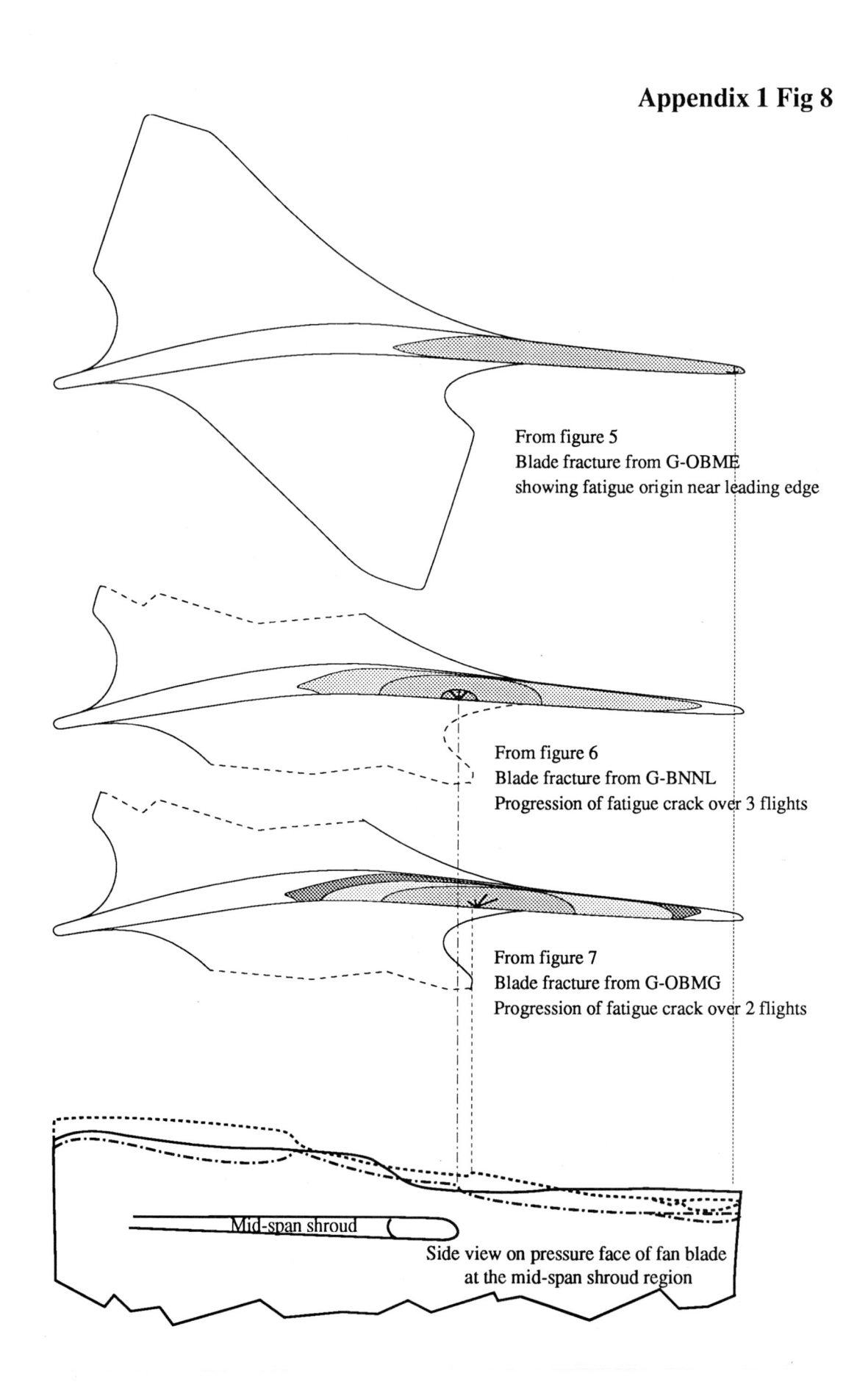

Mid-span shroud

Side view on pressure face of fan blade
at the mid-span shroud region

Comparison of fracture lines on 3 fan blades

APPENDIX 2

FIG 1: SHOWING HYBRID ELECTROMECHANICAL POINTER/LED COUNTER INSTRUMENTS USED FOR DISPLAY OF ENGINE PARAMETERS WITH VIBRATION INDICATORS ARROWED

APPENDIX 2

FIG. 2: SHOWING SOLID-STATE ELECTRONIC ENGINE INSTRUMENT SYSTEM (EIS), AS FITTED TO G-OBME, WITH VIBRATION INDICATORS ARROWED

APPENDIX 2   FIG 3

PRIMARY ENGINE DISPLAY   SECONDARY ENGINE/
                                      HYDRAULIC DISPLAY

ACTUAL SIZE

APPENDIX 2, FIG 4

Fan compartment detector – upper right hand (mounted on engine pylon)

Core compartment detector

Fan compartment detector – lower

Fan compartment detector – upper left hand

LOCATION OF FIRE/OVERHEAT DETECTION ELEMENTS

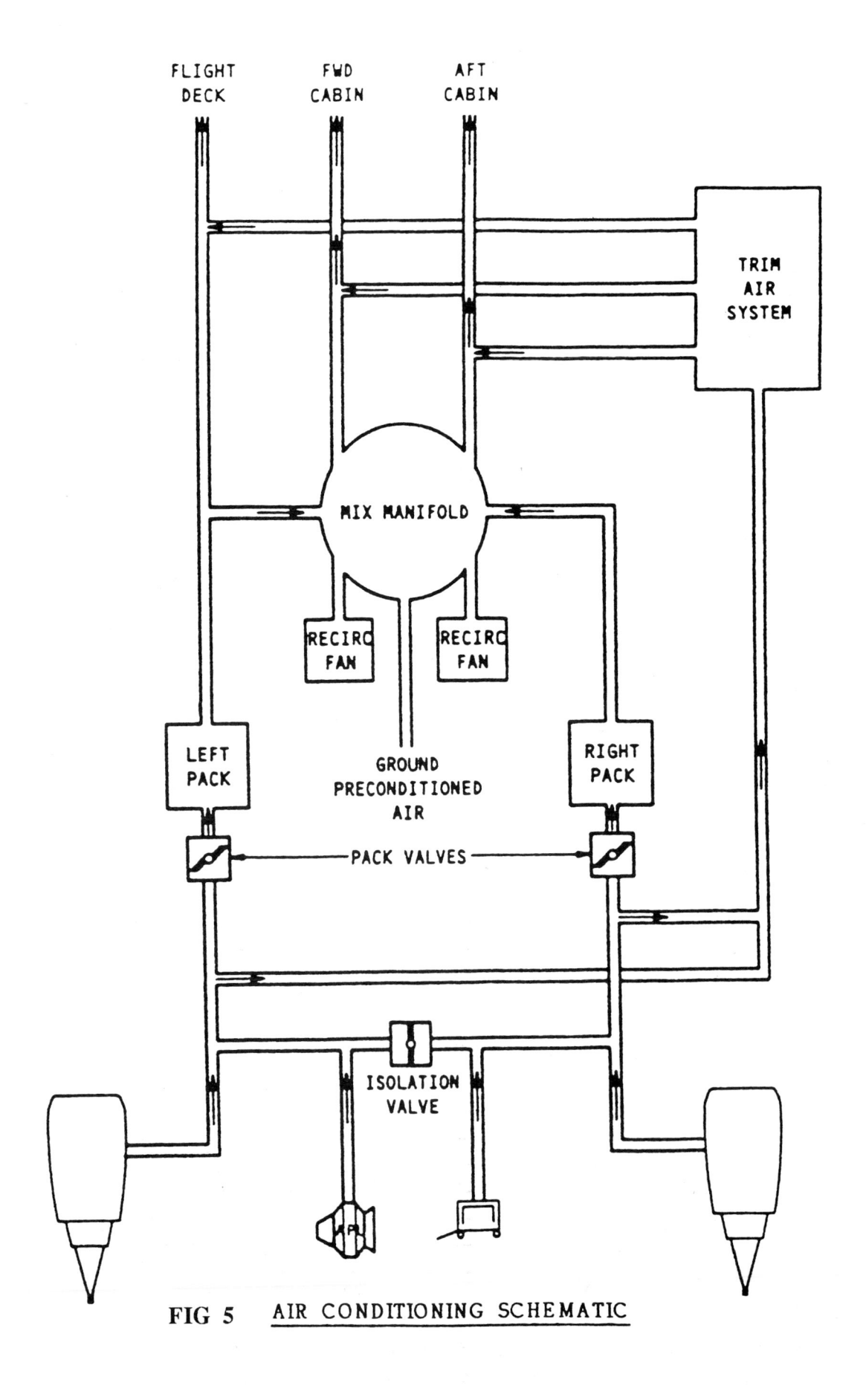

APPENDIX 2

FIG 5   AIR CONDITIONING SCHEMATIC

APPENDIX 2.6

Accident Flight ↓

FLIGHT ID	FF	FF	FF	FF	FF	FF	FF	FF	FF	FF
FLIGHT NUMBER	00	01	02	03	04	05	06	07	08	09
LEFT ENGINE	E1	E1	E1	E1	E1	E1	E1	E1	E1	E1
COMPRESSOR N1 VIBRATION	5.0	0.0	0.0	0.0	0.0	0.0	1.2	0.0	0.0	0.0
COMPRESSOR N2 VIBRATION	1.1	1.3	1.9	0.4	1.8	0.4	0.2	1.7	0.5	0.3
TURBINE N1 VIBRATION	5.0	0.0	0.0	0.0	0.0	0.0	0.2	0.0	0.0	0.0
TURBINE N2 VIBRATION	1.0	0.0	0.0	1.7	0.0	1.9	0.1	0.1	2.2	1.7
N1 SPEED	93	27	26	20	25	19	81	23	19	19
N2 SPEED	93	60	61	46	60	47	86	61	44	44
ELAPSED TIME	05	10	01	00	09	00	04	08	00	00
RIGHT ENGINE	E2	E2	E2	E2	E2	E2	E2	E2	E2	E2
COMPRESSOR N1 VIBRATION	0.0	0.0	0.0	1.2	0.6	0.6	0.4	0.4	0.0	0.0
COMPRESSOR N2 VIBRATION	1.1	1.4	1.2	0.0	0.4	0.3	0.1	0.3	1.2	1.8
TURBINE N1 VIBRATION	0.1	0.0	0.0	0.7	1.1	1.0	1.9	1.1	0.1	0.2
TURBINE N2 VIBRATION	0.2	0.1	0.0	0.0	0.4	0.4	0.2	0.3	0.2	0.2
N1 SPEED	22	22	21	55	96	96	99	96	25	22
N2 SPEED	60	59	59	79	98	97	94	97	60	60
ELAPSED TIME	00	00	12	05	02	01	03	01	00	00

FLIGHT ID	FF	FF	FF	FF	FF	FF	FF	FF	FF	FF
FLIGHT NUMBER	10	11	12	13	14	15	16	17	18	19
LEFT ENGINE	E1	E1	E1	E1	E1	E1	E1	E1	E1	E1
COMPRESSOR N1 VIBRATION	0.0	0.0	0.0	0.0	0.0	0.0	0.0	0.0	0.0	0.0
COMPRESSOR N2 VIBRATION	0.4	0.4	0.3	1.3	0.3	0.3	0.3	0.4	0.4	0.4
TURBINE N1 VIBRATION	0.0	0.0	0.0	0.0	0.0	0.0	0.0	0.0	0.0	0.0
TURBINE N2 VIBRATION	2.2	2.1	2.0	0.0	1.5	1.7	1.9	1.8	2.1	2.2
N1 SPEED	20	19	19	21	19	20	19	20	21	19
N2 SPEED	46	46	43	59	47	44	45	47	45	45
ELAPSED TIME	00	00	00	00	00	00	00	00	00	00
RIGHT ENGINE	E2	E2	E2	E2	E2	E2	E2	E2	E2	E2
COMPRESSOR N1 VIBRATION	0.0	0.0	0.0	0.0	0.4	0.0	0.5	0.4	0.5	0.0
COMPRESSOR N2 VIBRATION	1.2	1.4	1.4	1.7	0.0	1.4	0.4	0.0	0.1	1.3
TURBINE N1 VIBRATION	0.1	0.0	0.2	0.0	1.9	0.1	1.1	1.8	2.1	0.2
TURBINE N2 VIBRATION	0.2	0.1	0.1	0.1	0.1	0.2	0.3	0.2	0.0	0.2
N1 SPEED	25	23	22	23	40	23	96	99	40	24
N2 SPEED	60	59	60	59	94	60	97	95	93	60
ELAPSED TIME	00	09	00	09	03	00	04	03	06	00

Read-out of the last 20 flights recorded on G-OBME Airborne Vibration Monitor Solid State Memory. Values represent the peak experienced on each flight.

Appendix 2.7

Engine instrumentation

Layout

The design of engine instrumentation on multi-engined aircraft is inevitably a matter of compromise. The conventional and ergonomically accepted layout is for all instruments associated with a particular engine to be organised in a column, and for all instruments of the same type to be organised in a row. It is, moreover, clearly preferable for each column of instruments to be associated spatially with the throttle of the appropriate engine. This is the basic layout illustrated in Figure 1 and the desirability of using such a layout for the primary engine instruments is clear. Secondary engine information is not required on the front panel of the flight deck in those aircraft with three man crews, and the ideal layout of front panel engine instrumentation described above may thus be adopted.

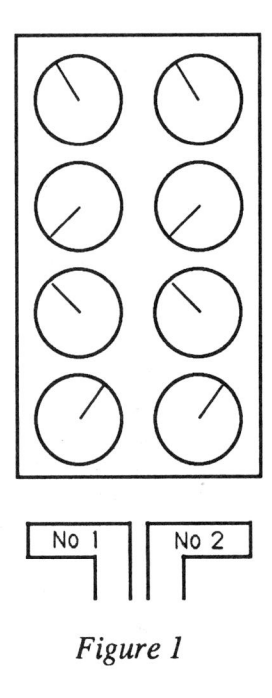

Figure 1

If the aircraft is provided with only two crew members, however, then the secondary engine instruments must be accommodated on the front panel as well. They cannot be accommodated by extending the height of the columns since panel height precludes such an option if the instruments are to be large enough to remain legible.

If the instruments are all to be located on the front panel, two possibilities are apparent. The first is to mount the secondary instruments to one side of the primary instruments as in Figure 2.

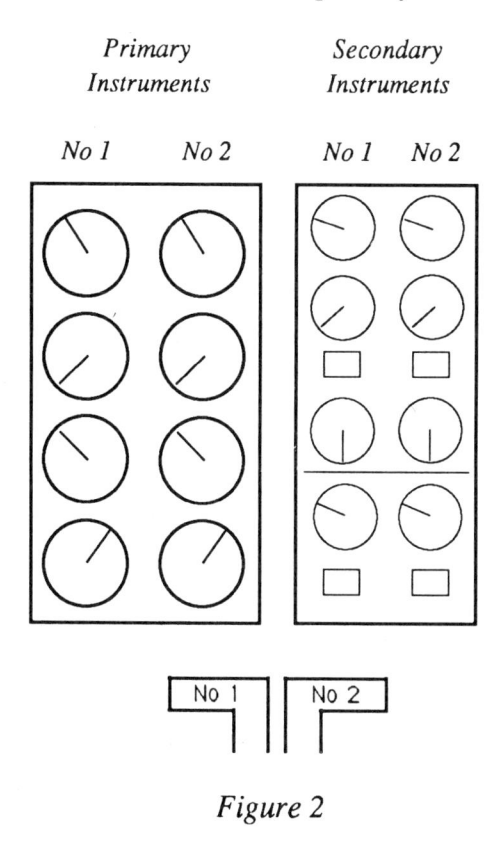

Figure 2

The second is to split the secondary instruments and mount them outboard of their respective primary instruments, as in Figure 3.

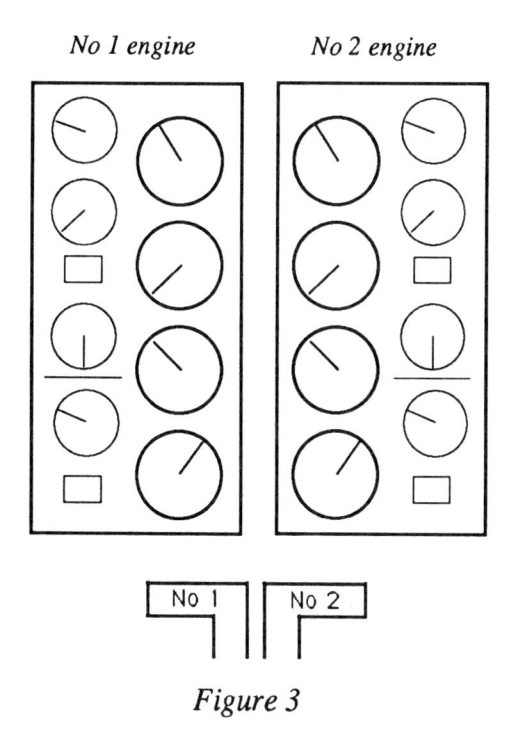

Figure 3

A-2

The advantage of the layout in Figure 3 is that the instruments for a given engine are all mounted together and are, if not spatially, at least cognitively, aligned with their associated power levers. This is achieved at the price of splitting the secondary instruments apart, with the associated possibility of disparate secondary readings going undetected.

Figure 2 achieves the goal of keeping the instruments paired together, and thus maximises the chances of disparate readings being detected, but does so at the price of splitting up the instruments associated with a given engine, and of losing the advantage of having all instruments cognitively aligned with their corresponding throttle levers.

Thus, Figure 3 could fairly be judged to maximise the probability that a given failure will be correctly identified by the crew as belonging to a given engine, at the possible cost of less efficient error detection on the secondary instruments, whereas Figure 2 may be judged as maximising the probability that disparate readings will be detected at the cost of degrading the probability that this detected failure will be associated by the crew with the correct engine.

The design of the EIS

The layout of the EIS in the Boeing 737 Series 300/400 conforms to Figure 2, which has been widely used without apparent difficulty in many two-engined, two-pilot aircraft. The illumination of the display, however, might aggravate the problem of perceived misalignment of the instruments with their respective throttles. On the hybrid instruments (LED counters with electro-mechanical pointers) fitted to other aircraft of this type, the faces of the instruments needed to be lit from in front to show the pointers, dials and scale marks. Such lighting does not, of course, illuminate only the legends and pointers on the instruments but also the general structure and limits of the display, so that the instruments could be argued to be viewed within a structured visual frame. In the EIS display, all symbology is edge-lit and set against a heavily constrasting background which, in an aircraft at night will be, to all intents and purposes, black. This may have the effect of enhancing the extent to which the instruments are seen as a single display rather than as two separate displays, and may degrade the extent to which deviant readings in, say columns 1 and 3 of the matrix could readily be associated with the No 1 engine.

The next most obvious and important change made between the hybrid system and the EIS is that the full-radius mechanical pointers have been changed to short LED pointers moving round the outsides of their scales. The mechanical pointers were relatively large, white and clearly linear devices, and their orientation on the display was immediately apparent. Not only was the absolute orientation of each pointer apparent but (and perhaps more importantly) it was readily apparent whether the pointers of each pair of instruments were parallel with one another. The pointers on the LED display are much shorter than the mechanical pointers, they are the same colour as the LED counters and they move in steps. They are much less conspicuous than the mechanical pointers, acting more as scale markers, and providing less immediate directional information. They are thus less well able to give the comparative information provided by the strong cue of parallelism of the mechanical pointers. This comparative information can be obtained with certainty only by interrogating each instrument to see if the LED pointers of each pair are at the same points on the scale or by comparing the readings of the pairs of counters.

Evaluation and testing

The entire function of any display on a flight deck is to transfer information from the aircraft to the pilot, and to do so in the way that will cause the pilot least workload and will be least likely to be interpreted wrongly. Although some principles, such as those discussed above, guide the design of displays, the only way of evaluating the adequacy of a display is by experiment and trial. It is therefore important that before any display is put into service, it is subjected not just to some form of acceptability judgement by company pilots, but to a structured assessment using average line pilots. Indeed, it could be argued that such assessments should be conducted using the least able pilots who are ever likely to use the display.

A display similar to the EIS was developed by Smith's Industries for use on the McDonnell Douglas MD88. It was held to differ from an earlier display which employed mechanical pointers, in that the colour coding of some dials was changed. The new display was evaluated by pilots employed by McDonnell Douglas and the Federal Aviation Administration (FAA). The evaluation was held to show that the new display provided clearly readable and interpretable information to the flight crew, showed whether the current state of powerplant operation was normal or abnormal, indicated the engine maximum/minimum safe operating range and showed whether the system(s) operation was being accomplished in a safe manner. These results were used by McDonnell Douglas to demonstrate to the FAA the acceptability of the new display as an equivalent means of compliance with current airworthiness regulations.

The EIS for the Boeing 737 was designed to represent a minimum change from the previous hybrid display and, accordingly, it was type certified by both the FAA and the CAA as fit for its purpose. The counters remained identical in size and colour but the dials of all instruments were reduced in size. The pointers were reduced in length by approximately two-thirds and placed on the outsides of the dials but the circumference swept by the needle tips (ie the instrument 'size') remained the same. The EIS display was deemed to have sufficient commonality with the hybrid display to circumvent the need for pilots to be separately rated for EIS-equipped models. It was tested for proper operation, compatibility and freedom from electrical interference but it was not evaluated for its efficiency in imparting information to pilots.

Although the desire for commonality is understandable, because a number of other factors were changed between the hybrid and the EIS displays, the apparent benefit of keeping size constant may have been offset or even negated by varying others such as illumination, contrast and pointer size. The desire to maintain consistency of display format while introducing new technology was responsible for the reduction in pointer size and conspicuity, and exemplifies a general problem. LED and CRT displays possess potential advantages over old technology instrumentation that may be exploited only if the display is designed afresh to exploit them. If a new technology display is designed simply to mimic the appearance of its precursors it may well fall into what is sometimes referred to as the 'electric horse' trap; the strengths of the old system are discarded because they cannot be duplicated, and the potential strengths of the new system are not exploited. Full length pointers cannot be represented on the LED system because the packing density of central LEDs cannot be achieved, and because symbology cannot be overlaid, and a potentially less satisfactory pointer is substituted.

It is reiterated that the general effectiveness of any new display may be judged only by trial and experiment, but even then some criterion of acceptability must be adopted. An obvious criterion in the case of engine instrumentation is that the new display should not prove less satisfactory to those pilots who use it than the display it replaces. When the EIS was introduced for use on the Boeing 737 no such tests were carried out.

Conclusions

Although there seems to be no question that the EIS display on the Boeing 737 provides accurate and reliable information to the crew, the overall layout of the displays, and the detailed implications of small LED pointers rather than the larger mechanical ones, and of edge-lit rather than reflective symbology do appear to require further consideration. These factors should not be ignored and the suitability of such new displays for use by airline pilots should be evaluated before they are brought into use.

Appendix 2.8

LATCH-UP CONDITION

At about the time of the accident to G-OBME, reports were starting to be received by the manufacturer that certain control modules were exhibiting unusual behaviour when subjected to interruptions in the 28V DC power supply. It appeared that the module became 'dormant' for various lengths of time following the interruption but with no fault indications apparent to the crew unless they performed the cockpit self-test, in which case the affected audio and visual warnings of overheat and fire failed to illuminate. Detailed investigation showed that the problem lay in a microcircuit from a particular vendor and units liable to latch-up could be thus identified . While the module manufacturer devised a modification to their equipment, Boeing issued an Operations Manual Bulletin No.89-2 dated 6 March 1989 to all operators. This essentially called for flight crews to perform a test of the Fire/Overheat detection system after initial power-up or after a power loss or transfer to No.2 generator bus. The time interval between power loss, or transfer, and the test was later revised to one minute in recognition of the fact that some units might not latch-up immediately. Should the system fail the test in flight, crews were advised to land at the nearest suitable airport. It has been noted that the behaviour of individual modules exhibiting latch-up tended to vary both with respect to the time taken for the condition to occur and its duration.

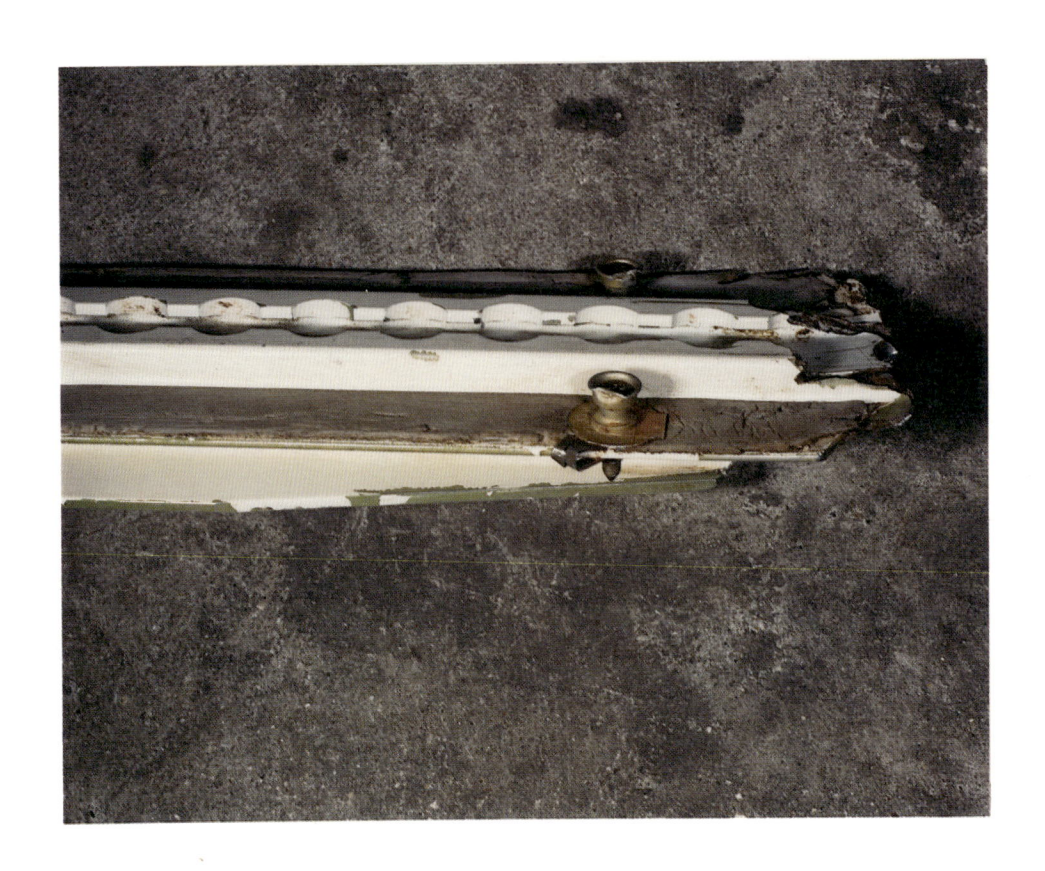

Appendix 3, figure 1 - Seat track, forward fuselage

Appendix 3, figure 2 - Seat track, aft fuselage

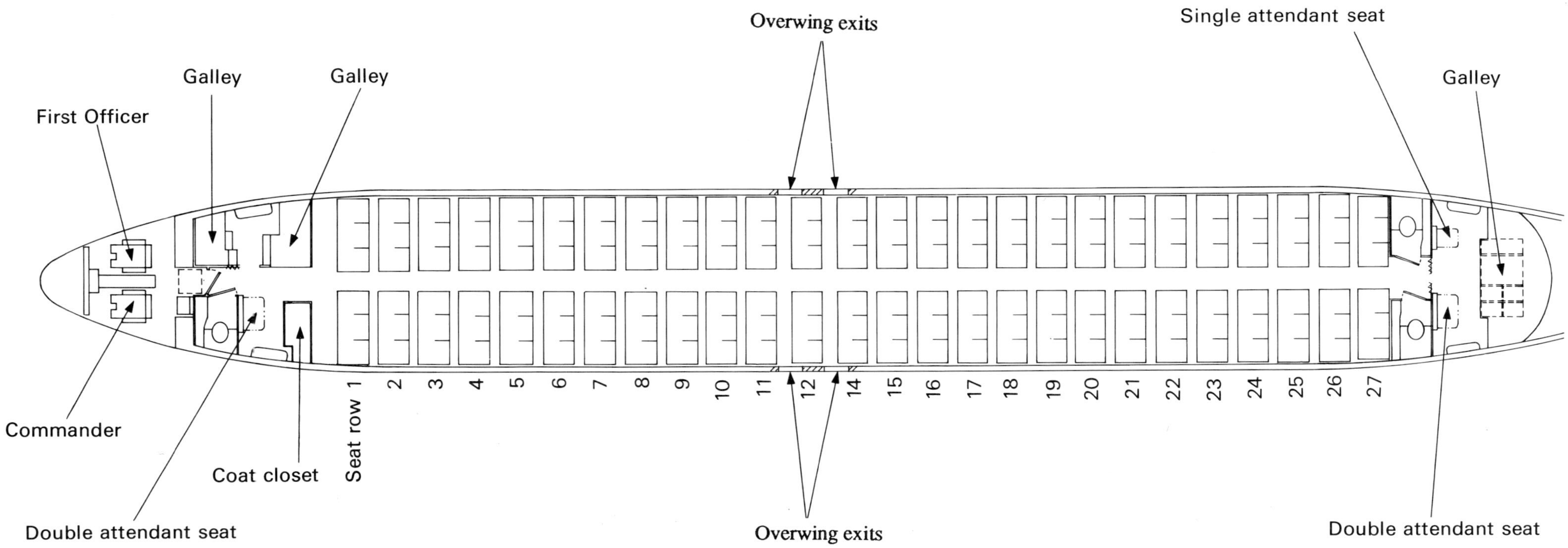

Appendix 3 Figure 3 G-OBME seating configuration

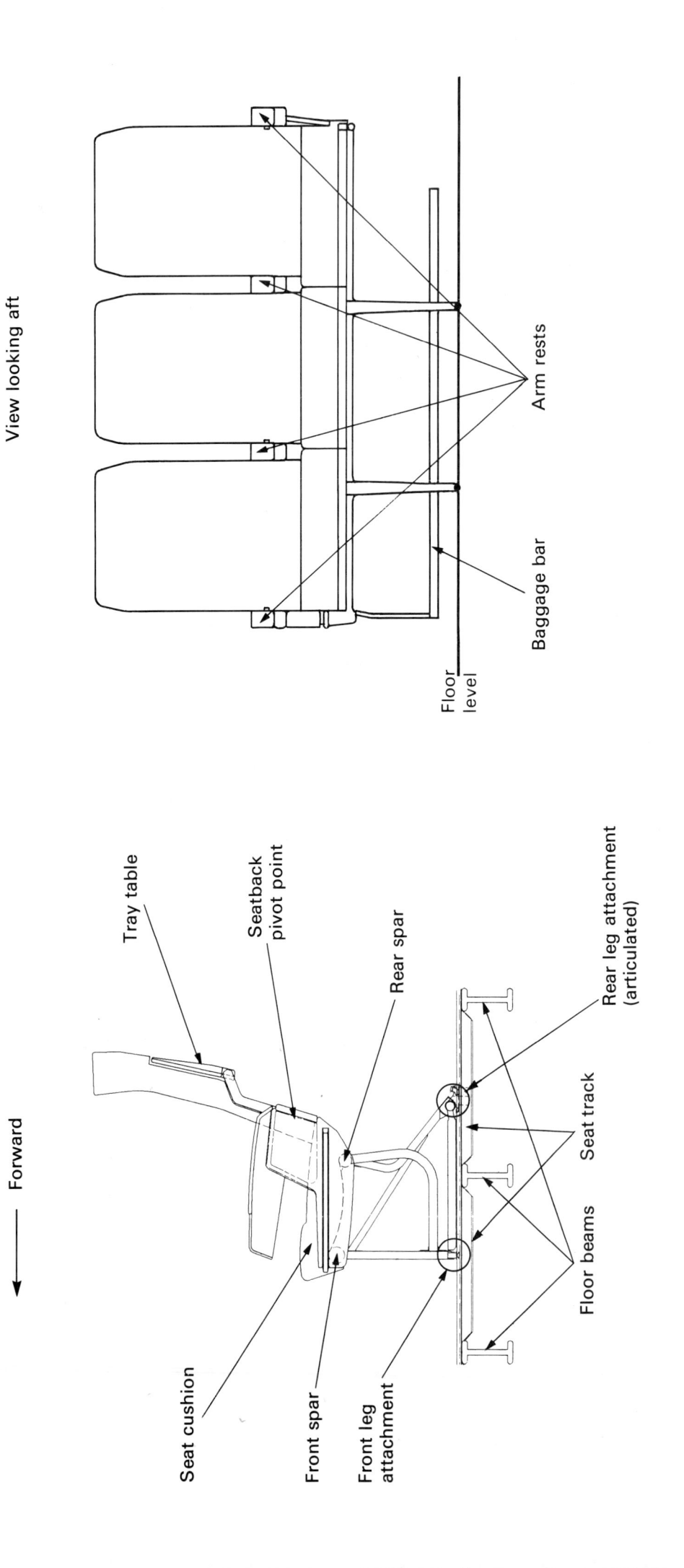

Appendix 3   Figure 4 Passenger triple seat

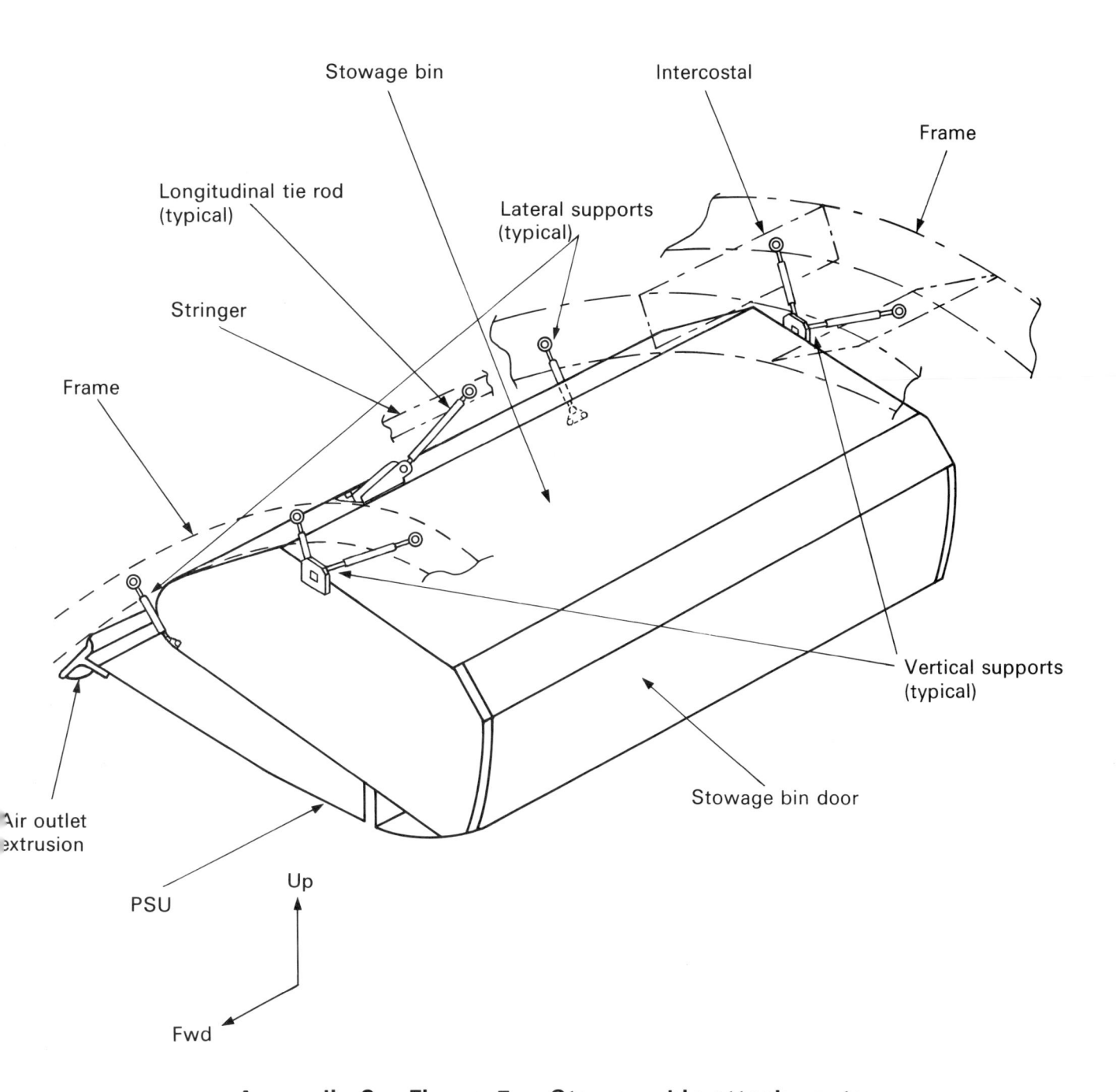

Appendix 3   Figure 5   Stowage bin attachments

Appendix 3 figure 6 - Impact sequence

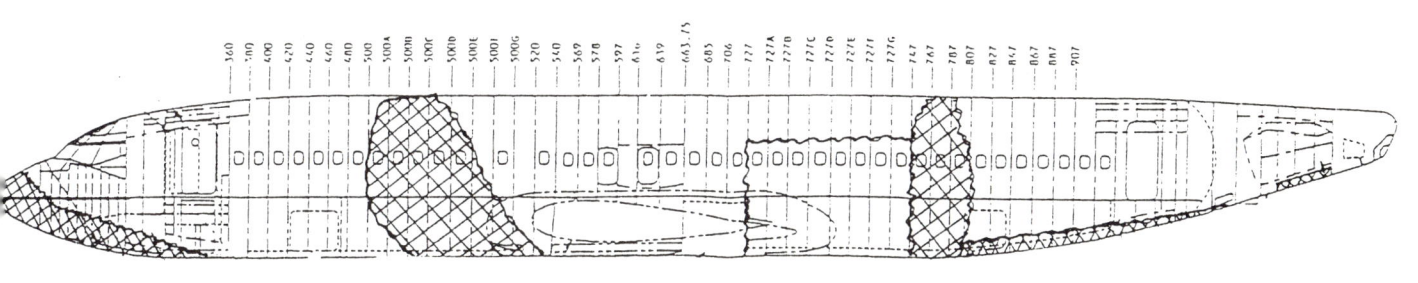

Appendix 3, figure 7 - Structural disruption

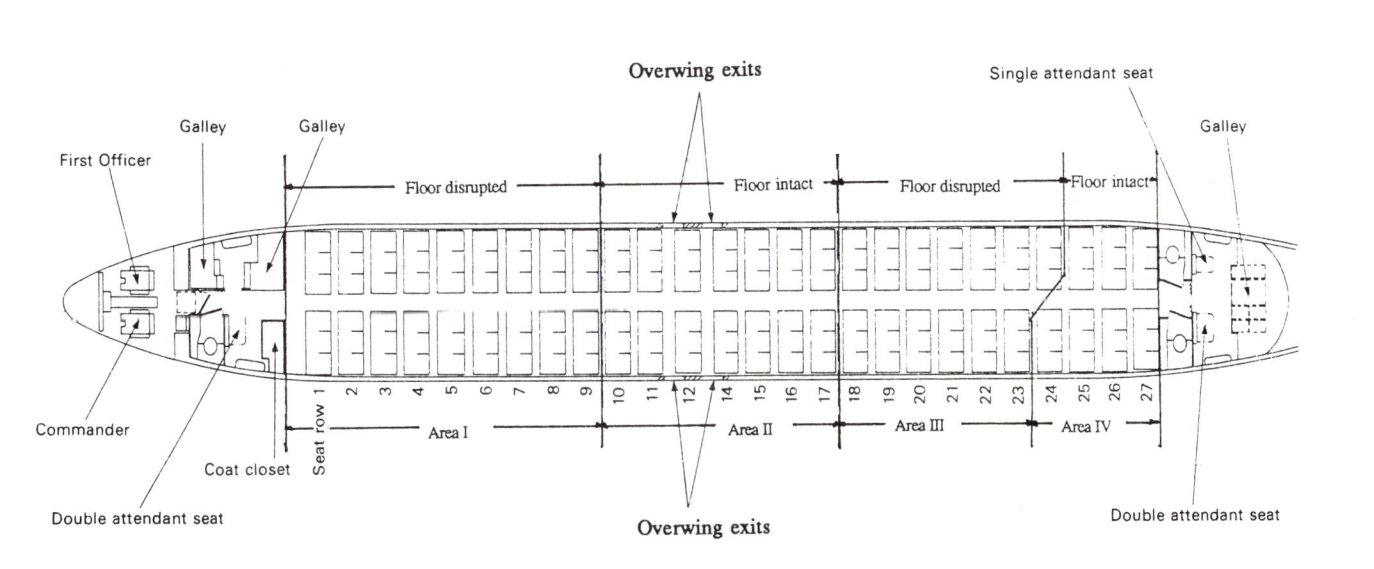

Area of cabin (fig. 7)	Triple Seats Row Nos.	Triples in area	Rear legs Attachment to track Identified	Attached	Detached	Front legs Attachment to front seat spar Identified	Fully attached	Partially attached	Detached	'U' - strap deformation Identified	Pristine	Deformed	Collapsed	Seat backs Attachment to seat Attached	Detached
I	1-9	18	33	27(82%)	6(18%)	35	17(49%)	12(34%)	6(17%)	35	4(11%)	18(51%)	13(37%)	46(85%)	8(15%)
II	10-17	14	28	28(100%)	0(0%)	28	23(82%)	5(18%)	0(0%)	27	5(19%)	2(7%)	20(74%)	56	0
III	18-23L/24R	13	25	18(72%)	7(28%)	24	7(29%)	13(54%)	4(16%)	24	5(21%)	14(58%)	5(21%)	(Fuselage buckle) 1 (Other) 17	20 1
IV	24L/25R-27	7	14	14(100%)	0(0%)	14	14(100%)	0(0%)	0(0%)	14	13(93%)	1(7%)	0(0%)	14	0

Appendix 3 figure 8 - Summary of passenger seat damage

Appendix 3, figure 9 - Seat 3L (area I)

Appendix 3, figure 10 - Seat 15L (area II)

Appendix 3, figure 11 - Seat 18L (area III)

Appendix 3, figure 12 - Seat 22R (area III)

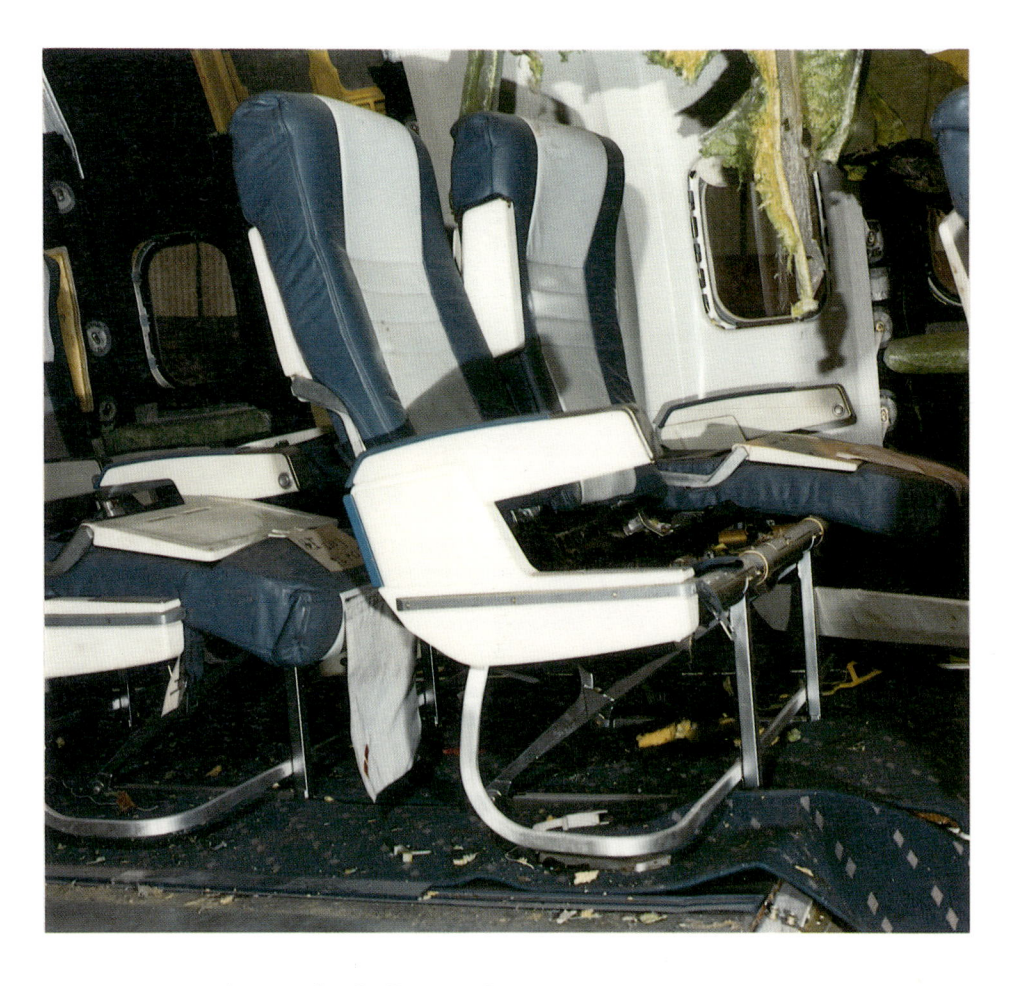

Appendix 3, figure 13 - Seat 25L (Area IV)

Appendix 3, figure 14 - Floor structure at station 867 (Area IV)

Appendix 3, figure 15 - Floor panel fasteners (area IV)

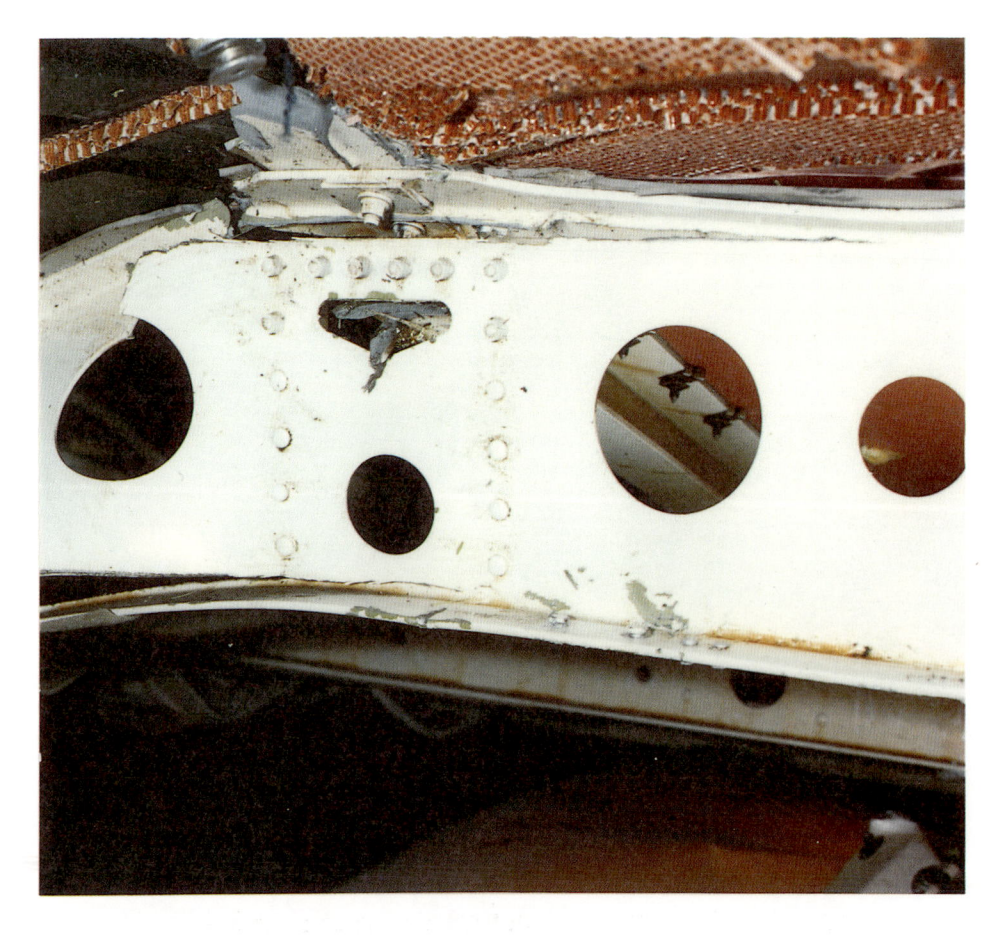

Appendix 3, figure 16 - Floor beam at station 807 (area IV)

Appendix 3, figure 17 - Seat track at station 727D (area III)

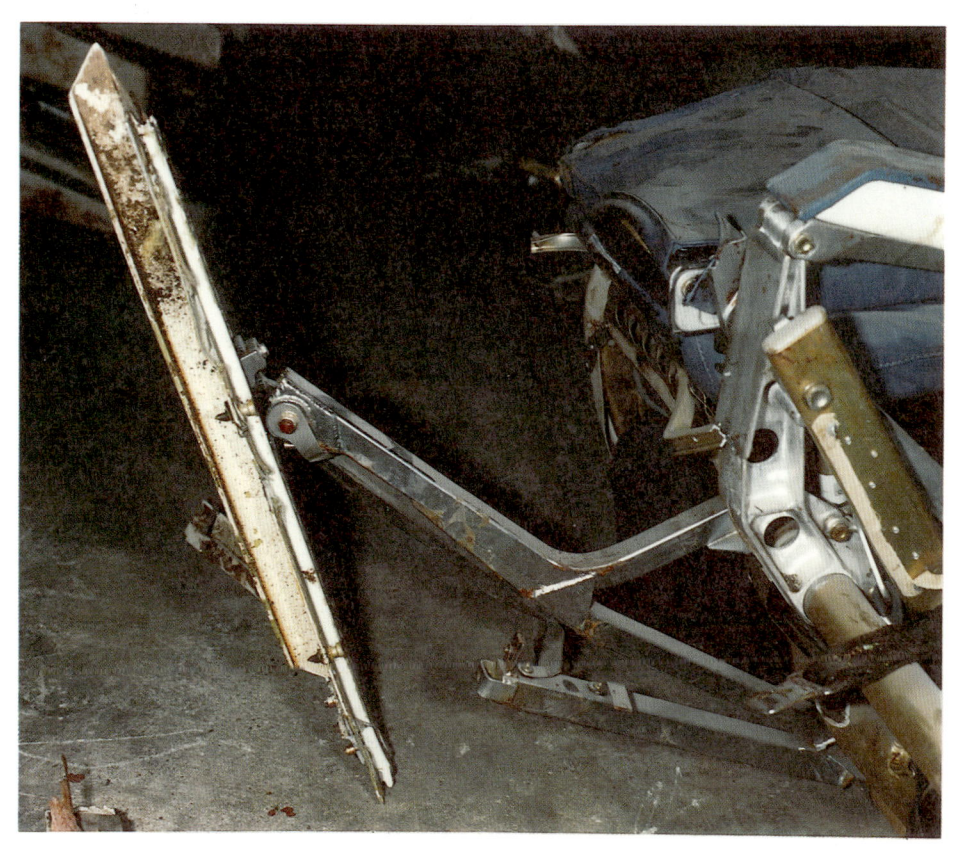

Appendix 3, figure 18 - Seat track and seat 5R (area I)

Appendix 3, figure 19 - Seat track and seat 3L (area I)

Appendix 3, figure 20 - Floor beam at station 460 (area I)

Appendix 3, figure 21 (a) - Stowage bin attachments

Appendix 3, figure 21 (b) - Stowage bins

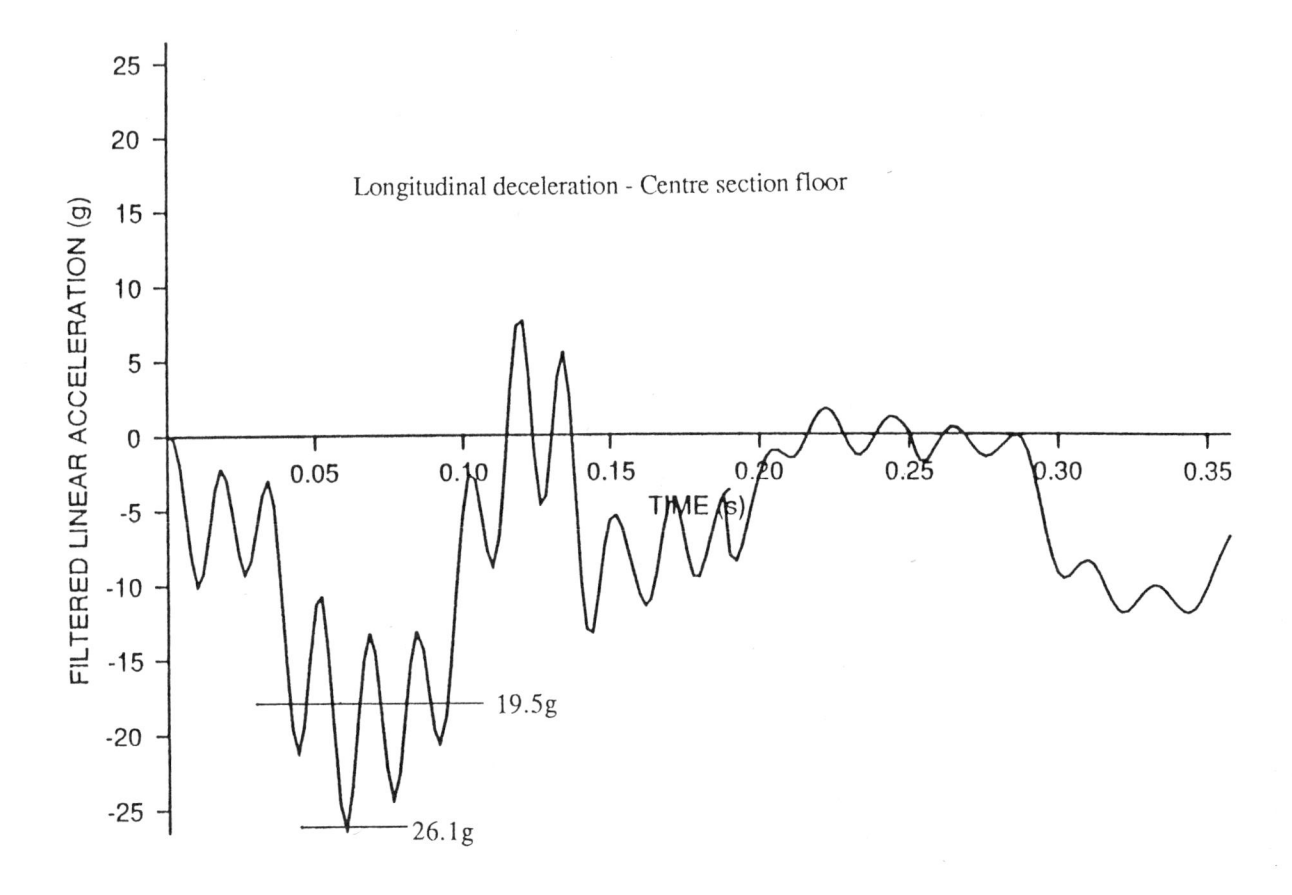

Appendix 3, figure 22 (a) - KRASH longitudinal deceleration - Run 2

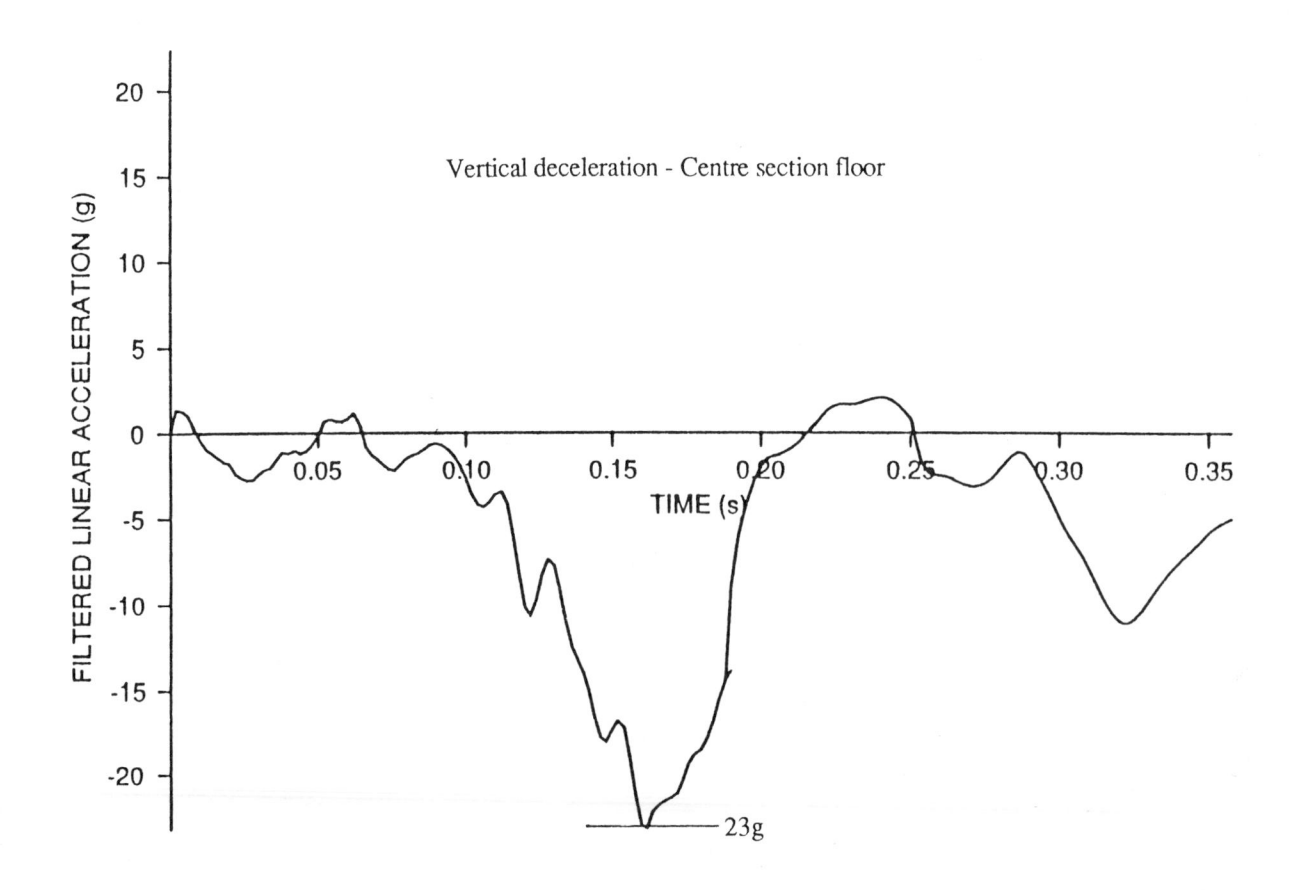

Appendix 3, figure 22 (b) - KRASH vertical deceleration - Run 2

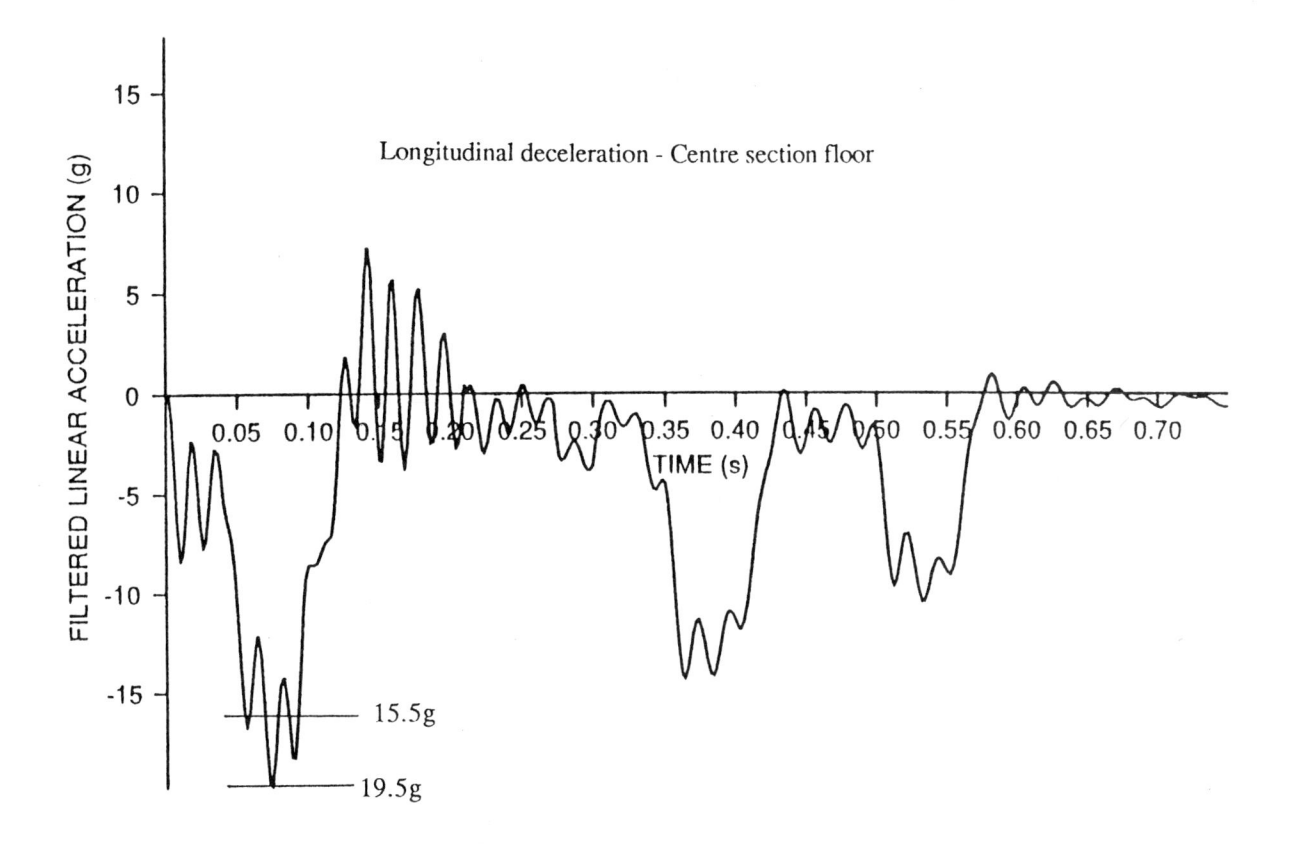

Appendix 3, figure 23 (a) - KRASH longitudinal deceleration - Run 3

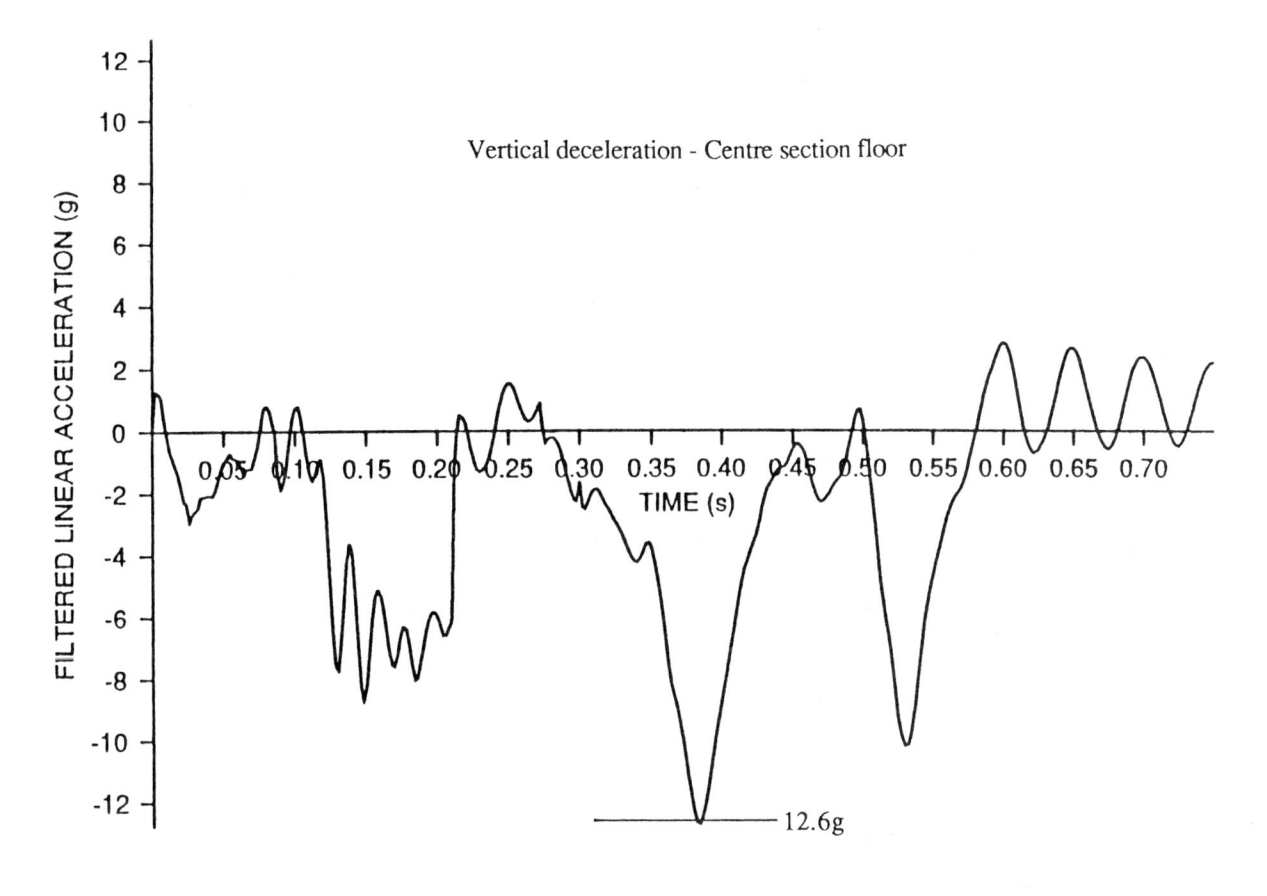

Appendix 3, figure 23 (b) - KRASH vertical deceleration - Run 3

No.	Date	Location	Type	Operator	Registration	Report	Comments
1)	11 Sept 1974	Charlotte, NC	DC9-31	Eastern	N8984E	AAR-75-9	82 SOB, 71 F
2)	27 Apr 1976	St. Thomas, VI	B727-95	American	N1963	AAR-77-1	89 SOB, 37 F
3)	16 Nov 1976	Denver, CO	DC9-41	Texas Int	N9104	AAR-77-10	86 SOB, 0 F
4)	14 Apr 1977	New Hope, GA	DC9-31	Southern	N1335U	AAR-78-3	85 SOB, 62 F
5)	25 Oct 1986	Charlotte, NC	B727-222	Piedmont	N752N	AAR-87-08	119 SOB, 0 F
6)	28 Dec 1978	Portland, OR	DC8-61	United	N8082U	AAR-79-7	189 SOB, 10 F (inc. 3 infants)
7)	31 Aug 1988	Dallas, TX	B727-232	Delta	N473DA	AAR-89-04	108 SOB, 14 F
8)	27 Dec 1973	Chattanooga, TN	DC9-32	Delta	N3323L	AAR-74-13	79 SOB, 0 F
9)	20 Dec 1972	Chicago, Il	CV880/DC9	Delta/N. Cent	N8807E/N954N	AAR-73-15	45 SOB, 10 F
10)	7 Aug 1975	Denver, CO	B727-224	Continental	N88777	AAR-76-14	134 SOB, 0 F
11)	24 Jun 1975	JFK, NY	B727-225	Eastern	N8845E	AAR-76-8	124 SOB, 112 F
12)	18 May 1972	Fort Lauderdale, FL	DC9-31	Eastern	N8961E	AAR-72-31	10 SOB, 0 F
13)	26 June 1978	Toronto, Ontario	DC9-32	Air Canada	CF-TLV	H80002	107 SOB, 2F

Appendix 3, figure 24 - Sample of North American jet transport accidents (paragraph 1.17.17)

APPENDIX 4, FIGURE 1

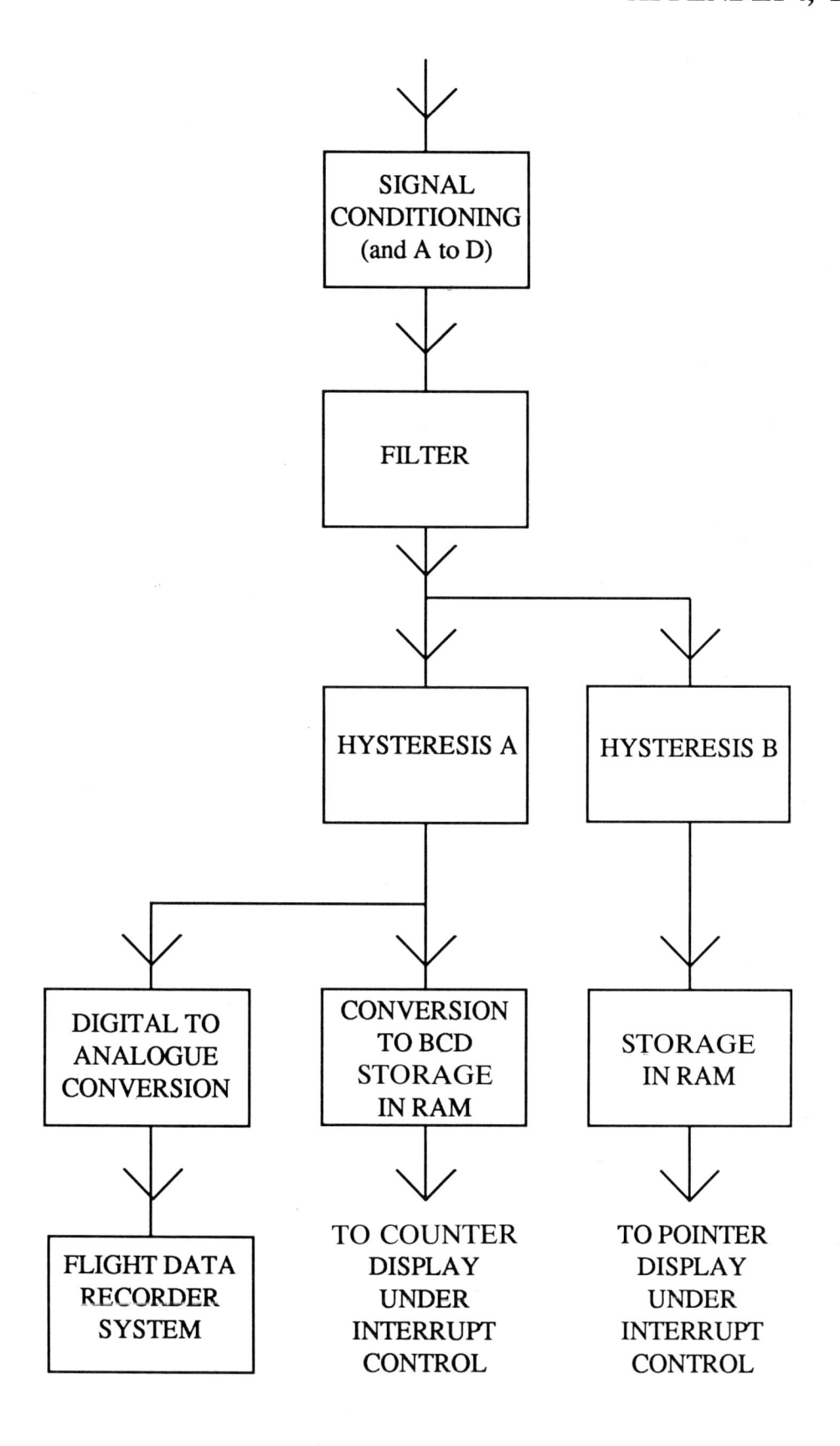

```
              |
              v
     +------------------+
     |      SIGNAL      |
     |   CONDITIONING   |
     |   (and A to D)   |
     +------------------+
              |
              v
     +------------------+
     |      FILTER      |
     +------------------+
              |
         +----+----+
         v         v
  +-----------+  +-----------+
  |HYSTERESIS |  |HYSTERESIS |
  |     A     |  |     B     |
  +-----------+  +-----------+
       |              |
   +---+---+          |
   v       v          v
+--------+ +--------+ +--------+
|DIGITAL | |CONVER- | |STORAGE |
|TO      | |SION TO | |IN RAM  |
|ANALOGUE| |BCD     | |        |
|CONVER- | |STORAGE | |        |
|SION    | |IN RAM  | |        |
+--------+ +--------+ +--------+
    |          |          |
    v          v          v
+--------+  TO COUNTER  TO POINTER
|FLIGHT  |   DISPLAY     DISPLAY
|DATA    |   UNDER       UNDER
|RECORDER|   INTERRUPT   INTERRUPT
|SYSTEM  |   CONTROL     CONTROL
+--------+
```

SIMPLIFIED BLOCK DIAGRAM OF EIS SIGNAL PATH

APPENDIX 4, fig 2

G-OBME TRACK PLOT

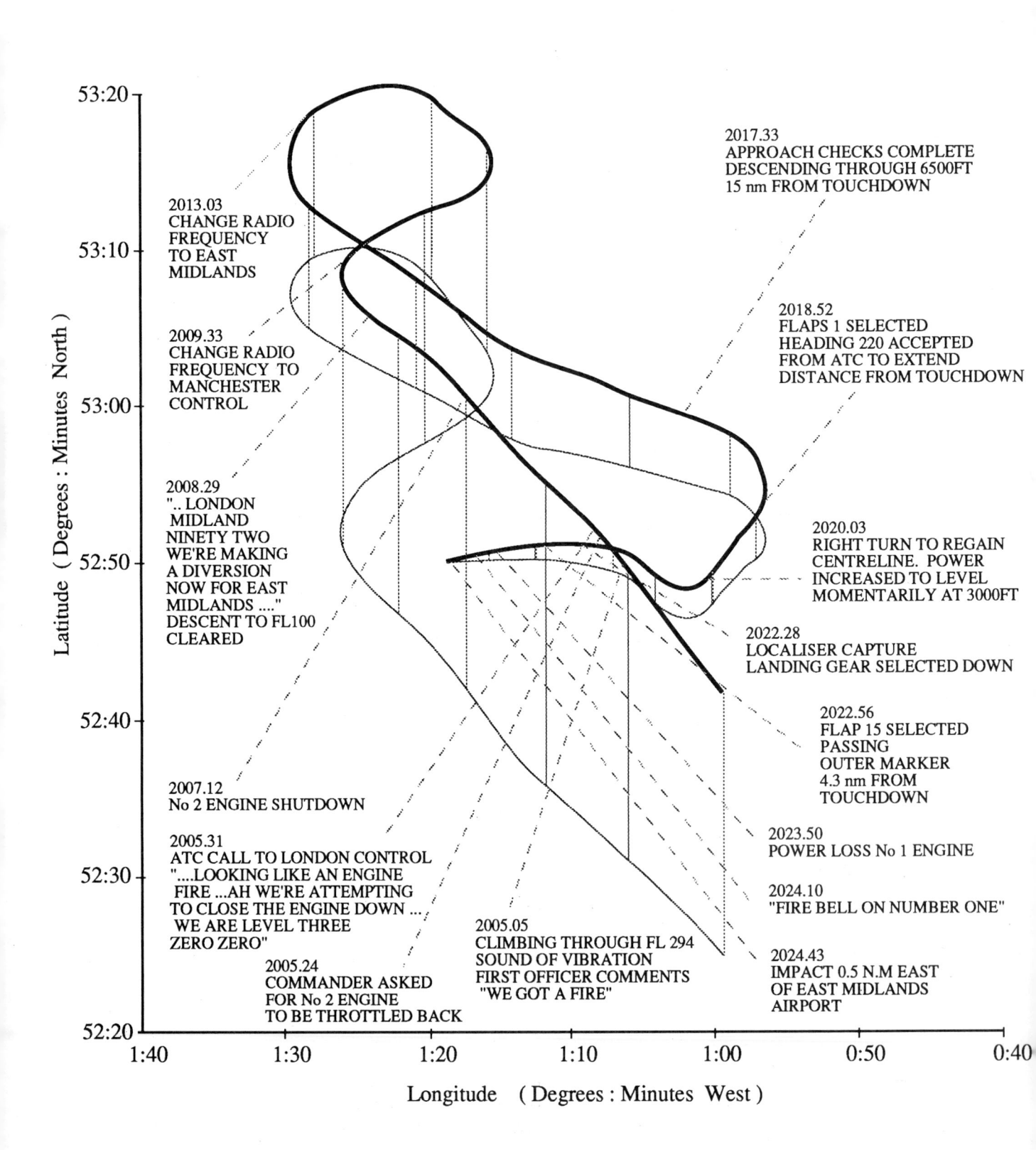

2017.33
APPROACH CHECKS COMPLETE
DESCENDING THROUGH 6500FT
15 nm FROM TOUCHDOWN

2013.03
CHANGE RADIO
FREQUENCY
TO EAST
MIDLANDS

2018.52
FLAPS 1 SELECTED
HEADING 220 ACCEPTED
FROM ATC TO EXTEND
DISTANCE FROM TOUCHDOWN

2009.33
CHANGE RADIO
FREQUENCY TO
MANCHESTER
CONTROL

2008.29
".. LONDON
MIDLAND
NINETY TWO
WE'RE MAKING
A DIVERSION
NOW FOR EAST
MIDLANDS ...."
DESCENT TO FL100
CLEARED

2020.03
RIGHT TURN TO REGAIN
CENTRELINE. POWER
INCREASED TO LEVEL
MOMENTARILY AT 3000FT

2022.28
LOCALISER CAPTURE
LANDING GEAR SELECTED DOWN

2022.56
FLAP 15 SELECTED
PASSING
OUTER MARKER
4.3 nm FROM
TOUCHDOWN

2007.12
No 2 ENGINE SHUTDOWN

2005.31
ATC CALL TO LONDON CONTROL
"....LOOKING LIKE AN ENGINE
FIRE ...AH WE'RE ATTEMPTING
TO CLOSE THE ENGINE DOWN ...
WE ARE LEVEL THREE
ZERO ZERO"

2023.50
POWER LOSS No 1 ENGINE

2024.10
"FIRE BELL ON NUMBER ONE"

2005.24
COMMANDER ASKED
FOR No 2 ENGINE
TO BE THROTTLED BACK

2005.05
CLIMBING THROUGH FL 294
SOUND OF VIBRATION
FIRST OFFICER COMMENTS
"WE GOT A FIRE"

2024.43
IMPACT 0.5 N.M EAST
OF EAST MIDLANDS
AIRPORT

Latitude (Degrees : Minutes North)

Longitude (Degrees : Minutes West)

APPENDIX 4 FIGURE 3

G-OBME ENGINE PARAMETERS FROM FLIGHT DATA RECORDER

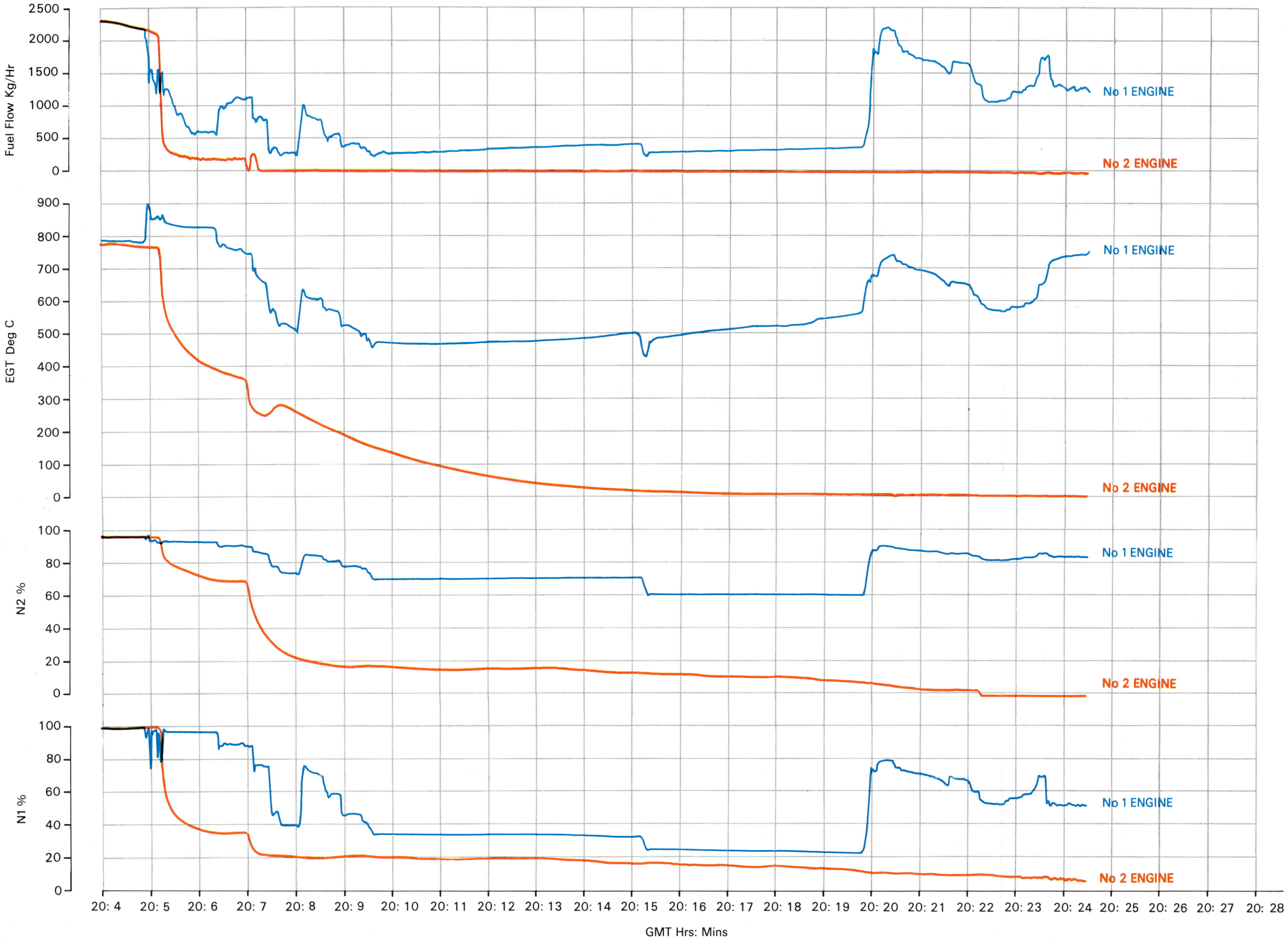

APPENDIX 4 FIGURE 4

G—OBME VIBRATION LEVELS

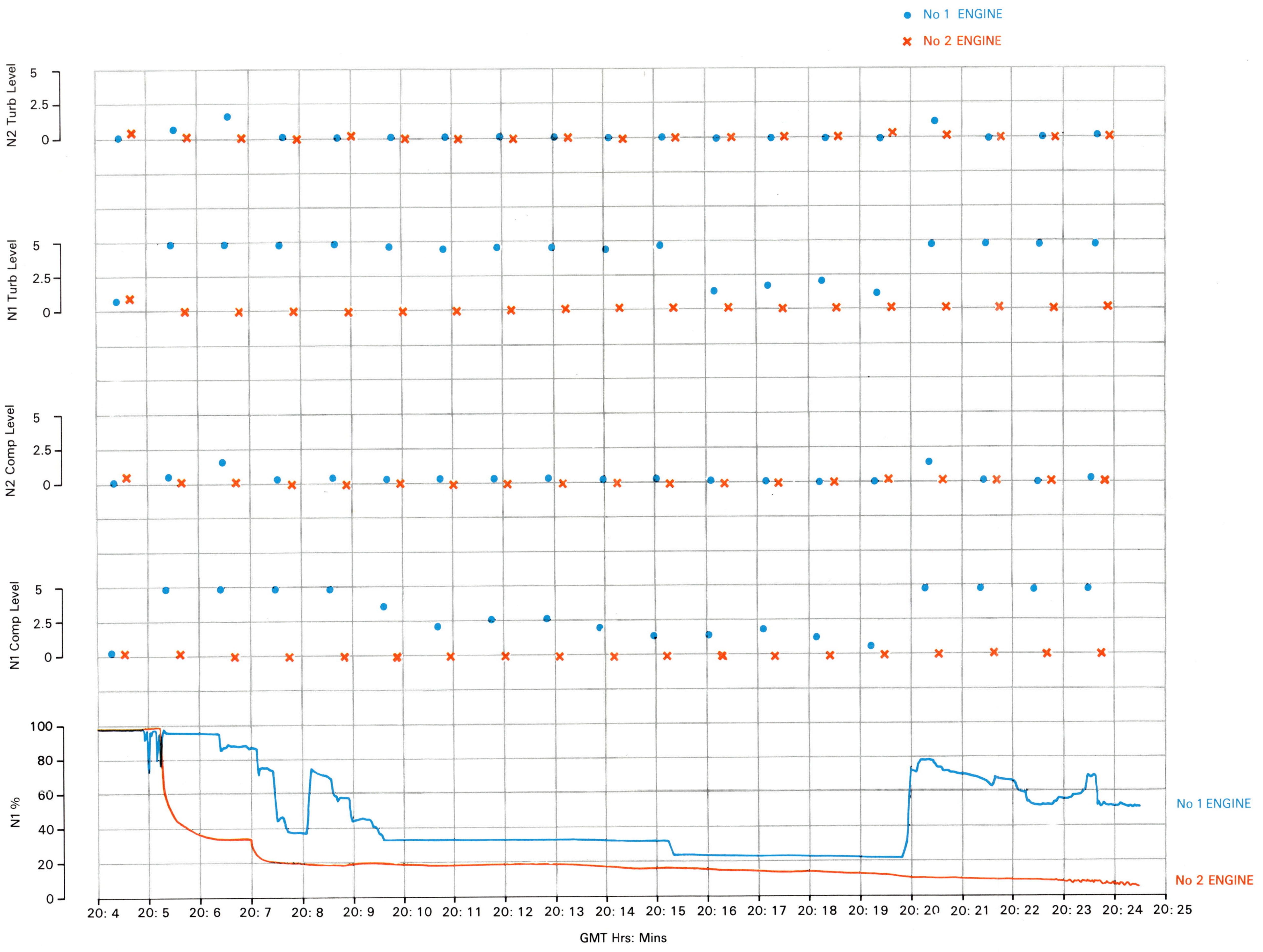

APPENDIX 4 FIGURE 5

G—OBME PRIMARY ENGINE PARAMETERS AT EVENT 1

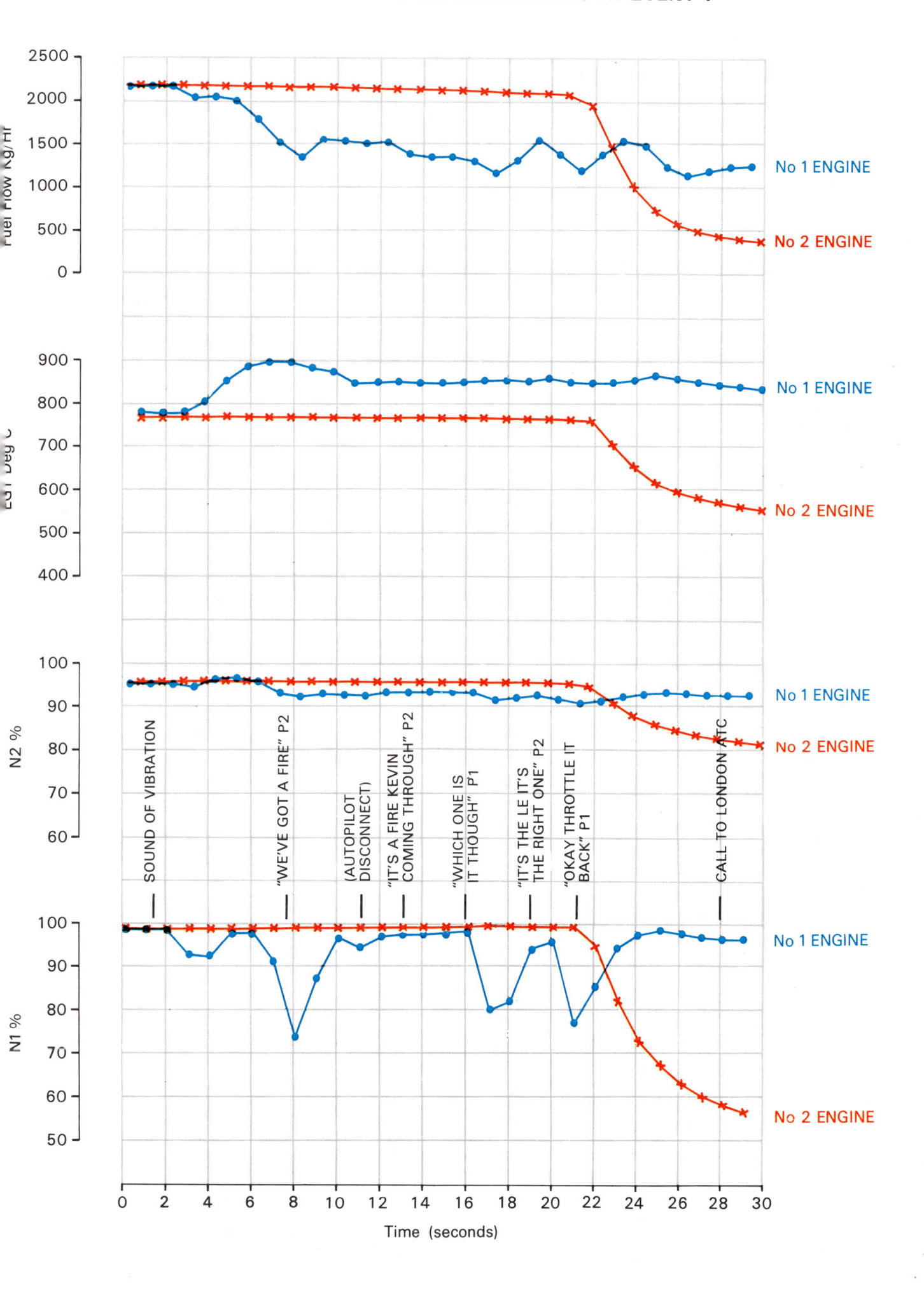

APPENDIX 4 FIGURE 6

G—OBME FINAL DATA FROM FLIGHT RECORDER

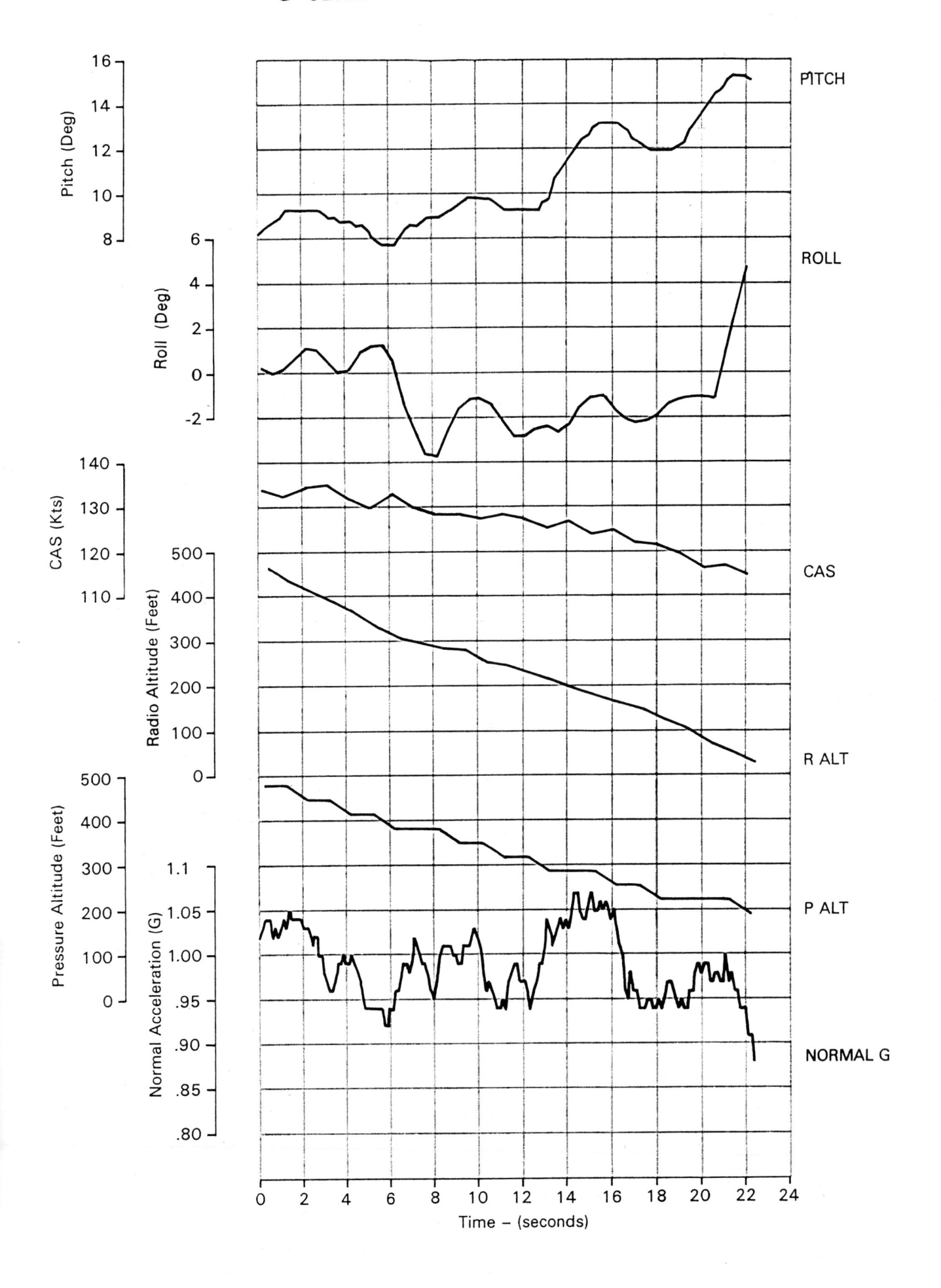

APPENDIX 4 FIGURE 7

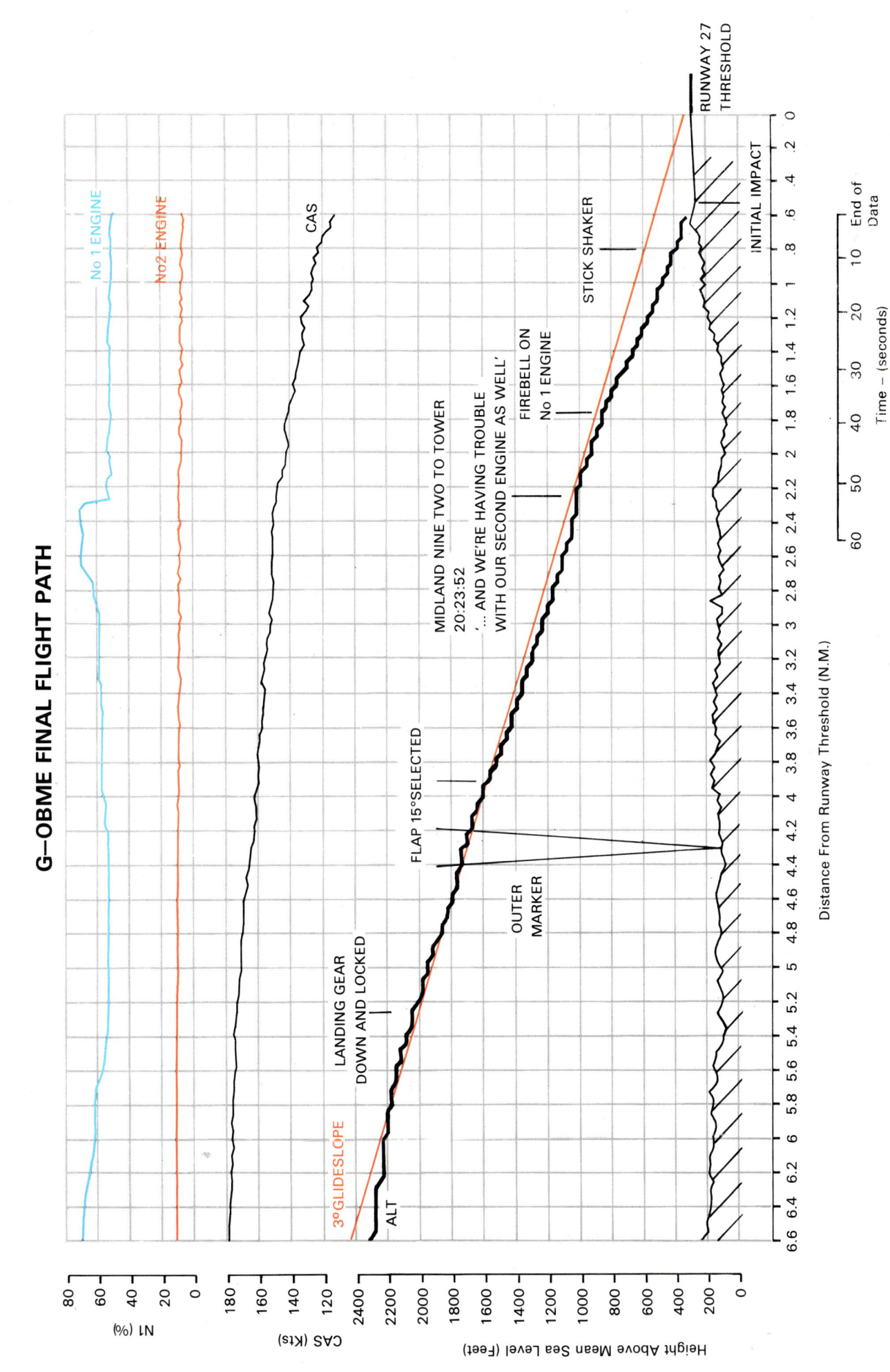

G-OBME FINAL FLIGHT PATH

APPENDIX 4, Fig 8

COMPARISON OF SIGNATURES BEFORE AND AFTER FIRST EVENT
(FROM CVR AREA MIC)

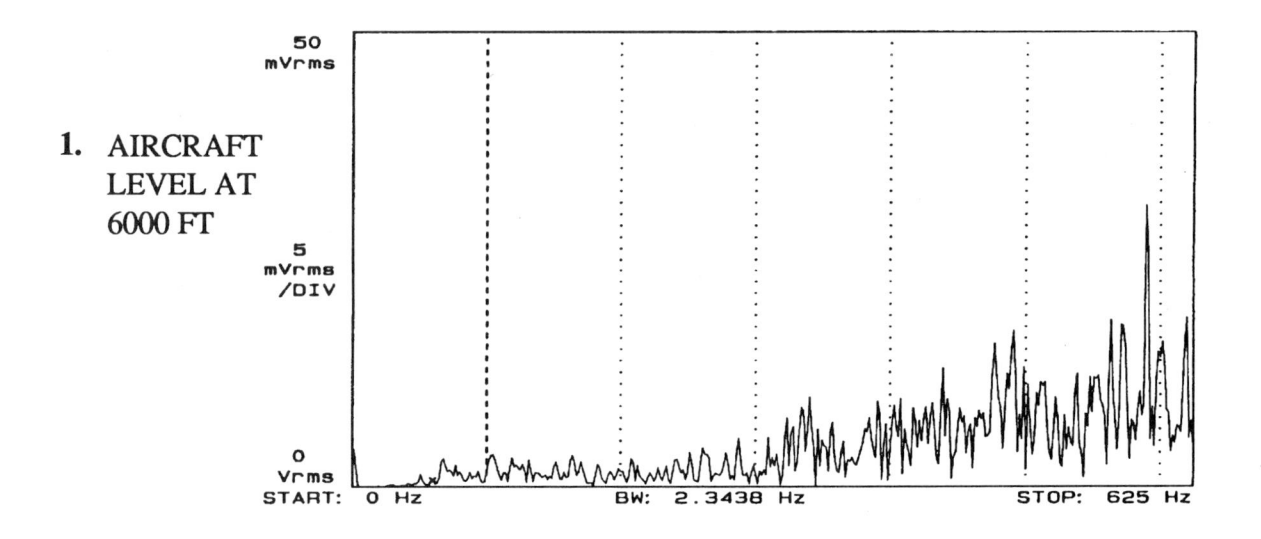

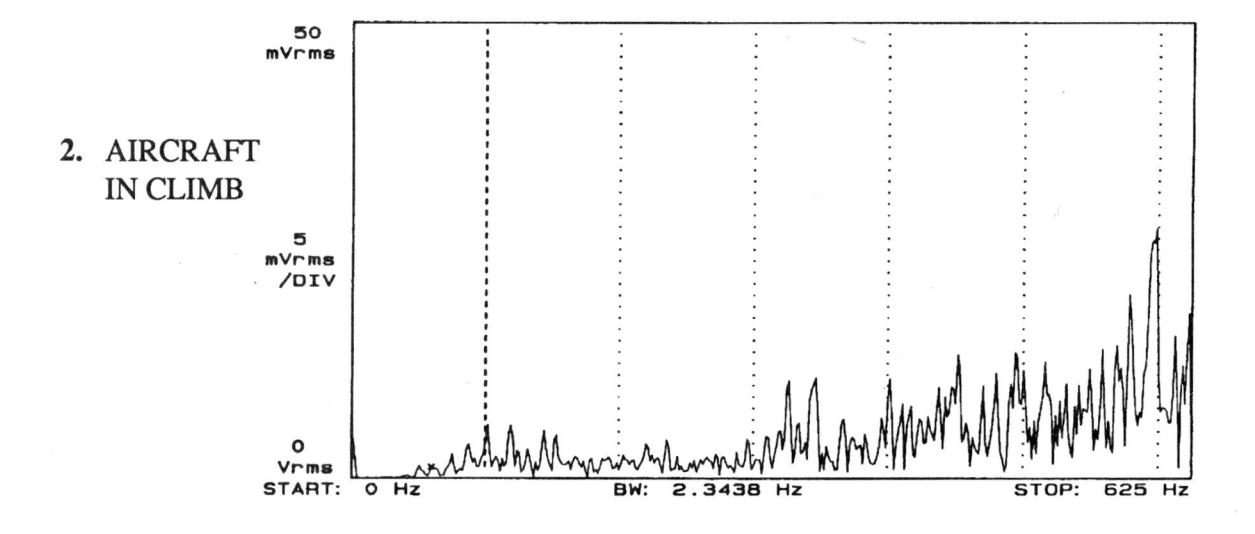

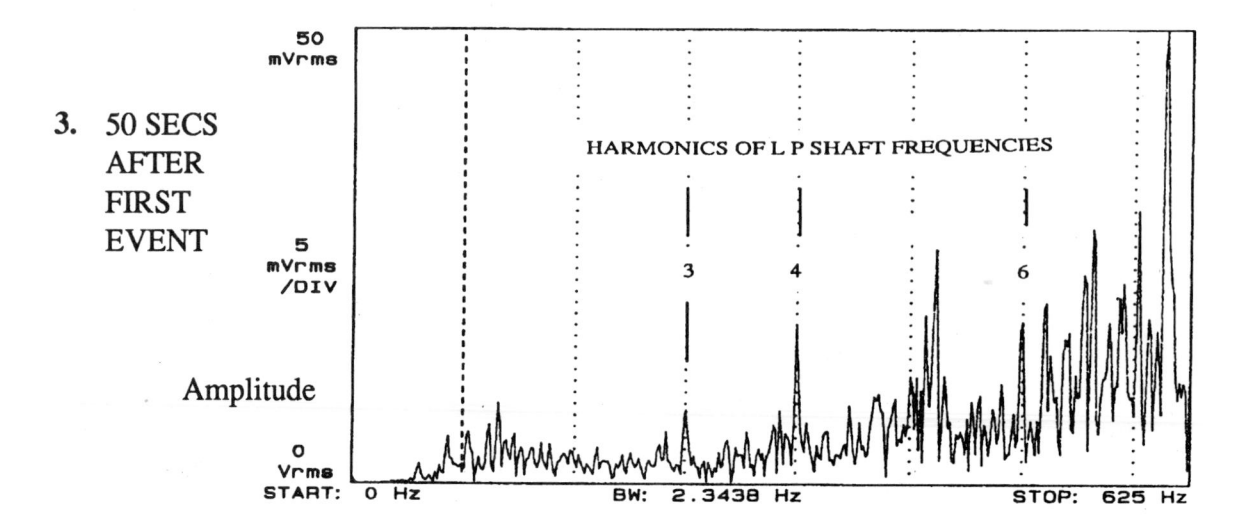

1. AIRCRAFT LEVEL AT 6000 FT

2. AIRCRAFT IN CLIMB

3. 50 SECS AFTER FIRST EVENT

HARMONICS OF L P SHAFT FREQUENCIES

Amplitude

Frequency

APPENDIX 4, Fig 9

COMPARISON OF SIGNATURES BEFORE AND AFTER SECOND EVENT
(FROM CVR AREA MIC)

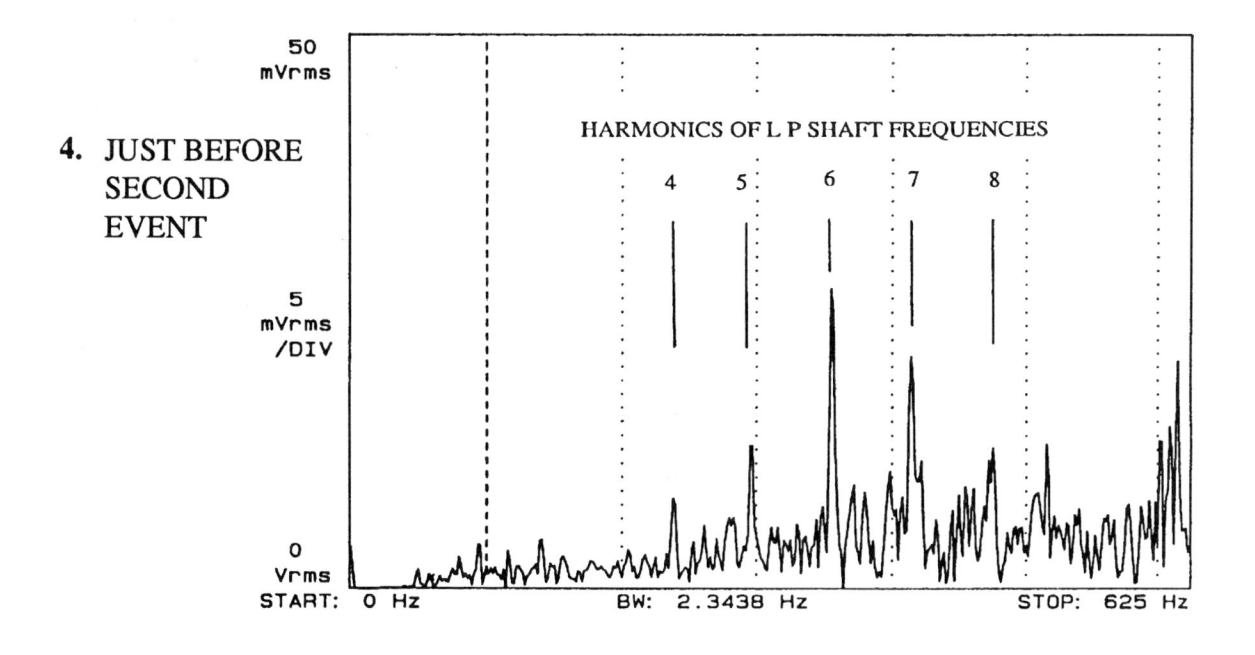

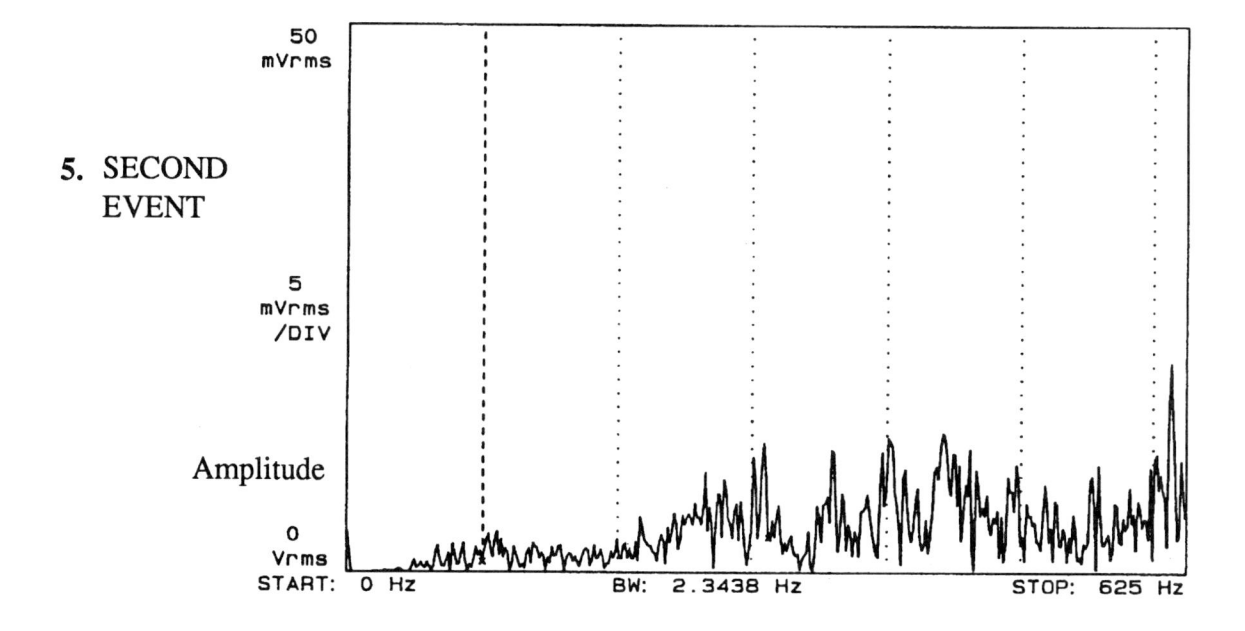

4. JUST BEFORE SECOND EVENT

HARMONICS OF L P SHAFT FREQUENCIES

5. SECOND EVENT

Amplitude

Frequency

APPENDIX 4, Fig. 10

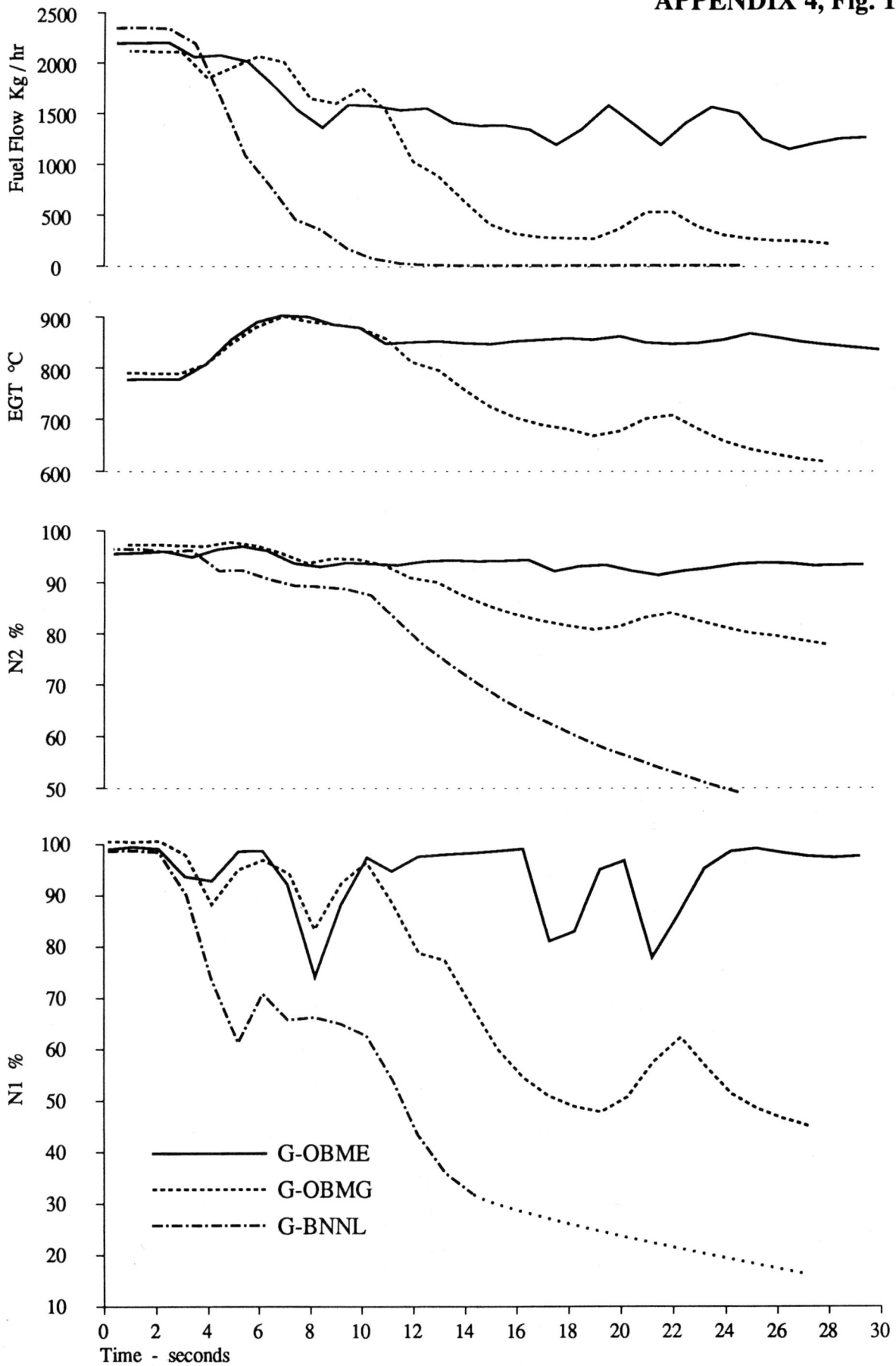

Comparison of engine parameter response following fan blade outer panel separation on three aircraft (G-OBME, G-OBMG, G-BNNL)

APPENDIX 4, Fig. 11

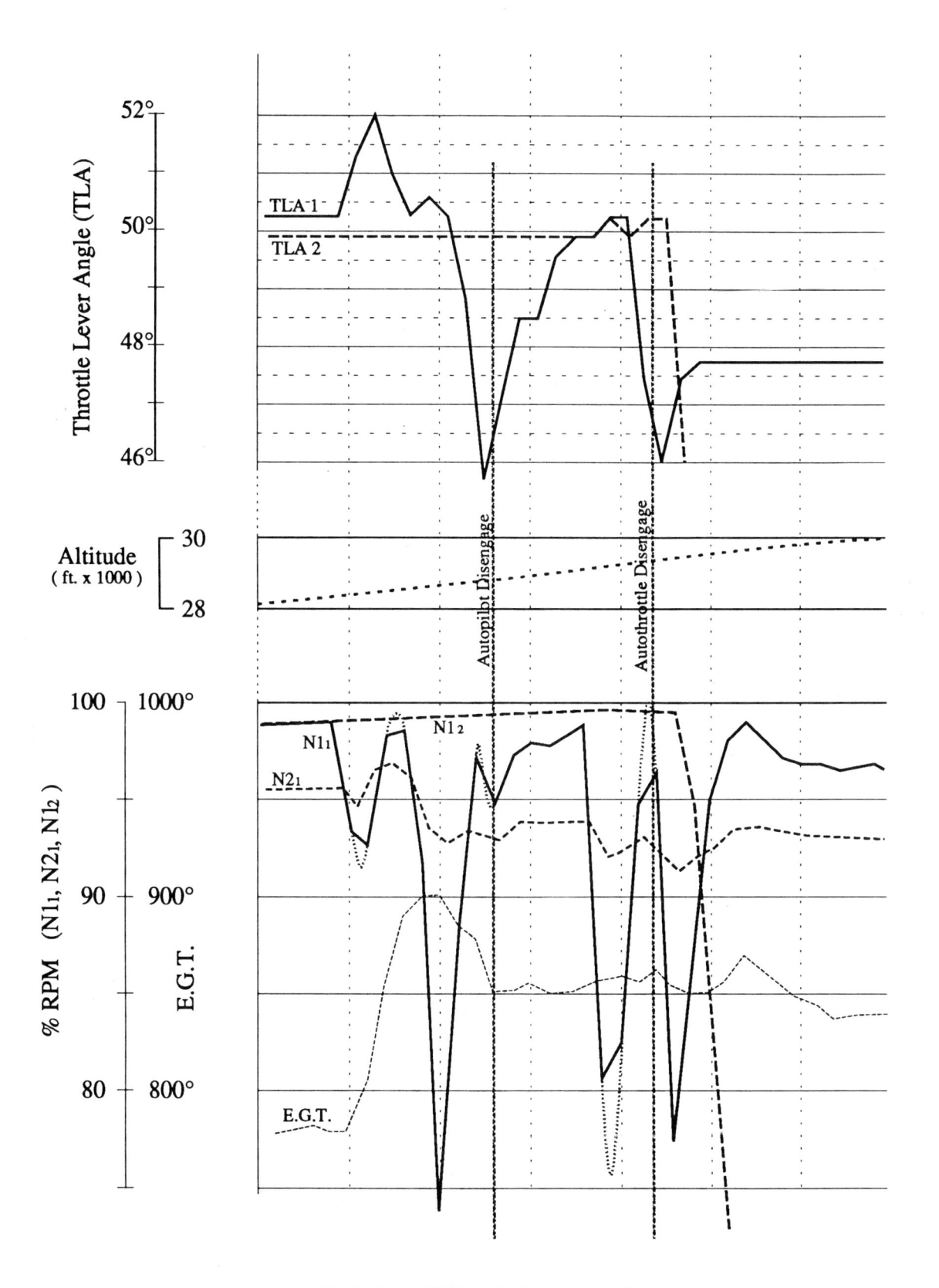

Variation of Throttle Lever Angle
related to engine parameters and altitude during Event 1

APPENDIX 5

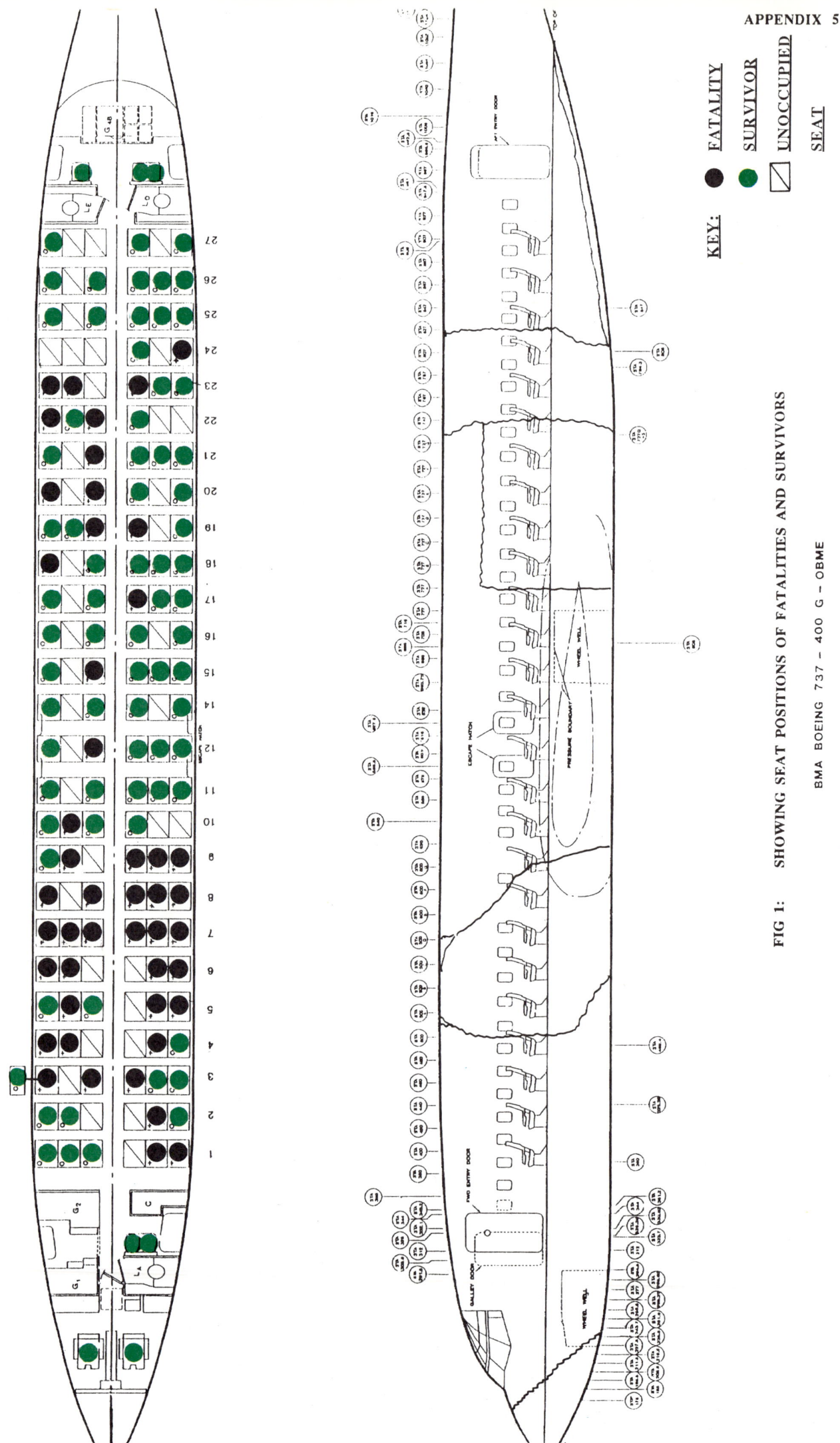

KEY: FATALITY ● SURVIVOR ● UNOCCUPIED SEAT ◪

FIG 1: SHOWING SEAT POSITIONS OF FATALITIES AND SURVIVORS

BMA BOEING 737 - 400 G - OBME

APPENDIX 5

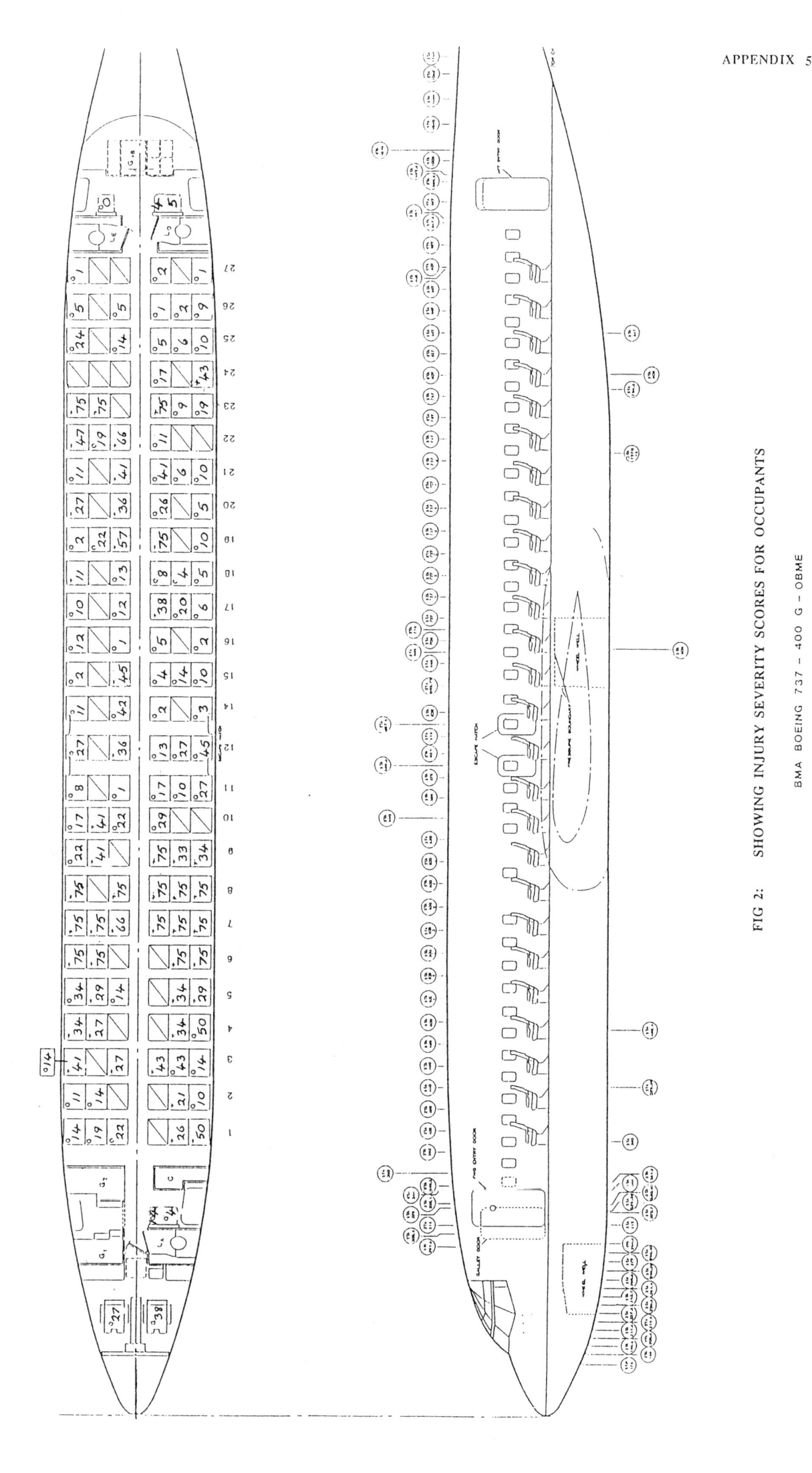

FIG 2: SHOWING INJURY SEVERITY SCORES FOR OCCUPANTS

BMA BOEING 737 - 400 G - OBME

APPENDIX 5

KEY:
- ■ I.S.S.>16
- ■ I.S.S.<16
- ◨ UNOCCUPIED SEAT

FIG 3: SHOWING DISTRIBUTION OF INJURY SEVERITY

BMA BOEING 737 – 400 G – OBME

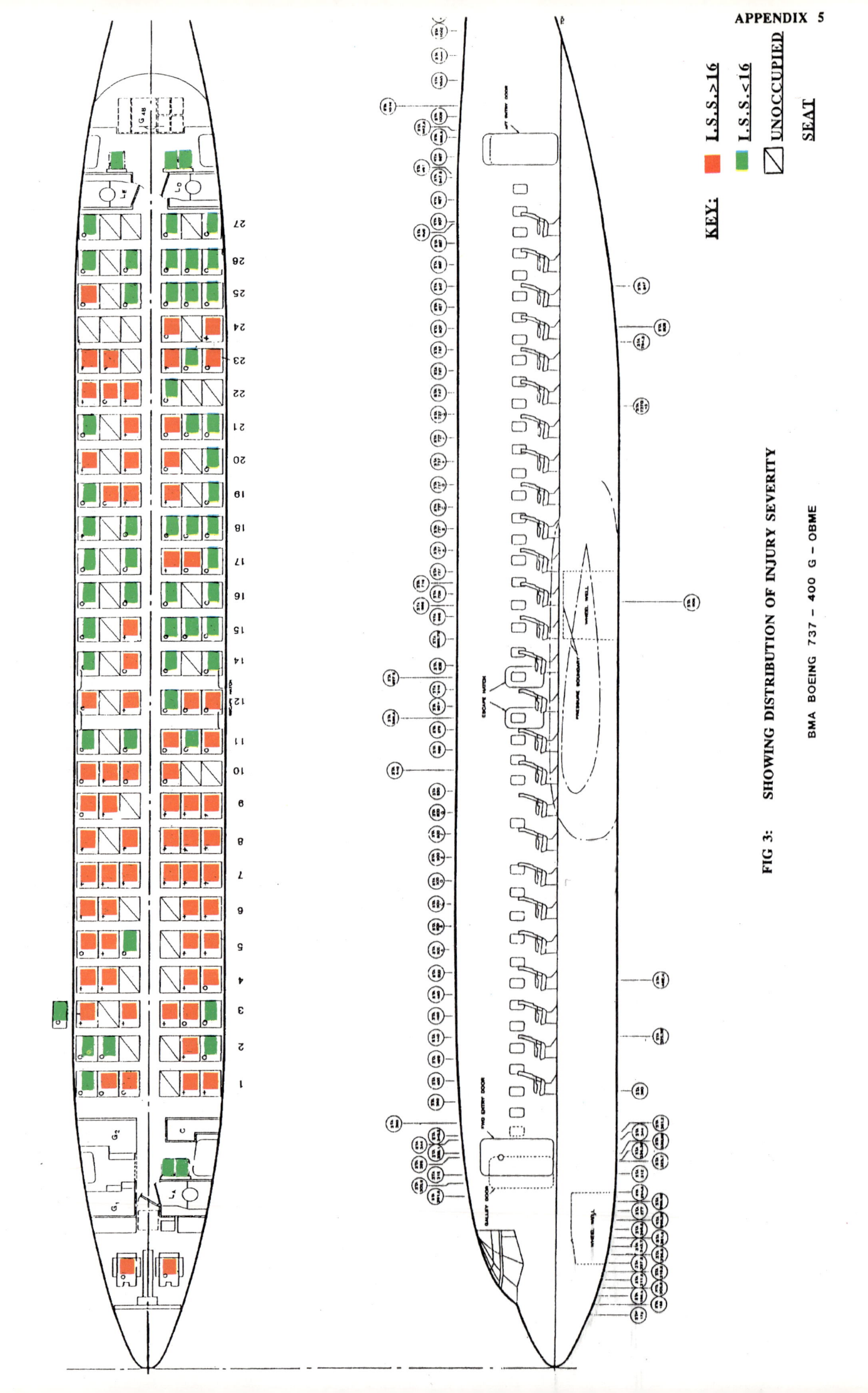

APPENDIX 5

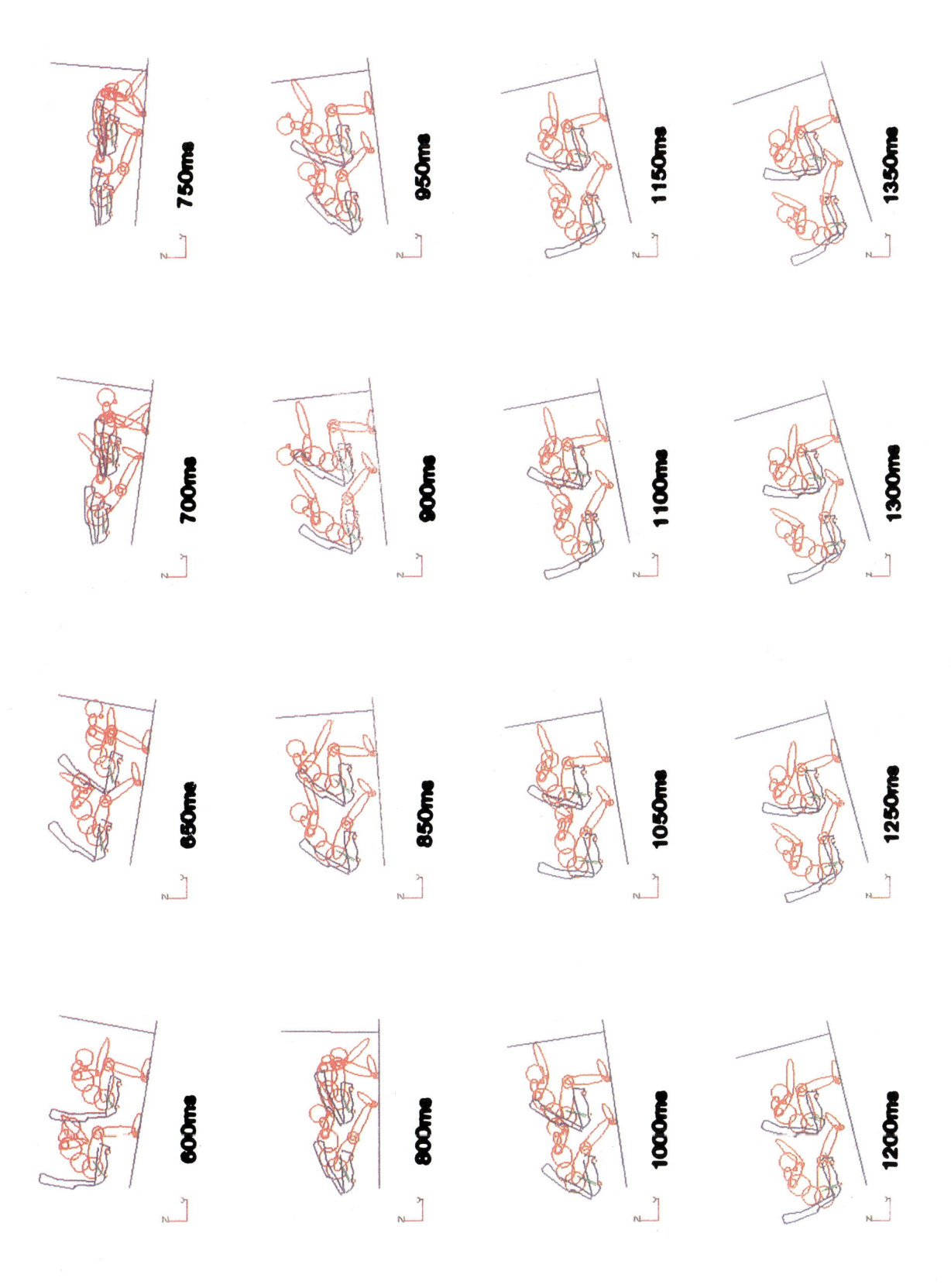

FIG 4: SHOWING COMPUTER SIMULATION OF IMPACT INDUCED OCCUPANT DISPLACEMENT, WITH LAP BELT RESTRAINT

APPENDIX 5

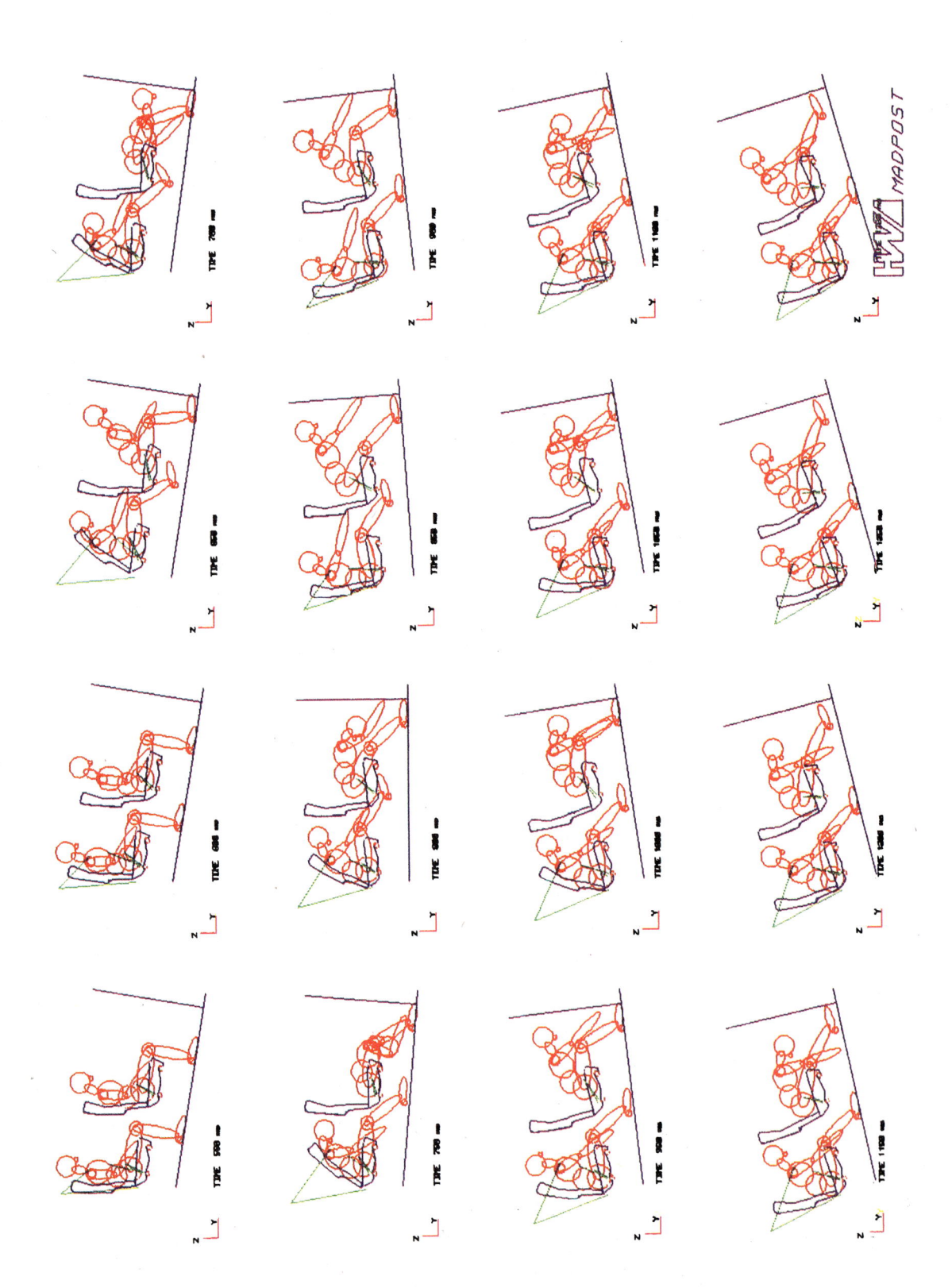

FIG 5: SHOWING COMPUTER SIMULATION OF IMPACT INDUCED OCCUPANT DISPLACEMENT, WITH LAP BELT AND UPPER TORSO RESTRAINT OF REAR OCCUPANT

APPENDIX 5

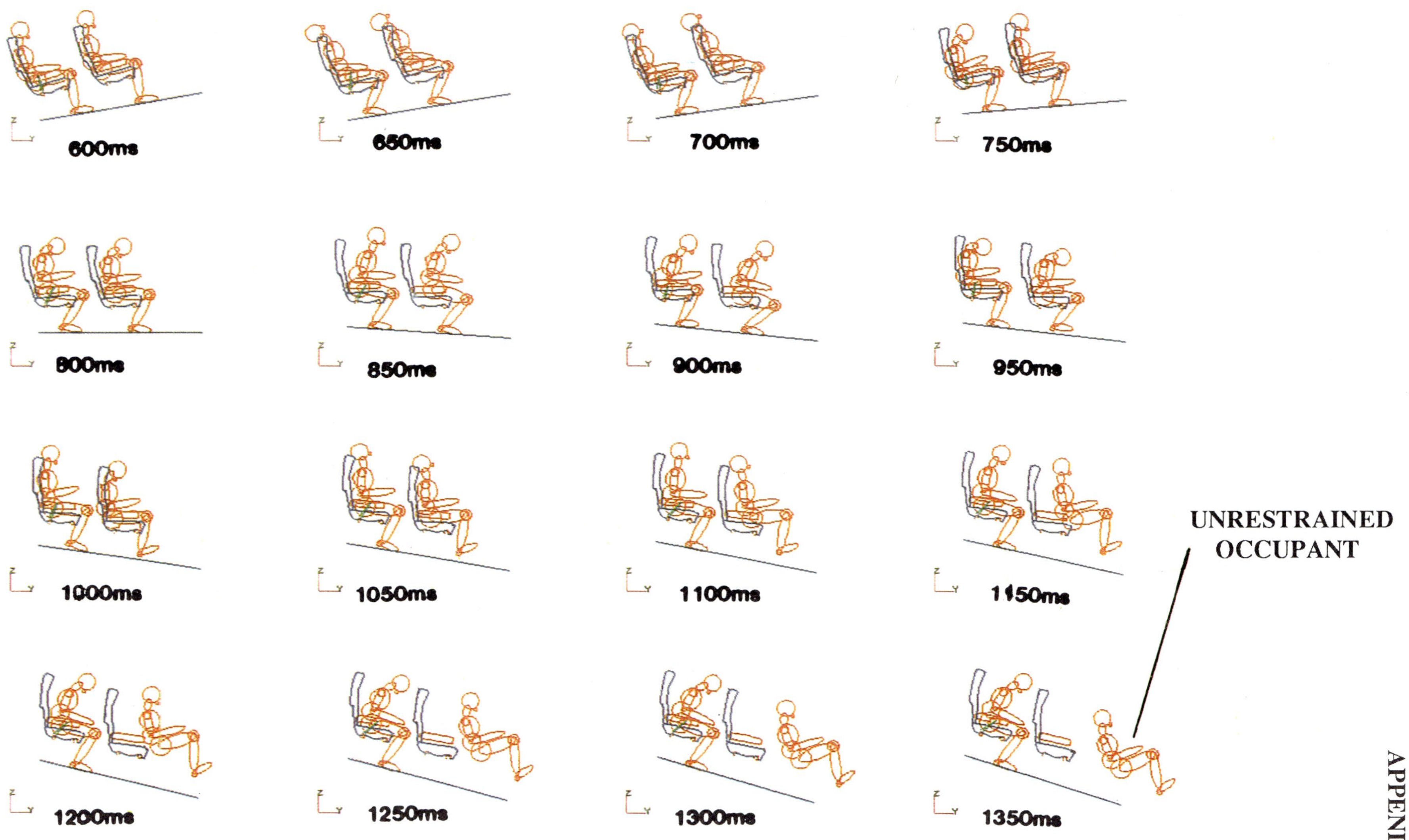

UNRESTRAINED OCCUPANT

FIG 6: SHOWING COMPUTER SIMULATION OF IMPACT INDUCED OCCUPANT DISPLACEMENT, WITH AFT-FACING SEAT (STANDARD SEAT)

Appendix 5.7

REFERENCES

1) Trent Regional Health Authority. "Aircraft Accident BD092, M1 Motorway/East Midlands Airport. Sunday 8th January 1989". Emergency Planning Ref JAC/C17/24.

2) Kirsh, G., Rowles, J.M. & Macey, A.C. Personal communication. NLDB Study Group. University Hospital Nottingham.

3) American Association for Automotive Medicine: The Abbreviated Injury Severity Score. 1985 revision. AAAM, 1985.

4) Baker, S.P., O'Neill, B., Haddon, W., Long, W.B. "The Injury Severity Score: A Method for Describing Patients with Multiple Injuries and Evaluating Emergency Care." J Trauma 1974, 14,3: 187.

5) White, D.B., Mumford, C., Rowles, J.M. & Firth, J.L., "Head Injuries in Survivors of the M1 Aircrash." Personal Communication. NLDB Study Group, University of Nottingham.

6) H.W. Structures Ltd. 1989. H.W. Structures Ltd, Leamington Spa, Warwickshire.

Air Accidents Investigation Branch
Department of Transport
Royal Aerospace Establishment
Farnborough
Hants GU14 6TD
Tel: 0252-510300

Air Accidents Investigation Branch

APPENDIX 6

THE DEPARTMENT OF TRANSPORT

AAIB Bulletin
SPECIAL

S 2/89

ACCIDENT TO BOEING 737-400 G-OBME AT KEGWORTH, LEICESTERSHIRE ON 8 JANUARY 1989

This bulletin contains a statement of the facts which have been determined up to the time of issue. It is published under Regulation 6 of the Civil Aviation (Investigation of Accidents) Regulations 1983 to inform the aviation industry and the public of the general circumstances of the accident. It must necessarily be regarded as tentative, and subject to alteration or correction if additional evidence becomes available. The bulletin is not an accident report - either final or interim.

On the 8 January the Chief Inspector of Accidents appointed Mr E J Trimble, a Principal Inspector of Accidents, to carry out an "Inspector's Investigation" in accordance with the regulations. Much work remains to be done before his report can be compiled. Following this he, as the Inspector, must invite and consider representations on the draft report from the parties involved (in accordance with Regulation 11) before it is completed for submission to the Secretary of State for Transport. Unless one of these parties asks for a Review Board (under Regulation 12) the report will then be published.

Thus nothing in this bulletin is to be taken as a final statement of the facts and circumstances of the accident, nor would it be right to draw any conclusions from it as to the cause(s) of the accident.

This bulletin can be reproduced without specific permission providing that the source is acknowledged.

This bulletin contains facts which have been determined up to the time of issue. This information is published to inform the aviation industry and the public of the general circumstances of accidents and must necessarily be regarded as tentative and subject to alteration or correction if additional evidence becomes available.

Extracts can be published without specific permission providing that the source is duly acknowledged.

©Crown copyright 1989

ISSN 0309-4278

Aircraft Type and Registration: Boeing 737-400, G-OBME

No & Type of Engines: 2 CFM 56-3C high by-pass turbo-fan engines

Year of Manufacture: 1988

Date and Time (UTC): 8 January 1989 at 2025 hrs

Location: Kegworth, near East Midlands Airport, Leicestershire

Type of Flight: Scheduled passenger

Persons on Board: Crew - 8 Passengers - 117 + 1 infant
Injuries: Crew - 7 (serious) Passengers - 47 (fatal).
  66 + 1 infant (serious)
 1 (minor) 4 (minor)

Nature of Damage: Aircraft destroyed

Commander's Licence: Airline Transport Pilot's Licence

Commander's Age: 43 years

Commander's Total Flying Experience: 13180 hours (of which 765 were on Boeing 737-300/400 types)

Information Source: AAIB Inspector's Investigation under the Civil Aviation (Investigation of Accidents) Regulations 1983

History of the Flight

The aircraft was engaged on a double shuttle between London Heathrow and Belfast. It landed at Heathrow at 1845 hrs after completing the first shuttle flight and took off again for Belfast at 1952 hrs with the first officer handling the aircraft. After take-off, the aircraft climbed initially to flight level (FL) 60, where it levelled off above a layer of stratocumulus cloud for two minutes, before receiving clearance to climb to FL 120. Soon afterwards, at 1958 hrs, clearance was passed for the aircraft to continue its climb to its cruising FL of 350 on a direct track to the Trent VOR (Very high frequency Omni-Range beacon).

At 2005.05 hrs, as the aircraft was approaching FL 290, the flight crew experienced moderate to severe vibration, a burning smell and smoke. The commander immediately took control of the aircraft, disengaging both the auto-pilot and the automatic throttle. The two pilots then diagnosed the symptoms of vibration and smoke as indicating a problem in the right engine and 20 seconds after the onset of the vibration, the commander instructed the first officer to throttle back the right engine. The commander later stated that the action of closing the right throttle reduced the smell and signs of smoke and that he remembered no continuation of the vibration after the right throttle was closed.

Immediately after throttling back the right engine, the first officer advised London Air Traffic Control (ATC) that the aircraft was at FL 300 and that they had an emergency situation which looked like an engine fire. When this message had been passed, the commander ordered the first officer to shut-down the engine; the flight crew were then engaged in ATC radio transmissions, stating their intention to divert to Castle Donington (East Midlands Airport). During this period a female cabin attendant used the cabin address system to advise the passengers to fasten their seat belts. The right engine was shut down 2 minutes and 7 seconds after the vibration began. By that time power had been reduced on the left engine, which continued to operate at comparatively low power. After the accident, the commander stated that during the remainder of the descent the indications from the engine instruments were such as to confirm that the emergency had been successfully concluded and that the left engine was operating normally. The recorded engine parameters associated with this stage of the flight are included in the section on "FDR and CVR evidence".

In the cabin, the passengers and the cabin attendants had heard an unusual noise accompanied by moderate to severe vibration. Some passengers had also been aware of what they described as smoke, but none were able to describe its colour or density. They described the smell of burning as "rubber", "oil" and "hot metal". Many had seen signs of fire from the left engine, which they described variously as "fire", "torching" or "sparks". Several of the cabin attendants described the noise as a low, repetitive "thudding", and one described how the vibration had been severe enough to shake the walls of the forward galley. Soon after the right engine had been shut-down, and in response to a cabin "chime" from the commander, the flight service manager (FSM) came to the flight deck. The commander asked him if they had had smoke in the cabin. He replied that they had. Later, after another statement from the FSM that the passengers were becoming concerned, the commander broadcast on the cabin address system that there was trouble with the right engine which had produced some smoke in the cabin, that the engine was now shut-down and that they could expect to land at East Midlands Airport in about 10 minutes. Passengers stated that the smell of smoke had dissipated by the time the commander made this announcement.

The right engine had been shut-down approximately 5 nm north-west of East Midlands Airport. Having cleared the aircraft to turn right and descend to FL 100, London ATC passed control to Manchester ATC, who passed headings for the aircraft to descend to the north west of East Midlands Airport, before vectoring it to the east of the airport to begin its approach to runway 27. ATC control of the aircraft was then transferred to Castle Donington Approach.

The approach then continued until the aircraft was on the localiser of the instrument landing system (ILS) for runway 27, with flaps lowered to 5°. At 2,000 ft the landing gear was lowered and, as the outer marker was passed at 4.3 nm from touchdown, 15° of flap was selected. One minute later, at 2023.50 hrs, when the aircraft was 2.4 nm from touchdown and at a height of 900 ft above ground level (agl), the left engine lost power with compressor speed reducing rapidly and high vibration levels. The commander told the first officer to relight (*ie* restart) the right engine. 17 seconds after the power loss, the fire warning system operated on the left engine. No power became available from the right engine before the aircraft struck the ground at 2024.43 hrs, 36 seconds after the fire warning.

The initial ground impact was in a nose-high attitude on level ground just to the east of the M1 motorway. The aircraft then passed through trees and suffered its second, and major, impact on the western (*ie* northbound) carriageway of the M1 and the lower part of the western embankment: this second impact occurred some 70 metres after the initial impact and 10 metres lower. The fuselage was extensively disrupted and the aircraft came to rest entirely on the wooded western embankment, approximately 900 metres from the threshold of runway 27 and displaced 50 metres to the right of the centreline of the approach lights.

Ground witnesses who saw the final approach of the aircraft saw clear evidence of fire associated with the left engine. The intake area of the engine was filled with yellow/orange fire and flames were observed streaming aft of the nacelle, pulsating in unison with "thumping noises" which emanated from this engine. Metallic "rattling" noises were also heard and flaming debris was observed falling from the region of the burning engine.

Wreckage examination

Examination of the fuselage showed that two major structural failures had occurred in the impact, one slightly forward of the wing leading-edge and one aft of the wing trailing-edge. These had respectively resulted in the fuselage nose section becoming detached from the centre section and the tail section buckling over, and to the right of, the centre section. The forward fuselage had therefore sustained a high degree of disruption in the passenger cabin, with floor structure, seats and furnishings becoming detached; similar damage had occurred around the aft fuselage failure. The floor structure and seating were much less disrupted in the centre (*ie* over-wing) section of the cabin and in the inverted tail section.

The Flight Data Recorder (FDR) and Cockpit Voice Recorder (CVR) were removed during the early morning of Monday 9 January and taken to AAIB Farnborough for readout and analysis.

The No.1 (left) engine showed evidence of fire damage, including that arising from ground fire. The left wing appeared to have contained its fuel, whereas the right wing had suffered sufficient impact damage to cause leakage of its fuel contents, which had run back down the embankment slope, on to the motorway.

The No.2 (right) engine showed no evidence of fire.

Fragments of engine fan blades from No.1 engine were found under the approach path, up to 3½ km east of the crash site.

The airframe wreckage was progressively removed from the site and transported to AAIB Farnborough during the period from the 10-14 January and the engines were transported directly to the manufacturer, CFMI at Villaroche in France on 13/14 January where they were the subject of detailed strip down examination, under AAIB supervision.

FDR and CVR evidence

The aircraft was equipped with a Sundstrand Universal Flight Data Recorder and a Fairchild A100 Cockpit Voice Recorder. Both were replayed satisfactorily at AAIB. The FDR read-out established that, as the aircraft was approaching FL 290, an event occurred which led to the No.1 (left) engine recording its maximum indicated vibration level ("5 units"), recordings of rapidly fluctuating fan speeds and fluctuating HP core speeds, with an associated rise in exhaust gas temperature (EGT) and fluctuation in fuel flow. Approximately 20 seconds after this occurrence, the No.2 (right) engine was throttled back, at which point the No.1 engine fan and core speeds settled down, although at slightly different values, with the indicated vibration level remaining at maximum and EGT markedly higher than before - ie 840°C, compared to 780°C previously. Prior to being throttled back, the No. 2 engine had been operating with steady engine indications, with a fan speed (N1) of 99%, HP compressor speed (N2) of 96%, EGT of 770°C and low vibration level ("0.5 units"). 1 minute and 47 seconds later, the No.2 engine was shut-down. It was apparent that the flight crew were aware of smoke on the flight deck and thought that they had a possible engine fire. There was no fire warning at this time.

The flight proceded under the control of London, Manchester, and finally Castle Donington ATC. The No.1 engine appeared to respond reasonably to applied throttle demands, although the engine was at "flight idle" for a considerable time (10 minutes).

At about 900 ft above ground level on the final approach, the No.1 engine fan speed dropped rapidly and EGT increased significantly with other engine parameters unchanged, and a maximum indicated vibration level. The No.1 engine lost considerable power and some 17 seconds later the fire warning bell sounded. About 36 seconds later the aircraft impacted with the ground.

Engine strip examination

Inspection of the fan assembly of the No.1 (left) engine showed extensive damage had occurred to the titanium alloy blades, with many associated damage-induced overstressing failures. One fan blade was found to have fractured outboard of the "mid-span shrouds", due to a progressive fatigue failure originating near the leading edge of this blade, adjacent the pressure face. This failure had released the outer "panel" (approximately 4 inches) of this blade. The cause of this fatigue failure, which was the only instance of fatigue fracture found amongst the fan blades, is being pursued.

The abradable seal material which surrounds the fan assembly would have been progressively removed by the damaged fan assembly, as would the rubberized seals surrounding the low pressure compressor "booster" section, due to out-of-balance running, and would have led to associated smoke products entering the air conditioning system.

Inspection of the No.1 engine revealed evidence consistent with the anticipated effects of this engine having run under severe out- of -balance conditions due to fan damage, with some damage to the high pressure compressor arising from fan debris ingestion. No failures were found within the core-module rotating assemblies.

Investigation of the source(s) and development of the airborne fire on the No.1 engine is still in progress. Evidence found to date is provisionally indicative of two areas of fire, one of which was located around the upper/outboard region of the exterior of the fan casing and the other which appears to have trailed from the thrust reverser duct on the left side. It is considered that the sources of both areas of fire were secondary to, and were induced by, the primary engine failure and subsequent continued operation with attendant high vibration.

Detailed investigation of the No.1 engine and its operating history will continue in an attempt to identify the cause of the fan blade fatigue and to explain fully the initiation and progression of the fire.

The No.2 (right) engine has been fully stripped and shows no evidence of pre-crash fire or failure.

Systems examination

Checks have been made of the wiring leading to the Engine Indicating System (EIS). These have confirmed that the indications of both primary and secondary engine parameters were displayed in the correct sense. The primary EIS display unit passed a full function and calibration check. The secondary EIS unit exhibited an obvious fault condition affecting the display of oil pressure, hydraulic pressure and oil quantity, but not the engine vibration indicators. The secondary EIS unit had suffered significant impact damage and the fault appears consistent with such damage. Since the Flight Data Recorder receives engine data (except vibration) from the EIS output to its display, it is implicit that such data was displayed by the EIS.

The Airborne Vibration Monitor unit (AVM), which feeds vibration signals from the engines to the EIS and FDR, was subjected to a full test schedule and, despite some minor external case damage, fully met the acceptance requirements. Both engine vibration indicators operated satisfactorily. The engine vibration indicators and FDR cannot register vibration levels higher than "5 units", since the AVM limits its output.

The Engine and APU fire detection module was severely damaged by impact, such that a functional test was not possible, and will require detailed inspection. Checks of the actual detector loops on the engines concluded that those not damaged beyond meaningful test by impact were capable of providing both overheat and fire detection warnings. The Engine and APU fire suppression bottles were found fully charged. There were no indications that an attempt had been made to discharge any extinguisher.

Further investigation of the systems aspects will include an appraisal of the EIS/Flight crew interface to evaluate the effectiveness of the presentation of engine indications to pilots. This evaluation will be assisted by the RAF Institute of Aviation Medicine Flight Skills Section.

Survival factors

A full evaluation of passenger and crew testimony and injury, combined with an analysis of the pathology, is being progressed. This information will be related to the crash-induced damage to the cabin structure and seating in order that the causes of injury are identified, with a view towards consideration of what improvements may be indicated to reduce injuries and maximise survivability in future accidents.

AAIB Safety Recommendations

Shortly after the accident, on the 11 January 1989, AAIB made 2 Safety Recommendations to the CAA. These were made at a stage in the investigation when it was known that the left engine had failed in-flight, but the reason for the in-flight shut-down of the right engine had not yet been established. In addition, it was considered prudent to address the possibility of a defective engine vibration or fire/overheat warning system although no evidence of such defect(s) had been found. The following precautionary Safety Recommendations were made to the CAA:

1. That the CAA consider increasing the frequency of existing engine inspections and engine health monitoring on Boeing 737-300 and Boeing 737-400 aircraft until the causes of the engine failure(s) are established.

2. That the CAA call for an examination of the Boeing 737-300 and Boeing 737-400 engine Fire/Overheat and Vibration monitoring circuitry for left/right engine sense.

As a result, the CAA issued letters to owners/operators Nos. 905 and 906 on 11 January 1989 which required (respectively) testing of the engine overheat/fire warning and vibration monitoring systems for "correct-sense" operation; and increased frequency of certain engine "health monitoring" checks on Boeing 737-300, 737-400 and Airbus 320 aircraft.

On 10 February 1989, the AAIB advised the CAA that the left engine had suffered a fatigue-failure of a fan blade and that there was no continuing justification for the increased inspections of the "oil-wetted" components of the CFM 65-3 and -5 engines. However, in view of the fan blade failure (the cause of which has not thus far been established) and AAIB caution concerning any possible means by which the fatigue strength of such fan blades may be inadvertently compromised, the following 2 Safety Recommendations were made to the CAA:

3. The Civil Aviation Authority, in conjunction with the engine manufacturer, consider instituting inspection procedures for the examination of the fan stage of CFM 56 engines to ensure the early detection of damage that could lead to the failure of a blade.

4. The Civil Aviation Authority review the advice given in the Boeing 737-400 Maintenance Manual concerning the excessive generation of heat during blending operations with power grinding and blending tools.

CFMI and Boeing issued letters to operators, emphasising the daily visual check on the engine inlet and fan blades and the detailed fan blade inspection at the aircraft "B check" (approximately every 750 hours). In addition, operators were recommended to review their policies and instructions for the maintenance and repair of CFM 56 fan blades, with particular emphasis on adhering strictly to the limits and procedures detailed in the aircraft maintenance manual for fan blade repair.

On 23 February 1989, the AAIB made a further 3 Safety Recommendations to the CAA:

5. The CAA take action to advise pilots of Boeing 737-300/400 aircraft, and of other types with engines which have similar characteristics, that when instances of engine-induced high vibration occur, they may be accompanied by associated smoke and/or smells of burning entering the flight deck and/or cabin through the air-conditioning system, due merely to blade tip contact between fan/compressor rotating assemblies and the associated abradable seals.

6. The CAA request the Boeing Airplane Company to produce amendments to the existing aircraft flight manuals and checklists to indicate what actions should be taken when engine-induced high vibration occurs, accompanied by smoke and/or the smell of burning entering the flight deck and/or cabin.

7. The CAA review the current attitude of pilots to the engine vibration indicators on Boeing 737-300/400 aircraft and other applicable types with turbo-fan engines, with a view towards providing flight crews with an indication of the pertinence of such vibration instruments when certain engine malfunctions or failures occur.